Hands-On Machine Learning with JavaScript

Solve complex computational web problems
using machine learning

Burak Kanber

BIRMINGHAM - MUMBAI

Hands-On Machine Learning with JavaScript

Commissioning Editor: Sunith Shetty
Acquisition Editor: Vinay Argekar
Content Development Editor: Aaryaman Singh
Technical Editor: Sayli Nikalje
Copy Editors: Safis Editing
Project Coordinator: Manthan Patel
Proofreader: Safis Editing
Indexer: Mariammal Chettiyar
Graphics: Tania Dutta
Production Coordinator: Aparna Bhagat

First published: May 2018

Production reference: 1250518

Published by Packt Publishing Ltd.
Livery Place
35 Livery Street
Birmingham
B3 2PB, UK.

ISBN 978-1-78899-824-6

www.packtpub.com

`mapt.io`

Mapt is an online digital library that gives you full access to over 5,000 books and videos, as well as industry leading tools to help you plan your personal development and advance your career. For more information, please visit our website.

Why subscribe?

- Spend less time learning and more time coding with practical eBooks and Videos from over 4,000 industry professionals

- Improve your learning with Skill Plans built especially for you

- Get a free eBook or video every month

- Mapt is fully searchable

- Copy and paste, print, and bookmark content

PacktPub.com

Did you know that Packt offers eBook versions of every book published, with PDF and ePub files available? You can upgrade to the eBook version at `www.PacktPub.com` and as a print book customer, you are entitled to a discount on the eBook copy. Get in touch with us at `service@packtpub.com` for more details.

At `www.PacktPub.com`, you can also read a collection of free technical articles, sign up for a range of free newsletters, and receive exclusive discounts and offers on Packt books and eBooks.

Contributors

About the author

Burak Kanber is an entrepreneur and engineer with nearly 20 years of experience developing software. After completing graduate school at The Cooper Union, Burak joined a marketing technology startup as co-founder and CTO. Machine learning was not as accessible as it is today, so from 2010–2012 he wrote a series of articles that taught ML to web developers from first principles. His *ML in JS* series has since been enjoyed by over a million readers.

Burak is also the co-author of *Genetic Algorithms in Java Basics*, published by Apress in 2015.

I have been writing about ML in JS for years, and I would like to thank Packt and their team for the opportunity to bring this book to market. I would also like to thank my wife Kimberly for her endless support, love, and patience, especially during the countless hours I spent in my own little world writing this book. I'll never stop trying to make you proud.

About the reviewer

Paulo Pires is a geographical engineer who, in his early thirties, decided to apply his skills in business intelligence. He started working in Webdetails seven years ago and specialized in frontend dashboards with CTools, Pentaho, HTML, JavaScript and its libraries, CSS, and some backend ETL. Currently, he is a senior consultant.

As a hobby, he likes to explore new technologies, and lately he has been playing with Home Automation with Node.js, Sonoff sensors, and Mosquitto broker.

Packt is searching for authors like you

If you're interested in becoming an author for Packt, please visit `authors.packtpub.com` and apply today. We have worked with thousands of developers and tech professionals, just like you, to help them share their insight with the global tech community. You can make a general application, apply for a specific hot topic that we are recruiting an author for, or submit your own idea.

Table of Contents

Preface   1

Chapter 1: Exploring the Potential of JavaScript   9
  Why JavaScript?   9
  Why machine learning, why now?   12
  Advantages and challenges of JavaScript   14
  The CommonJS initiative   15
  Node.js   16
  TypeScript language   18
  Improvements in ES6   19
    Let and const   20
    Classes   21
    Module imports   22
    Arrow functions   23
    Object literals   25
    The for...of function   26
    Promises   26
    The async/await functions   27
  Preparing the development environment   28
    Installing Node.js   29
    Optionally installing Yarn   29
    Creating and initializing an example project   30
    Creating a Hello World project   30
  Summary   33

Chapter 2: Data Exploration   35
  An overview   35
  Feature identification   38
    The curse of dimensionality   39
    Feature selection and feature extraction   41
    Pearson correlation example   44
  Cleaning and preparing data   47
    Handling missing data   48
      Missing categorical data   48
      Missing numerical data   49
    Handling noise   49
    Handling outliers   55
    Transforming and normalizing data   59
  Summary   66

Chapter 3: Tour of Machine Learning Algorithms 67
    Introduction to machine learning 68
    Types of learning 68
        Unsupervised learning 70
        Supervised learning 73
            Measuring accuracy 74
            Supervised learning algorithms 77
        Reinforcement learning 81
    Categories of algorithms 82
        Clustering 82
        Classification 83
        Regression 83
        Dimensionality reduction 83
        Optimization 84
        Natural language processing 84
        Image processing 85
    Summary 85

Chapter 4: Grouping with Clustering Algorithms 87
    Average and distance 89
    Writing the k-means algorithm 91
        Setting up the environment 92
        Initializing the algorithm 93
        Testing random centroid generation 98
        Assigning points to centroids 100
        Updating centroid locations 102
        The main loop 106
    Example 1 – k-means on simple 2D data 107
    Example 2 – 3D data 114
    k-means where k is unknown 117
    Summary 123

Chapter 5: Classification Algorithms 125
    k-Nearest Neighbor 126
        Building the KNN algorithm 127
            Example 1 – Height, weight, and gender 132
            Example 2 – Decolorizing a photo 136
    Naive Bayes classifier 141
        Tokenization 144
        Building the algorithm 145
        Example 3 – Movie review sentiment 155
    Support Vector Machine 160
    Random forest 169
    Summary 175

Chapter 6: Association Rule Algorithms 177
  The mathematical perspective 179
  The algorithmic perspective 182
  Association rule applications 184
  Example – retail data 186
  Summary 191

Chapter 7: Forecasting with Regression Algorithms 193
  Regression versus classification 194
  Regression basics 195
  Example 1 – linear regression 200
  Example 2 – exponential regression 204
  Example 3 – polynomial regression 210
  Other time-series analysis techniques 213
    Filtering 214
    Seasonality analysis 217
    Fourier analysis 219
  Summary 221

Chapter 8: Artificial Neural Network Algorithms 223
  Conceptual overview of neural networks 224
  Backpropagation training 229
  Example - XOR in TensorFlow.js 232
  Summary 241

Chapter 9: Deep Neural Networks 243
  Convolutional Neural Networks 244
    Convolutions and convolution layers 245
    Example – MNIST handwritten digits 250
  Recurrent neural networks 257
    SimpleRNN 258
    Gated recurrent units 263
    Long Short-Term Memory 265
  Summary 268

Chapter 10: Natural Language Processing in Practice 269
  String distance 271
  Term frequency - inverse document frequency 273
  Tokenizing 279
  Stemming 286
  Phonetics 288
  Part of speech tagging 290
  Word embedding and neural networks 292
  Summary 294

Chapter 11: Using Machine Learning in Real-Time Applications   297
  Serializing models   298
    Training models on the server   299
    Web workers   301
    Continually improving and per-user models   303
  Data pipelines   305
    Data querying   306
    Data joining and aggregation   309
    Transformation and normalization   310
    Storing and delivering data   314
  Summary   316

Chapter 12: Choosing the Best Algorithm for Your Application   319
  Mode of learning   321
  The task at hand   324
  Format, form, input, and output   326
  Available resources   328
  When it goes wrong   330
  Combining models   332
  Summary   334

Other Books You May Enjoy   337

Index   341

Preface

I started my first deep dive into **machine learning (ML)** back in 2008 when I was developing algorithms for adaptive traction control systems for electric cars. Shortly thereafter, I moved out of the mechanical engineering field and co-founded a marketing technology startup. Within a few weeks, I realized how important ML was going to be for me and my company, and I decided to read every book and paper on ML that I could find.

I spent the next couple of years with my nose to the grindstone, reading dozens of textbooks and hundreds of academic papers, writing every algorithm I could find from scratch, and slowly developing an intuition and philosophy around ML.

During that period, I discovered a few things about the ML ecosystem that I wasn't too happy with. There was a strong culture of gatekeeping at the time. The idea of writing ML in a language other than Python was considered absurd. There was a sentiment that only people who had gone to school to study ML could possibly be successful in the field. Much of the publicly available reading material, such as blog articles and tutorials online, was written in a distinctly mathematical tone, thereby alienating readers who were unfamiliar with linear algebra and vector calculus.

At the same time, I was teaching a **JavaScript (JS)** programming bootcamp and many of my students—self-taught web developers—expressed an interest in ML. It was difficult for me to point them in the right direction; their only option at the time was to move to Python.

This was frustrating to me because I knew that my students were smart enough to grasp ML, and I also knew that ML didn't need to be confined to Python. I also got the sense that many of the developers using the popular Python libraries didn't actually understand the mechanism of the algorithms and would run into problems when trying to implement them. The gatekeeping had backfired and only served to reduce this powerful family of algorithms into black boxes that were applied carelessly by developers that were discouraged from digging deeper and learning more.

I wanted to prove to the world that ML could be taught to anyone and written in any language, so I started writing a series of articles called *Machine Learning in JavaScript*. The articles taught ML algorithms from first principles, free of jargon and with a focus on implementation rather than mathematical description.

I chose JS for a few reasons. First, the lack of ML libraries in JS would force my readers to write their own implementations and discover for themselves that ML isn't magic, just code. Second, JS hadn't truly come into its own yet (Node.js didn't exist at the time) and was generally considered a poor choice of programming language for serious problems, but I wanted to prove that ML could be written in *any* language. Finally, I wanted to use a language that most web developers, particularly self-taught developers, would be comfortable with. Choosing a backend language such as PHP or Java would mean excluding a large portion of developers, so I chose the language that every web developer knows: JS.

The series, though dated now, was a hit. Over a million people have read my articles, and I have heard from many readers that my articles inspired them to start on a new path; I consider this among my greatest professional successes.

This book is a humble and modern update to my *Machine Learning in JavaScript* series. Much has changed since 2008. JS is now the most popular programming language, and ML is being rapidly democratized. Developers can use AWS or Google Cloud to summon immense computational resources with a single API call, and the smartphones of today rival the processing power of desktop computers from a decade ago.

Similarly to my old article series, this book will teach you ML algorithms from first principles. We'll focus on developing the concepts and implementations of ML without straying too far into the mathematical description. Unlike the old series, however, the JS landscape of today actually has ML libraries and implementations available. At times, therefore, we will write our own algorithms and at other times we will rely on existing libraries.

The goal of this book is not to teach you every ML algorithm that exists, nor to make you an expert in any one algorithm. Instead, my goal is to teach you, an experienced web developer, what you need to know to get started and get comfortable with ML so that you can begin your own educational journey with confidence.

Who this book is for

This book is for experienced JS developers who want to get started with ML. In general, I will assume that you are a competent JS developer with little to no experience with ML or mathematics beyond what you would learn in high school. In terms of JS abilities, you should already be familiar with the basic concepts of algorithms, modular code, and data transformations. I also assume that you can read JS code and understand both the intent and the mechanism.

This book is not intended for novice programmers, though you still may be able to get something out of it. This book is also not intended for readers who are already comfortable with ML, as most of the content will be familiar to you—though there may be some small nuggets of wisdom that could be helpful to you in these pages.

This book is perfect for you if you want to step into the ML landscape but don't know where to start in a vast and confusing ecosystem. Whether you're looking to make a shift in your career or simply learning something new, I believe you will find this book helpful.

What this book covers

Chapter 1, *Exploring the Potential of JavaScript*, takes a look at the JavaScript programming language, its history, ecosystem, and applicability to ML problems.

Chapter 2, *Data Exploration*, discusses the data that underlies and powers every ML algorithm, and the various things you can do to preprocess and prepare your data for an ML application.

Chapter 3, *A Tour of Machine Learning Algorithms*, takes you on a brief tour of the ML landscape, partitioning it into categories and families of algorithms, much as the gridlines on a map help you navigate unfamiliar terrain.

Chapter 4, *Grouping with Clustering Algorithms*, implements our first ML algorithms, with a focus on clustering algorithms that automatically discover and identify patterns within data in order to group similar items together.

Chapter 5, *Classification Algorithms*, discusses a broad family of ML algorithms that are used to automatically classify data points with one or more labels, such as spam/not spam, positive or negative sentiment, or any number of arbitrary categories.

Chapter 6, *Association Rule Algorithms*, looks at several algorithms used to make associations between data points based on frequency of co-occurrence, such as products that are often bought together on e-commerce stores.

Chapter 7, *Forecasting with Regression Algorithms*, looks at time series data, such as server load or stock prices, and discusses various algorithms that can be used to analyze patterns and make predictions for the future.

Chapter 8, *Artificial Neural Network Algorithms*, teaches you the foundations of neural networks, including their core concepts, architecture, training algorithms, and implementations.

Chapter 9, *Deep Neural Networks*, digs deeper into neural networks and explores various exotic topologies that can solve problems such as image recognition, computer vision, speech recognition, and language modeling.

Chapter 10, *Natural Language Processing in Practice*, discusses the overlap of natural language processing with ML. You learn several common techniques and tactics that you can use when applying machine learning to natural language tasks.

Chapter 11, *Using Machine Learning in Real-Time Applications*, discusses various practical approaches to deploying ML applications on production environments, with a particular focus on the data pipeline process.

Chapter 12, *Choosing the Best Algorithm for Your Application*, goes back to the basics and discusses the things you must consider in the first stages of a ML project, with a particular focus on choosing the best algorithm or set of algorithms for a given application.

To get the most out of this book

If you haven't programmed in JS in a while, it would be best for you to give yourself a refresher before you get started. In particular, the examples in this book will use ES6/ES2015 syntax; I will give you a tour of the new syntax in the first chapter, but you may also want to become familiar with it on your own.

If you don't have Node.js installed yet, you'll want to install that now. The examples in this book were written using Node.js version 9.6.0, though I expect most of the examples to work for any Node.js version greater than 8 and for Node.js version 10 as well.

You will not need much education in math to get through this book, but I assume that you paid attention to your high school math courses. If you don't remember much probability, statistics, or algebra, you may want to refresh yourself on those topics, as they are prevalent in ML. While I have tried my best to avoid deep dives into advanced mathematical concepts, I will indeed have to present some in this book so that you at least get a level of comfort with math and the willingness to research some select mathematical concepts on your own.

Download the example code files

You can download the example code files for this book from your account at
`www.packtpub.com`. If you purchased this book elsewhere, you can visit
`www.packtpub.com/support` and register to have the files emailed directly to you.

You can download the code files by following these steps:

1. Log in or register at `www.packtpub.com`.
2. Select the **SUPPORT** tab.
3. Click on **Code Downloads & Errata**.
4. Enter the name of the book in the **Search** box and follow the onscreen
   instructions.

Once the file is downloaded, please make sure that you unzip or extract the folder using the
latest version of:

- WinRAR/7-Zip for Windows
- Zipeg/iZip/UnRarX for Mac
- 7-Zip/PeaZip for Linux

The code bundle for the book is also hosted on GitHub at `https://github.com/`
`PacktPublishing/Hands-On-Machine-Learning-with-JavaScript`. In case there's an
update to the code, it will be updated on the existing GitHub repository.

We also have other code bundles from our rich catalog of books and videos available
at `https://github.com/PacktPublishing/`. Check them out!

Download the color images

We also provide a PDF file that has color images of the screenshots/diagrams used in this
book. You can download it here: `https://www.packtpub.com/sites/default/files/`
`downloads/HandsOnMachineLearningwithJavaScript_ColorImages.pdf`.

Conventions used

There are a number of text conventions used throughout this book.

`CodeInText`: Indicates code words in text, database table names, folder names, filenames, file extensions, pathnames, dummy URLs, user input, and Twitter handles. Here is an example: "Use the command line, your favorite IDE, or your file browser to create a directory somewhere on your machine called `MLinJSBook`, with a subdirectory called `Ch1-Ex1`."

A block of code is set as follows:

```
var items = [1, 2, 3 ];
for (var index in items) {
var item = items[index];
...
  }
```

When we wish to draw your attention to a particular part of a code block, the relevant lines or items are set in bold:

```
['landscape.jpeg', 'lily.jpeg', 'waterlilies.jpeg'].forEach(filename => {
  console.log("Decolorizing " + filename + '...');
  decolorize('./files/' + filename)
    .then(() => console.log(filename + " decolorized"));
});
```

Any command-line input or output is written as follows:

```
$ node --version
V9.4.0
```

Bold: Indicates a new term, an important word, or words that you see onscreen.

 Warnings or important notes appear like this.

 Tips and tricks appear like this.

Get in touch

Feedback from our readers is always welcome.

General feedback: Email `feedback@packtpub.com` and mention the book title in the subject of your message. If you have questions about any aspect of this book, please email us at `questions@packtpub.com`.

Errata: Although we have taken every care to ensure the accuracy of our content, mistakes do happen. If you have found a mistake in this book, we would be grateful if you would report this to us. Please visit `www.packtpub.com/submit-errata`, selecting your book, clicking on the Errata Submission Form link, and entering the details.

Piracy: If you come across any illegal copies of our works in any form on the Internet, we would be grateful if you would provide us with the location address or website name. Please contact us at `copyright@packtpub.com` with a link to the material.

If you are interested in becoming an author: If there is a topic that you have expertise in and you are interested in either writing or contributing to a book, please visit `authors.packtpub.com`.

Reviews

Please leave a review. Once you have read and used this book, why not leave a review on the site that you purchased it from? Potential readers can then see and use your unbiased opinion to make purchase decisions, we at Packt can understand what you think about our products, and our authors can see your feedback on their book. Thank you!

For more information about Packt, please visit `packtpub.com`.

Exploring the Potential of JavaScript

1

We will cover the following topics in this chapter:

- Why JavaScript?
- Why machine learning, why now?
- Advantages and challenges of JavaScript
- The CommonJS initiative
- Node.js
- TypeScript language
- Improvements in ES6
- Preparing the development environment

Why JavaScript?

I started writing about **machine learning (ML)** in JavaScript in 2010. At the time, Node.js was brand new and JavaScript was just beginning to come into its own as a language. For much of the history of the internet, JavaScript had been seen as a toy language, used to create simple dynamic interactions on web pages.

The perception of JavaScript began to change in 2005 with the release of the **Prototype JavaScript Framework**, which aimed to simplify AJAX requests and help developers deal with cross-browser `XMLHttpRequest`. The Prototype Framework also introduced the familiar dollar function as an alias for `document.getElementById` : `$("myId")`, for instance.

One year later, John Resig released the wildly popular jQuery library. At the time of writing, `w3techs.com` reports that jQuery is used on 96% of websites whose JavaScript libraries are known to them (which accounts for 73% of all websites). jQuery worked to make common JavaScript operations cross-browser compatible and easy to achieve, bringing important tools such as AJAX requests, **Document Object Model (DOM)** traversal and manipulation, and animations to web developers everywhere.

Then, in 2008, the Chrome web browser and the Chrome V8 JavaScript engine were released. Chrome and V8 introduced a marked performance improvement over older browsers: JavaScript was now fast, owing in large part to the V8 engine's innovative just-in-time compiler that builds machine code directly from JavaScript.

JavaScript became more popular as jQuery and Chrome took over the web. Developers historically have never loved JavaScript as a programming language, but with jQuery in the picture, running on a fast and modern browser, it became clear that JavaScript was an underutilized tool and capable of much more than it had been used for previously.

In 2009, the JavaScript developer community decided to break JavaScript free from the web browser environment. The CommonJS initiative was launched early that year, and Node.js followed after a few months. CommonJS modules' goal was to develop a standard library and improve the ecosystem for JavaScript so that it could be used outside of the browser environment. As part of this effort, CommonJS standardized a module-loading interface that allowed developers to build libraries that they could share with others.

The release of Node.js in mid-2009 rocked the JavaScript world by giving JavaScript developers a new paradigm to consider: JavaScript as a server-side language. Packing the Chrome V8 engine under the hood made Node.js surprisingly fast, though the V8 engine doesn't deserve all of the credit for the software's performance. The Node.js instance uses an event loop to process requests, so it can handle a large number of concurrent connections despite being single-threaded.

The novelty of JavaScript on the server, its surprising performance, and the early introduction of the npm registry which let developers publish and discover modules, attracted thousands of developers. The standard library published with Node.js was primarily low-level I/O APIs, and developers raced to see who could publish the first good HTTP request wrapper, the first easy-to-use HTTP server, the first high-level image processing library, and so on. The rapid early growth of the JavaScript ecosystem generated confidence in developers who were reluctant to adopt the new technology. JavaScript, for the first time, was being seen as a real programming language, rather than just something we tolerated because of web browsers.

While JavaScript as a programming platform was maturing, the Python community was busy working on ML, in part inspired by Google's success in the market. The foundational and very popular number processing library, NumPy, was released in 2006, though it had existed in one form or another for a decade prior. A ML library called **scikit-learn** was released in 2010, and that was the moment I decided to start teaching ML to JavaScript developers.

The popularity of ML in Python and the ease of building and training models with tools, such as scikit-learn, astounded me and many others. In my eyes, the surge in popularity caused an ML bubble; because models were so easy to build and run, I found that many developers didn't actually understand the mechanics of the algorithms and techniques they were using. Many developers lamented their underperforming models, not understanding that they themselves were the weak link in the chain.

Machine learning at the time had been seen as mystical, magical, academic, accessible only to a select few geniuses, and only accessible to Python developers. I felt differently. Machine learning is just a category of algorithms with no magic involved. Most of the algorithms are actually easy to understand and reason about!

Rather than showing developers how to import Bayes in Python, I wanted to show developers how to build the algorithms from scratch, an important step in building intuition. I also wanted my students to largely ignore the popular Python libraries that existed at the time, because I wanted to reinforce the notion that ML algorithms can be written in any language and Python is not required.

I chose JavaScript as my teaching platform. To be perfectly honest, I chose JavaScript in part because it was considered a *bad* language by many at that time. My message was *machine learning is easy, you can even do it in JavaScript!* Fortunately for me, Node.js and JavaScript were both becoming incredibly popular, and my early articles on ML in JavaScript were read by over a million curious developers in the following years.

I also chose JavaScript in part because I didn't want ML to be seen as a tool only accessible to academics, or computer scientists, or even college graduates. I believed, and still believe, that these algorithms can be thoroughly understood by any competent developer, given enough practice and repetition. I chose JavaScript because it allowed me to reach a new audience of frontend and full-stack web developers, many of whom were self-taught or had never studied computer science formally. If the goal was to demystify and democratize the field of ML, I felt it was much better to reach the web developer community rather than the backend Python programmer community, which as a whole was already more comfortable with ML at the time.

Python has always been and remains the language of choice for ML, in part due to the maturity of the language, in part due to the maturity of the ecosystem, and in part due to the positive feedback loop of early ML efforts in Python. Recent developments in the JavaScript world, however, are making JavaScript more attractive to ML projects. I think we will see a major ML renaissance in JavaScript within a few years, especially as laptops and mobile devices become ever more powerful and JavaScript itself surges in popularity.

Why machine learning, why now?

Several ML techniques have been around since before computers themselves, but many of the modern ML algorithms we use today were discovered all the way back in the 1970s and 1980s. They were interesting but not practical then, and were confined largely to academia.

What changed to give ML its massive rise in popularity? First, computers finally got fast enough to run non-trivial neural networks and large ML models. And then two things happened: Google and **Amazon Web Services** (**AWS**). Google proved the value of ML to the market in a very visible manner, and then AWS made scalable computing and storage resources readily available (AWS democratized it and created new competition).

Google PageRank, the ML algorithm powering Google Search, taught us all about business applications of ML. Sergei and Larry, the founders of Google, told the world that the massive success of their search engine and resultant advertising business was the PageRank algorithm: a relatively straightforward linear algebra equation, with a massive matrix.

 Note that neural networks are also relatively straightforward linear algebra equations with a massive matrix.

That was ML in all its glory; big data giving big insight which translates into a major market success. This got the world economically interested in ML.

AWS, with the launch of EC2 and hourly billing, democratized compute resources. Researchers and early-stage start ups were now able to launch large computing clusters quickly, train their models, and scale the cluster back down, avoiding the need for large capital expenditures on beefy servers. This created new competition and an inaugural generation of ML-focused start ups, products, and initiatives.

ML has recently had another surge in popularity, both in the developer and business communities. The first generation of ML-focused start ups and products have now come to maturity and are proving the value of ML in the market, and in many cases these companies are closing in on or have overtaken their competitors. The desire of companies to remain competitive in their market drove up the demand for ML solutions.

The late 2015 introduction of Google's neural network library, **TensorFlow**, energized developers by democratizing neural networks much in the same way that EC2 democratized computing power. Additionally, those first-generation start ups that focused on developers have also come to maturity, and now we can make a simple API request to AWS or **Google Cloud Platform (GCP)** that runs an entire pretrained **Convolutional Neural Network (CNN)** on an image, and tells me if I'm looking at a cat, a woman, a handbag, a car, or all four at once.

As ML is democratized it will slowly lose its competitive value, that is, companies will no longer be able to use ML to jump leaps and bounds ahead of the competition, because their competition will also be using ML. Everyone in the field is now using the same algorithms, and competition becomes a data war. If we want to keep competing on technology, if we want to find the next 10x improvement, then we'll either need to wait for, or preferably cause, the next big technological breakthrough.

If ML had not been such a success in the market, that would have been the end of the story. All the important algorithms would be known to all, and the fight would move to who can gather the best data, put walls around their garden, or exploit their ecosystem the best.

But introducing a tool such as TensorFlow into the market changed all of that. Now, neural networks have been democratized. It's surprisingly easy to build a model, train and run it on a GPU, and generate real results. The academic fog surrounding neural networks has been lifted, and now tens of thousands of developers are playing around with techniques, experimenting, and refining. This will launch a second major wave of ML popularity, particularly focused on neural networks. The next generation of ML and neural network-focused start ups and products is being born right now, and when they come to maturity in a few years, we should see a number of significant breakthroughs, as well as breakaway companies.

Each new market success we see will create demand for ML developers. The increase of the talent pool and democratization of technology causes technology breakthroughs. Each new technology breakthrough hits the market and creates new market successes, and the cycle will continue while the field itself advances at an accelerating pace. I think, for purely economic reasons, that we really are headed for an **artificial intelligence (AI)** boom.

Advantages and challenges of JavaScript

Despite my optimism towards the future of ML in JavaScript, most developers today would still choose Python for their new projects, and nearly all large-scale production systems are developed in Python or other languages more typical to ML.

JavaScript, like any other tool, has its advantages and disadvantages. Much of the historic criticism of JavaScript has focused on a few common themes: strange behavior in type coercion, the prototypical object-oriented model, difficulty organizing large codebases, and managing deeply nested asynchronous function calls with what many developers call *callback hell*. Fortunately, most of these historic gripes have been resolved by the introduction of **ES6**, that is, **ECMAScript 2015**, a recent update to the JavaScript syntax.

Despite the recent language improvements, most developers would still advise against using JavaScript for ML for one reason: the ecosystem. The Python ecosystem for ML is so mature and rich that it's difficult to justify choosing any other ecosystem. But this logic is self-fulfilling and self-defeating; we need brave individuals to take the leap and work on real ML problems if we want JavaScript's ecosystem to mature. Fortunately, JavaScript has been the most popular programming language on GitHub for a few years running, and is growing in popularity by almost every metric.

There are some advantages to using JavaScript for ML. Its popularity is one; while ML in JavaScript is not very popular at the moment, the language itself is. As demand for ML applications rises, and as hardware becomes faster and cheaper, it's only natural for ML to become more prevalent in the JavaScript world. There are tons of resources available for learning JavaScript in general, maintaining Node.js servers, and deploying JavaScript applications. The **Node Package Manager** (**npm**) ecosystem is also large and still growing, and while there aren't many very mature ML packages available, there are a number of well built, useful tools out there that will come to maturity soon.

Another advantage to using JavaScript is the universality of the language. The modern web browser is essentially a portable application platform which allows you to run your code, basically without modification, on nearly any device. Tools like **electron** (while considered by many to be bloated) allow developers to quickly develop and deploy downloadable desktop applications to any operating system. Node.js lets you run your code in a server environment. React Native brings your JavaScript code to the native mobile application environment, and may eventually allow you to develop desktop applications as well. JavaScript is no longer confined to just dynamic web interactions, it's now a general-purpose, cross-platform programming language.

Finally, using JavaScript makes ML accessible to web and frontend developers, a group that historically has been left out of the ML discussion. Server-side applications are typically preferred for ML tools, since the servers are where the computing power is. That fact has historically made it difficult for web developers to get into the ML game, but as hardware improves, even complex ML models can be run on the client, whether it's the desktop or the mobile browser.

If web developers, frontend developers, and JavaScript developers all start learning about ML today, that same community will be in a position to improve the ML tools available to us all tomorrow. If we take these technologies and democratize them, expose as many people as possible to the concepts behind ML, we will ultimately elevate the community and seed the next generation of ML researchers.

The CommonJS initiative

In 2009, a Mozilla engineer named Kevin Dangoor realized that server-side JavaScript needed a lot of help in order to be useful. The concept of server-side JavaScript had already existed, but wasn't very popular due to a number of limitations, particularly in terms of the JavaScript ecosystem.

In a blog post written in January of 2009, Dangoor cited a few examples of where JavaScript needed some help. He wrote that the JavaScript ecosystem would need a standard library and standard interfaces for things such as file and database access. Additionally, the JavaScript environment needed a way to package, publish, and install libraries and dependencies for others to use, and also needed a package repository to host all of the aforementioned.

Out of all of this came the **CommonJS** initiative, whose most notable contribution to the JavaScript ecosystem is the CommonJS module format. If you've done any work with Node.js, you're probably already familiar with CommonJS: your `package.json` file is written in the CommonJS modules package specification format, and writing code like `var app = require('./app.js')` in one file with `module.exports = App` in `app.js` is using the CommonJS module specification.

The standardization of modules and packages paved the way for a significant boost in JavaScript popularity. Developers were now able to use modules to write complex applications spanning many files, without polluting the global namespace. Package and library developers were able to build and publish new libraries of higher levels of abstraction than JavaScript's standard library. Node.js and npm would shortly grab onto these concepts and build a major ecosystem around package sharing.

Node.js

The release of Node.js in 2009 is possibly the single most important moment in JavaScript's history, though it would not have been possible without the release of the Chrome browser and Chrome's V8 JavaScript engine in the previous year.

Those readers who remember the launch of Chrome also recognize why Chrome dominated the browser wars: Chrome was fast, it was minimalist, it was modern, it was easy to develop for, and JavaScript itself ran much faster on Chrome than on other browsers.

Behind Chrome is the open source Chromium project, which in turn developed the **V8** JavaScript engine. The innovation that V8 brought to the JavaScript world was its new execution model: instead of interpreting JavaScript in real time, V8 contains a JIT compiler that turns JavaScript directly into native machine code. This gambit paid off, and the combined effect of its stellar performance and its open source status led others to co-opt V8 for their own purposes.

Node.js took the V8 JavaScript engine, added an event-driven architecture around it, and added a low-level I/O API for disk and file access. The event-driven architecture turned out to be a critical decision. Other server-side languages and technologies, such as PHP, typically used a thread pool to manage concurrent requests, with each thread itself blocking while processing the request. Node.js is a single-threaded process, but using an event loop avoids blocking operations and instead favors asynchronous, callback-driven logic. While the single-threaded nature of Node.js is considered by many to be a drawback, Node.js was still able to handle many concurrent requests with good performance, and that was enough to bring developers to the platform.

A few months later, the npm project was released. Building on top of the foundational work that CommonJS achieved, npm allowed package developers to publish their modules to a centralized registry (called the **npm registry**), and allowed package consumers to install and maintain dependencies with the npm command-line tool.

Node.js likely would not have broken into the mainstream if not for npm. The Node.js server itself provided the JavaScript engine, the event loop, and a few low-level APIs, but as developers work on bigger projects they tend to want higher-level abstractions. When making HTTP requests or reading files from disk, developers don't always want to have to worry about binary data, writing headers, and other low-level issues. The npm and the npm registry let the developer community write and share their own high-level abstractions in the form of modules other developers could simply install and `require()`.

Unlike other programming languages which typically have high-level abstractions built in, Node.js was allowed to focus on providing the low-level building blocks and the community took care of the rest. The community stepped up by building excellent abstractions such as the `Express.js` web application framework, the `Sequelize ORM`, and hundreds of thousands of other libraries ready to be used after just a simple `npm install` command.

With the advent of Node.js, JavaScript developers with no prior server-side language knowledge were now able to build entire full-stack applications. The frontend code and backend code could now be written in the same language, by the same developers.

Ambitious developers were now building entire applications in JavaScript, though they ran into a few issues and solutions along the way. Single-page applications fully written in JavaScript became popular, but also became difficult to template and organize. The community responded by building frameworks such as **Backbone.js** (the spiritual predecessor to frameworks such as Angular and React), **RequireJS** (a CommonJS and AMD module loader), and templating languages such as **Mustache** (a spiritual predecessor to JSX).

When developers ran into issues with SEO on their single-page applications, they invented the concept of **isomorphic applications**, or codes that could be rendered both server side (so that web spiders could index the content) and client side (to keep the application fast and JavaScript-powered). This led to the invention of more JavaScript frameworks such as **MeteorJS**.

Eventually, JavaScript developers building single-page applications realized that often, their server-side and database requirements were lightweight, requiring just authentication, and data storage, and retrieval. This led to the development of *serverless* technologies or **database-as-a-service (DBaaS)** platforms such as **Firebase**, which in turn laid out a path for mobile JavaScript applications to become popular. The Cordova/PhoneGap project appeared around the same time, allowing developers to wrap their JavaScript code in a native iOS or Android WebView component and deploy their JavaScript applications to the mobile app stores.

For our purposes throughout this book, we'll be relying on Node.js and npm very heavily. Most of the examples in this book will use ML packages available on npm.

TypeScript language

The development and sharing of new packages on npm was not the only result of JavaScript's popularity. JavaScript's increasing usage as a primary programming language caused many developers to lament the lack of IDE and language tooling support. Historically, IDEs were more popular with developers of compiled and statically-typed languages such as C and Java, as it's easier to parse and statically analyze those types of languages. It wasn't until recently that great IDEs started appearing for languages such as JavaScript and PHP, while Java has had IDEs geared towards it for many years.

Microsoft wanted better tooling and support for their large-scale JavaScript projects, but there were a few issues with the JavaScript language itself that got in the way. In particular, JavaScript's dynamic typing (the fact that `var number` could start its life as the integer **5**, but then be assigned to an object later) precludes using static analysis tools to ensure type safety, and also makes it difficult for an IDE to find the correct variable or object to autocomplete with. Additionally, Microsoft wanted a class-based object-oriented paradigm with interfaces and contracts, but JavaScript's object-oriented programming paradigm was based on **prototypes**, not classes.

Microsoft therefore invented the TypeScript language in order to support large-scale JavaScript development efforts. TypeScript introduced classes, interfaces, and static typing to the language. Unlike Google's Dart, Microsoft made sure TypeScript would always be a strict superset of JavaScript, meaning that all valid JavaScript is also valid TypeScript. The TypeScript compiler does static type checking at compile time, helping developers catch errors early. Support for static typing also helps IDEs interpret code more accurately, making for a nicer developer experience.

Several of TypeScript's early improvements to the JavaScript language have been made irrelevant by ECMAScript 2015, or what we call ES6. For instance, TypeScript's module loader, class syntax, and arrow function syntax have been subsumed by ES6, and TypeScript now simply uses the ES6 versions of those constructs; however, TypeScript still brings static typing to JavaScript, which ES6 wasn't able to accomplish.

I bring up TypeScript here because, while we won't be using TypeScript in the examples in this book, some of the examples of ML libraries we examine here are written in TypeScript.

For instance, one example found on the `deeplearn.js` tutorials page shows code that looks like the following:

```
const graph = new Graph();
// Make a new input in the graph, called 'x', with shape [] (a Scalar).
const x: Tensor = graph.placeholder('x', []);
// Make new variables in the graph, 'a', 'b', 'c' with shape [] and
```

```
    random
// initial values.
const a: Tensor = graph.variable('a', Scalar.new(Math.random()));
const b: Tensor = graph.variable('b', Scalar.new(Math.random()));
const c: Tensor = graph.variable('c', Scalar.new(Math.random()));
```

The syntax looks like ES6 JavaScript except for the new colon notation seen in `const x:
Tensor = ...` : this code is telling the TypeScript compiler that the `const x` must be an
instance of the `Tensor` class. When TypeScript compiles this code, it first checks that
everywhere x is used expects a `Tensor` (it will throw an error if not), and then it simply
discards the type information when compiling to JavaScript. Converting the preceding
TypeScript code to JavaScript is as simple as removing the colon and the `Tensor` keyword
from the variable definition.

You are welcome to use TypeScript in your own examples as you follow along with this
book, however, you will have to update the build process that we set up later to support
TypeScript.

Improvements in ES6

The ECMAScript committee, which defines the specification for the JavaScript language
itself, released a new specification called ECMAScript 6/ECMAScript 2015 in June 2015. The
new standard, called **ES6** for short, was a major revision of the JavaScript programming
language and added a number of new paradigms intended to make development of
JavaScript programs easier.

While ECMAScript defines the specification for the JavaScript language, the actual
implementation of the language is dependent on the browser vendors and the maintainers
of the various JavaScript engines. ES6 by itself is only a guideline, and because the browser
vendors each have their own timeline for implementing new language features, the
JavaScript language and the JavaScript implementations diverged slightly. Features defined
by ES6, such as classes, were not available in the major browsers, but developers wanted to
use them anyway.

Enter **Babel**, the JavaScript transpiler. Babel can read and parse different JavaScript flavors
(such as ES6, ES7, ES8, and React JSX) and convert it or compile it into browser-standard
ES5. Even today, the entirety of ES6 has not yet been implemented by the browser vendors,
so Babel remains an essential tool for developers wishing to write ES6 code.

The examples in this book will use ES6. If you're not yet familiar with the newer syntax,
here are a few of the major features you'll see used throughout this book.

Let and const

In ES5 JavaScript, we use the `var` keyword to define variables. In most cases, `var` can simply be replaced with `let`, with the major difference between the two constructs being the scoping of the variable with respect to blocks. The following example from **MDN web docs**, or previously **Mozilla Developer Network** (`https://developer.mozilla.org/en-US/docs/Web/JavaScript/Reference/Statements/let`), demonstrates the subtle difference between the two:

```
function varTest() {
  var x = 1;
  if (true) {
    var x = 2;  // same variable!
    console.log(x);  // 2
  }
  console.log(x);  // 2
}

function letTest() {
  let x = 1;
  if (true) {
    let x = 2;  // different variable
    console.log(x);  // 2
  }
  console.log(x);  // 1
}
```

So, while you must use additional caution in cases like the preceding one, in most cases you can simply replace `var` with `let`.

The `const` keyword, unlike `let`, defines a variable as a constant; that is, you cannot reassign a variable initialized with `const` at a later date. For example, the following code causes an error with a message similar to `invalid assignment to const a`:

```
const a = 1;
a = 2;
```

On the other hand the same code, using `var` or `let` to define a, would run successfully.

Note that if a is an object, you are allowed to modify object properties of a.

The following code will run successfully:

```
const obj = {};
obj.name = 'My Object';
```

However, attempting to redefine objects such as in `obj = {name: "other object"}` would cause an error.

I find that in most programming contexts, `const` is typically more appropriate than `let`, as most variables you use never need to be redefined. My recommendation is to use `const` as much as you can, and use `let` only when you have a reason to redefine the variable later.

Classes

One very welcome change in ES6 is the addition of classes and class inheritance. Previously, object-oriented programming in JavaScript required prototypical inheritance, which many developers found unintuitive, like the following ES5 example:

```
var Automobile = function(weight, speed) {
    this.weight = weight;
    this.speed = speed;
}
Automobile.prototype.accelerate = function(extraSpeed) {
    this.speed += extraSpeed;
}
var RaceCar = function (weight, speed, boost) {
    Automobile.call(this, weight, speed);
    this.boost = boost;
}
RaceCar.prototype = Object.create(Automobile.prototype);
RaceCar.prototype.constructor = RaceCar;
RaceCar.prototype.accelerate = function(extraSpeed) {
  this.speed += extraSpeed + this.boost;
}
```

In the preceding code, extending an object requires calling the parent class in the child's `constructor` function, creating a clone of the parent's prototype object, and overriding the parent's prototype constructor with the child's prototype constructor. These steps were seen as unintuitive and burdensome by most developers.

Using ES6 classes, however, the code will look like this:

```
class Automobile {
 constructor(weight, speed) {
   this.weight = weight;
   this.speeed = speed;
 }
 accelerate(extraSpeed) {
   this.speed += extraSpeed;
 }
}
class RaceCar extends Automobile {
 constructor(weight, speed, boost) {
   super(weight, speed);
   this.boost = boost;
 }
 accelerate(extraSpeed) {
   this.speed += extraSpeed + this.boost;
 }
}
```

The preceding syntax is more in line with what we'd expect from object-oriented programming, and also makes inheritance much simpler.

It's important to note that under the hood, ES6 classes still use JavaScript's prototypical inheritance paradigm. Classes are just syntactic sugar on top of the existing system, so there is no significant difference between these two approaches other than clean code.

Module imports

ES6 also defines a module import and export interface. With the older CommonJS approach, modules are exported using the `modules.export` construct, and modules are imported with the `require(filename)` function. The ES6 approach looks a little different. In one file, define and export a class, as shown in the following code:

```
Class Automobile {
...
}
export default Automobile
```

And in another file, import the class, as shown in the following code:

```
import Automobile from './classes/automobile.js';
const myCar = new Automobile();
```

At present, Babel compiles ES6 modules to the same format as CommonJS modules, so you can use either the ES6 modules syntax or the CommonJS modules syntax if you're using Babel.

Arrow functions

One quirky, useful, but somewhat annoying aspect of ES5 JavaScript is its heavy use of callbacks that run asynchronously. You are probably intimately familiar with jQuery code that looks something like this:

```
$("#link").click(function() {
  var $self = $(this);
  doSomethingAsync(1000, function(resp) {
    $self.addClass("wasFaded");
    var processedItems = resp.map(function(item) {
      return processItem(item);
    });
    return shipItems(processedItems);
  });
});
```

We're forced to create a variable called $self because the original this context is lost in our inner anonymous function. We also have a lot of boilerplate and difficult-to-read code due to needing to create three separate anonymous functions.

Arrow function syntax is both syntactic sugar that helps us write anonymous functions with a shorter syntax, and also a functional update that preserves the context of this inside an arrow function.

For instance, the preceding code may be written in ES6 as follows:

```
$("#link").click(function() {
  dozsSomethingAsync(1000, resp => {
    $(this).addClass("wasFaded");
    const processedItems = resp.map(item => processItem(Item));
    return shipItems(processedItems);
  });
});
```

You can see in the preceding code that we no longer need a $self variable to preserve this, and our call to .map is much simpler, no longer requiring the function keyword, parentheses, curly braces, or a return statement.

Now let's look at some equivalent functions. Let's look at the following code:

```
const double = function(number) {
  return number * 2;
}
```

The preceding code would be similar to:

```
const double = number => number * 2;
// Is equal to:
const double = (number) => { return number * 2; }
```

In the aforementioned examples, we can omit the parentheses around the number parameter because the function only requires one parameter. If the function required two parameters, we would be required to add parentheses as in the next example. Additionally, if the body of our function only requires one line, we can omit the function body curly braces and omit the return statement.

Let's look at another equivalence, with multiple parameters, as shown in the following code:

```
const sorted = names.sort(function (a, b) {
  return a.localeCompare(b);
});
```

The preceding code would be similar to:

```
const sorted = names.sort((a, b) => a.localeCompare(b));
```

I find that arrow functions make themselves most useful in situations like the preceding one, when you're doing data transformations, especially where using Array.map, Array.filter, Array.reduce, and Array.sort calls with straightforward function bodies. Arrow functions are less useful in jQuery because of jQuery's tendency to give you data using the this context, which you don't receive with anonymous arrow functions.

Object literals

ES6 makes some improvements to object literals. There are several improvements, but the one you'll see most is the implicit naming of object properties. In ES5 it would be as follows:

```
var name = 'Burak';
var title = 'Author';
var object = {name: name, title: title};
```

In ES6, if the property name and the variable name are the same as the preceding one, you can simplify it to the following:

```
const name = 'Burak';
const title = 'Author';
const object = {name, title};
```

Additionally, ES6 introduces the object spread operator, which simplifies shallow object merges. For instance, take a look at the following code in ES5:

```
function combinePreferences(userPreferences) {
 var defaultPreferences = {size: 'large', mode: 'view'};
 return Object.assign({}, defaultPreferences, userPreferences);
}
```

The preceding code will create a new object from `defaultPreferences`, and merge in properties from `userPreferences`. Passing an empty object to the `Object.assign` instance first parameter ensures that we create a new object rather than overwriting `defaultPreferences` (which isn't an issue in the preceding example, but is an issue in real-life use cases).

And now, let's take a look at the same in ES6:

```
function combinePreferences(userPreferences) {
 var defaultPreferences = {size: 'large', mode: 'view'};
 return {...defaultPreferences, ...userPreferences};
}
```

This approach does the same as the ES5 example, but is quicker and easier to read in my opinion than the `Object.assign` method. Developers familiar with React and Redux, for instance, often use the object spread operator when managing reducer state operations.

The for...of function

The `for` loops over arrays in ES5 are often achieved using the `for (index in array)` syntax, which looks something like this:

```
var items = [1, 2, 3 ];
for (var index in items) {
var item = items[index];
...
  }
```

And ES6 adds the `for...of` syntax, which saves you a step, as you can see from the following code:

```
const items = [1, 2, 3 ];
for (const item of items) {
  ...
  }
```

Promises

Promises, in one form or another, have been available in JavaScript for a while. All jQuery users are familiar with the idea. A **promise** is a reference to a variable that is generated asynchronously and may become available in the future.

The ES5 way of doing things, if you weren't already using some sort of third-party promise library or jQuery's deferred's, was to accept a callback function to an asynchronous method and run the callback upon successful completion, as shown in the following code:

```
function updateUser(user, settings, onComplete, onError) {
  makeAsyncApiRequest(user, settings, function(response) {
    if (response.isValid()) {
      onComplete(response.getBody());
    } else {
      onError(response.getError())
    }
  });
}
updateUser(user, settings, function(body) { ... }, function(error) { ...
});
```

In ES6, you may return a `Promise` which encapsulates the asynchronous request and either gets resolved or rejected, as shown in the following code:

```
function updateUser(user, settings) {
  return new Promise((resolve, reject) => {
    makeAsyncApiRequest(user, settings, function(response) {
      if (response.isValid()) {
        resolve(response.getBody());
      } else {
        reject(response.getError())
      }
    });
  });
}
updateUser(user, settings)
  .then(
    body => { ... },
    error => { ... }
  );
```

The real power of promises is that they can be passed around as objects, and promise handlers can be chained.

The async/await functions

The `async` and `await` keywords are not an ES6 feature but rather an ES8 feature. While promises bring huge improvements to the way we deal with asynchronous calls, promises also are susceptible to lots of method chaining, and in some cases force us to use asynchronous paradigms when we really just want to write a function that acts asynchronously but reads as if it were a synchronous function.

Now let's take a look at the following example from MDN's asynchronous function reference page (`https://developer.mozilla.org/en-US/docs/Web/JavaScript/Reference/Statements/async_function`):

```
function resolveAfter2Seconds() {
  return new Promise(resolve => {
    setTimeout(() => {
      resolve('resolved');
    }, 2000);
  });
}
async function asyncCall() {
  console.log('calling');
```

```
    var result = await resolveAfter2Seconds();
    console.log(result);
    // expected output: "resolved"
}
asyncCall();
```

The `resolveAfter2Seconds` function is a normal JavaScript function that returns an ES6 promise. The magic is in the `asyncCall` function, which is marked by the `async` keyword. Inside `asyncCall`, we invoke `resolveAfter2Seconds` with the `await` keyword, rather than using the more familiar promise `.then(result =>` `console.log(result))` construct we'd normally use in ES6. The `await` keyword makes our `async` function wait for the promise to resolve before continuing, and returns the result of the `Promise` directly. In this manner, `async/await` can convert asynchronous functions that use promises to read like synchronous functions, which should help keep deeply nested promise calls and asynchronous function stats neat and easy to read.

The `async` and `await` features are part of ES8, not ES6, so when we set up Babel in a few minutes we'll need to be sure to include all new versions of EMCAScript in our configuration, not just ES6.

Preparing the development environment

The examples in this book will use both the web browser environment and the Node.js environment. While Node.js Version 8 and higher has support for ES6+, not all browser vendors have complete support yet for ES6+ features, and we will therefore be using Babel to transpile all of our code regardless.

This book will try its best to use the same project structure for all examples, whether they're executed on the command line in Node.js or run in the browser. Because we're attempting to standardize this project structure, not every project will use all of the features we set up in this section.

The tools you will need are:

- Your favorite code editor, such as Vim, Emacs, Sublime Text, or WebStorm
- An up-to-date web browser such as Chrome or Firefox
- Node.js Version 8 LTS or higher; this book will use version 9.4.0 for all examples
- The Yarn package manager (optional; you may use npm instead)
- Various build tools such as Babel and Browserify

Installing Node.js

If you're a macOS user, the easiest way to install Node.js is through a package manager such as **Homebrew** or **MacPorts**. For best compatibility with the examples in this book, install Node.js version 9.4.0 or greater.

Windows users can also use the **Chocolatey** package manager to install Node.js, otherwise you may follow the instructions on the Node.js current download page: https://nodejs. org/en/.

Linux users should be careful if installing Node.js through their distribution's package manager, as the shipped version of Node.js may be a much older version. If your package manager uses a version older than V8, you may either add a repository to your package manager, build from source, or install from binary, as appropriate for your system.

Once you've installed Node.js, ensure that it runs and is the correct version by running `node --version` from the command line. The output will look like the following:

```
$ node --version
V9.4.0
```

This is also a good time to test that npm also works:

```
$ npm --version
5.6.0
```

Optionally installing Yarn

Yarn is a package management tool similar to and compatible with npm, though I find it is faster and easier to work with. If using Homebrew on macOS, you may simply install it using `brew install yarn`; otherwise follow the instructions found on Yarn's installation guide page (https://yarnpkg.com/en/docs/install#windows-stable).

If you want to use npm instead of Yarn, you may; both respect the same format for `package.json`, though they have slightly different syntaxes for commands such as `add`, `require`, and `install`. If you're using npm instead of Yarn, simply replace the commands with the correct function; the package names used will all be the same.

Creating and initializing an example project

Use the command line, your favorite IDE, or your file browser to create a directory somewhere on your machine called `MLinJSBook`, with a subdirectory called `Ch1-Ex1`.

Navigate your command line to the `Ch1-Ex1` folder, and run the command `yarn init`, which like `npm init` will create a `package.json` file and prompt you for basic information. Respond to the prompts, answering appropriately. You will not be publishing this package so the answers aren't too important, however, when prompted for the application's entry point, type in `dist/index.js`.

Next, we need to install a few build tools that we'll use for the majority of our example projects:

- `babel-core`: The Babel transpiler core
- `babel-preset-env`: The Babel parser preset that parses ES6, ES7, and ES8 code
- `browserify`: A JavaScript bundler which can compile multiple files into a single file
- `babelify`: The Babel plugin for Browserify

Install these as development environment requirements by issuing the following command:

```
yarn add -D babel-cli browserify babelify babel-preset-env
```

Creating a Hello World project

To test that everything is building and running, we'll create a very simple two-file Hello World project and add our build script.

First, create two subdirectories under your `Ch1-Ex1` folder: `src` and `dist`. We'll use this convention for all projects: `src` will contain JavaScript source code, `dist` will contain built source code and any additional assets (images, CSS, HTML files, and so on) required by the project.

In the `src` folder, create a file called `greeting.js` with the following code:

```
const greeting = name => 'Hello, ' + name + '!';
export default greeting;
```

Then create another file called `index.js` with the following:

```
import greeting from './greeting';
console.log(greeting(process.argv[2] || 'world'));
```

This small application tests whether we can use basic ES6 syntax and module loading, as well as access command-line arguments given to Node.js.

Next, open up the `package.json` file in `Ch1-Ex1`, and add the following section to the file:

```
"scripts": {
 "build-web": "browserify src/index.js -o dist/index.js -t [ babelify -
  -presets [ env ] ]",
 "build-cli": "browserify src/index.js --node -o dist/index.js -t [
  babelify --presets [ env ] ]",
 "start": "yarn build-cli && node dist/index.js"
},
```

This defines three simple command-line scripts:

- `Build-web` uses Browserify and Babel to compile everything that `src/index.js` touches into a single file called `dist/index.js`
- `Build-cli` is similar to `build-web`, except it also uses Browserify's node option flag; without this option we would not be able to access command-line arguments given to Node.js
- `Start` is intended only for CLI/Node.js examples, and both builds and runs the source code

Your `package.json` file should now look something like the following:

```
{
"name": "Ch1-Ex1",
"version": "0.0.1",
"description": "Chapter one example",
"main": "src/index.js",
"author": "Burak Kanber",
"license": "MIT",
"scripts": {
  "build-web": "browserify src/index.js -o dist/index.js -t [ babelify --
presets [ env ] ]",
  "build-cli": "browserify src/index.js --node -o dist/index.js -t [
babelify --presets [ env ] ]",
  "start": "yarn build-cli && node dist/index.js"
},
"dependencies": {
  "babel-core": "^6.26.0",
```

```
  "babel-preset-env": "^1.6.1",
  "babelify": "^8.0.0",
  "browserify": "^15.1.0"
}}
```

Let's put this simple application through a few tests. First, make sure that `yarn build-cli` works. You should see something like the following:

```
$ yarn build-cli
yarn run v1.3.2
$ browserify src/index.js --node -o dist/index.js -t [ babelify --presets [
env ] ]
Done in 0.59s.
```

At this point, confirm that the `dist/index.js` file has been built, and try running it directly, using the following code:

```
$ node dist/index.js
Hello, world!
```

Also try passing in your name as an argument to the command, using the following code:

```
$ node dist/index.js Burak
Hello, Burak!
```

Now, let's try the `build-web` command, as shown in the following code. Because this command omits the `node` option, we expect that our argument will not work:

```
$ yarn build-web
yarn run v1.3.2
$ browserify src/index.js -o dist/index.js -t [ babelify --presets [ env ]
]
Done in 0.61s.
$ node dist/index.js Burak
Hello, world!
```

Without the `node` option, our arguments are not forwarded to the script, and it defaults to saying `Hello, world!`, which is the expected result here.

Finally, let's test our `yarn start` command, using the following code, to make sure it builds the CLI version of the application and also forwards our command-line arguments, using the following code:

```
$ yarn start "good readers"
yarn run v1.3.2
$ yarn build-cli && node dist/index.js 'good readers'
$ browserify src/index.js --node -o dist/index.js -t [ babelify --presets [
```

```
env ] ]
Hello, good readers!
Done in 1.05s.
```

The `yarn start` command successfully built the CLI version of the application and forwarded our command-line arguments to the program.

We will try our best to use the same structure for each of the examples in this book, however, pay attention to the beginning of each chapter as each example may require some additional setup work.

Summary

In this chapter, we've discussed the important moments of JavaScript's history as applied to ML, starting from the launch of Google (https://www.google.com/) and finishing up at the end of 2017 with the release of Google's deeplearn.js library.

We've discussed some advantages to using JavaScript for machine learning, and also some of the challenges we're facing, particularly in terms of the machine learning ecosystem.

We then took a tour of the most important recent developments in the JavaScript language, and had a brief introduction to ES6, the newest stable JavaScript language specification.

Finally, we set up an example development environment using Node.js, the Yarn package manager, Babel, and Browserify—tools that we will use throughout the rest of the book in our examples.

In the next chapter, we'll begin exploring and processing the data itself.

Data Exploration 2

The single most important thing for a beginner to know about **machine learning** (**ML**) is that *machine learning is not magic*. Taking a large dataset and naively applying a neural network to it will not automatically give you earth-shaking insights. ML is built on top of sound and familiar mathematical principles, such as probability, statistics, linear algebra, and vector calculus—voodoo not included (though some readers may liken vector calculus to voodoo)!

We will be covering the following topics in this chapter:

- An overview
- Variable identification
- Cleaning of data
- Transformation
- Types of analysis
- Missing values treatment
- Outlier treatment

An overview

One misconception I would like to dispel early on is that implementing the ML algorithm itself is the bulk of the work you'll need to do to accomplish some task. If you're new to this, you may be under the impression that 95% of your time should be spent on implementing a neural network, and that the neural network is solely responsible for the results you get. Build a neural network, put data in, magically get results out. What could be easier?

The reality of ML is that the algorithm you use is only as good as the data you put into it. Furthermore, the results you get are only as good as your ability to process and interpret them. The age-old computer science acronym **GIGO** fits well here: *Garbage In, Garbage Out*.

When implementing ML techniques, you must also pay close attention to their preprocessing and postprocessing of data. Data preprocessing is required for many reasons, and is the focus of this chapter. Postprocessing relates to your interpretation of the algorithm's output, whether your confidence in the algorithm's result is high enough to take action on it, and your ability to apply the results to your business problem. Since postprocessing of results strongly depends on the algorithm in question, we'll address postprocessing considerations as they come up in our specific examples throughout this book.

Preprocessing of data, like postprocessing of data, often depends on the algorithm used, as different algorithms have different requirements. One straightforward example is image processing with **Convolutional Neural Networks (CNNs)**, covered in a later chapter. All images processed by a single CNN are expected to have the same dimensions, or at least the same number of pixels and the same number of color channels (RGB versus RGBA versus grayscale, and so on). The CNN was configured to expect a specific number of inputs, and so every image you give to it must be preprocessed to make sure it complies with the neural network's expectations. You may need to resize, scale, crop, or pad input images before feeding them to the network. You may need to convert color images to grayscale. You may need to detect and remove images that have been corrupted from your dataset.

Some algorithms simply won't work if you attempt to give them the wrong input. If a CNN expects 10,000 grayscale pixel intensity inputs (namely an image that's 100 x 100 pixels), there's no way you can give it an image that's sized 150 x 200. This is a best-case scenario for us: the algorithm fails loudly, and we are able to change our approach before attempting to use our network.

Other algorithms, however, will fail silently if you give them bad input. The algorithm will appear to be working, and even give you results that look reasonable but are actually wholly inaccurate. This is our worst-case scenario: we think the algorithm is working as expected, but in reality we're in a GIGO situation. Just think about how long it will take you to discover that the algorithm is actually giving you nonsensical results. How many bad business decisions have you made based on incorrect analysis or poor data? These are the types of situations we must avoid, and it all starts at the beginning: making sure the data we use is appropriate for the application.

Most ML algorithms make assumptions about the data they process. Some algorithms expect data to be of a given size and shape (as in neural networks), some algorithms expect data to be bucketed, some algorithms expect data to be normalized over a range (between 0 and 1 or between -1 and +1), some algorithms are resilient to missing values and others aren't. It is ultimately your responsibility to understand what assumptions the algorithm makes about your data, and also to align the data with the expectations of the algorithm.

For the most part, the aforementioned relates to the format, shape, and size of data. There is another consideration: the quality of the data. A data point may be perfectly formatted and aligned with the expectations of an algorithm, but still be *wrong*. Perhaps someone wrote down the wrong value for a measurement, maybe there was an instrumentation failure, or maybe some environmental effect has contaminated or tainted your data. In these cases the format, shape, and size may be correct, but the data itself may harm your model and prevent it from converging on a stable or accurate result. In many of these cases, the data point in question is an **outlier**, or a data point that doesn't seem to fit within the set.

Outliers exist in real life, and are often valid data. It's not always apparent by looking at the data by itself whether an outlier is valid or not, and we must also consider the context and algorithm when determining how to handle the data. For instance, let's say you're running a meta-analysis that relates patients' height to their heart performance and you've got 100 medical records available to analyze. One of the patients is listed with a height of 7'3" (221 cm). Is this a typo? Did the person who recorded the data actually mean 6'3" (190 cm)? What are the odds that, of only 100 random individuals, one of them is actually that tall? Should you still use this data point in your analysis, even though it will skew your otherwise very clean-looking results? What if the sample size were 1 million records instead of only 100? In that case, it's much more likely that you did actually select a very tall person. What if the sample size were only 100, but they were all NBA players?

As you can see, dealing with outliers is not straightforward. You should always be hesitant to discard data, especially if in doubt. By discarding data, you run the risk of creating a self-fulfilling prophecy by which you've consciously or subconsciously selected only the data that will support your hypothesis, even if your hypothesis is wrong. On the other hand, using legitimately bad data can ruin your results and prevent progress.

In this chapter, we will discuss a number of different considerations you must make when preprocessing data, including data transformations, handling missing data, selecting the correct parameters, handling outliers, and other forms of analysis that will be helpful in the data preprocessing stage.

Feature identification

Imagine that you are responsible for placing targeted product advertisements on an e-commerce store that you help run. The goal is to analyze a visitor's past shopping trends and select products to display that will increase the shopper's likelihood to make a purchase. Given then the gift of foresight, you've been collecting 50 different metrics on all of your shoppers for months: you've been recording past purchases, the product categories of those purchases, the price tag on each purchase, the time on site each user spent before making a purchase, and so on.

Believing that ML is a silver bullet, believing that more data is better, and believing that more training of your model is better, you load all 50 dimensions of data into an algorithm and train it for days on end. When testing your algorithm you find that its accuracy is very high when evaluating data points that you've trained the algorithm on, but also find that the algorithm fails spectacularly when evaluating against your validation set. Additionally, the model has taken a very long time to train. What went wrong here?

First, you've made the assumption that all of your 50 dimensions of data are relevant to the task at hand. It turns out that not all data is relevant. ML is great at finding patterns within data, but not all data actually contains patterns. Some data is random, and other data is not random but is also uninteresting. One example of uninteresting data that fits a pattern might be the time of day that the shopper is browsing your site on: users can only shop while they're awake, so most of your users shop between 7 a.m. and midnight. This data obviously follows a pattern, but may not actually affect the user's purchase intent. Of course, there may indeed be an interesting pattern: perhaps night owls tend to make late-night impulse purchases—but maybe not.

Second, using all 50 dimensions and training your model for a long period of time may cause overfitting of your model: instead of being able to generalize behavioral patterns and making shopping predictions, your overfitted model is now very good at identifying that a certain behavior represents Steve Johnson (one specific shopper), rather than generalizing Steve's behavior into a widely applicable trend. This overfit was caused by two factors: the long training time and the existence of irrelevant data in the training set. If one of the dimensions you've recorded is largely random and you spend a lot of time training a model on that data, the model may end up using that random data as an identifier for a user rather than filtering it out as a non-trend. The model may learn that, when the user's time on site is exactly 182 seconds, they will purchase a product worth $120, simply because you've trained the model on that data point many thousands of times in the training process.

Let's consider a different example: face identification. You've got thousands of photos of peoples' faces and want to be able to analyze a photo and determine who the subject is. You train a CNN on your data, and find that the accuracy of your algorithm is quite low, only being able to correctly identify the subject 60% of the time. The problem here may be that your CNN, working with raw pixel data, has not been able to automatically identify the features of a face that actually matter. For instance, Sarah Jane always takes her selfies in her kitchen, and her favorite spatula is always on display in the background. Any other user who also happens to have a spatula in the picture may be falsely identified as Sarah Jane, even if their faces are quite different. The data has overtrained the neural network to recognize spatulas as Sarah Jane, rather than actually looking at the user's face.

In both of these examples, the problem starts with insufficient preprocessing of data. In the e-commerce store example, you have not correctly identified the features of a shopper that actually matter, and so have trained your model with a lot of irrelevant data. The same problem exists in the face detection example: not every pixel in the photograph represents a person or their features, and in seeing a reliable pattern of spatulas the algorithm has learned that Sarah Jane is a spatula.

To solve both of these problems, you will need to make better selections of the features that you give to your ML model. In the e-commerce example, it may turn out that only 10 of your 50 recorded dimensions are relevant, and to fix the problem you must identify what those 10 dimensions are and only use those when training your model. In the face detection example, perhaps the neural network should not receive raw pixel intensity data but instead facial dimensions such as *nose bridge length, mouth width, distance between pupils, distance between pupil and eyebrow, distance between earlobes, distance from chin to hairline*, and so on. Both of these examples demonstrate the need to select the most relevant and appropriate features of your data. Making the appropriate selection of features will serve to improve both the speed and accuracy of your model.

The curse of dimensionality

In ML applications, we often have high-dimensional data. If we're recording 50 different metrics for each of our shoppers, we're working in a space with 50 dimensions. If we're analyzing grayscale images sized 100 x 100, we're working in a space with 10,000 dimensions. If the images are RGB-colored, the dimensionality increases to 30,000 dimensions (one dimension for each color channel in each pixel in the image)!

This problem is called the **curse of dimensionality**. On one hand, ML excels at analyzing data with many dimensions. Humans are not good at finding patterns that may be spread out across so many dimensions, especially if those dimensions are interrelated in counter-intuitive ways. On the other hand, as we add more dimensions we also increase the processing power we need to analyze the data, and we also increase the amount of training data required to make meaningful models.

One area that clearly demonstrates the curse of dimensionality is **natural language processing (NLP)**. Imagine you are using a Bayesian classifier to perform sentiment analysis of tweets relating to brands or other topics. As you will learn in a later chapter, part of data preprocessing for NLP is tokenization of input strings into **n-grams**, or groups of words. Those n-grams are the features that are given to the Bayesian classifier algorithm.

Consider a few input strings: `I love cheese`, `I like cheese`, `I hate cheese`, `I don't love cheese`, `I don't really like cheese`. These examples are straightforward to us, since we've been using natural language our entire lives. How would an algorithm view these examples, though? If we are doing a 1-gram or **unigram** analysis—meaning that we split the input string into individual words—we see `love` in the first example, `like` in the second, `hate` in the third, `love` in the fourth, and `like` in the fifth. Our unigram analysis may be accurate for the first three examples, but it fails on the fourth and fifth because it does not learn that `don't love` and `don't really like` are coherent statements; the algorithm is only looking at the effects of individual words. This algorithm runs very quickly and requires little storage space, because in the preceding example there are only seven unique words used in the four phrases above (`I`, `love`, `cheese`, `like`, `hate`, `don't`, and `really`).

You may then modify the tokenization preprocessing to use `bigrams`, or 2-grams—or groups of two words at a time. This increases the dimensionality of our data, requiring more storage space and processing time, but also yields better results. The algorithm now sees dimensions like `I love` and `love cheese`, and can now also recognize that `don't love` is different from `I love`. Using the bigram approach the algorithm may correctly identify the sentiment of the first four examples but still fail for the fifth, which is parsed as `I don't`, `don't really`, `really like`, and `like cheese`. The classification algorithm will see `really like` and `like cheese`, and incorrectly relate that to the positive sentiment in the second example. Still, the bigram approach is working for 80% of our examples.

You might now be tempted to upgrade the tokenization once more to capture trigrams, or groups of three words at a time. Instead of getting an increase in accuracy, the algorithm takes a nosedive and is unable to correctly identify anything. We now have too many dimensions in our data. The algorithm learns what `I love cheese` means, but no other training example includes the phrase `I love cheese` so that knowledge can't be applied in any way. The fifth example parses into the trigrams `I don't really,` `don't really like,` and `really like cheese`—none of which have ever been encountered before! This algorithm ends up giving you a 50% sentiment for every example, because there simply isn't enough data in the training set to capture all of the relevant combinations of trigrams.

This is the curse of dimensionality at play: the **trigram** approach may indeed give you better accuracy than the bigram approach, but only if you have a huge training set that provides data on all the different possible combinations of three words at a time. You also now need a tremendous amount of storage space because there are a much larger number of combinations of three words than there are of two words. Choosing the preprocessing approach will therefore depend on the context of the problem, the computing resources available, and also the training data available to you. If you have a lot of training data and tons of resources, the trigram approach may be more accurate, but in more realistic conditions, the bigram approach may be better overall, even if it does misclassify some tweets.

The preceding discussion relates to the concepts of **feature selection**, **feature extraction**, and **dimensionality**. In general, our goal is to *select* only relevant features (ignore shopper trends that aren't interesting to us), *extract* or *derive* features that better represent our data (by using facial measurements rather than photograph pixels), and ultimately *reduce dimensionality* such that we use the fewest, most relevant dimensions we can.

Feature selection and feature extraction

Both feature selection and feature extraction are techniques used to reduce dimensionality, though they are slightly different concepts. Feature selection is the practice of using only variables or features that are relevant to the problem at hand. In general, feature selection looks at individual features (such as `time on site`) and makes a determination of the relevance of that single feature. Feature extraction is similar, however feature extraction often looks at multiple correlated features and combines them into a single feature (like looking at hundreds of individual pixels and converting them into a **distance between pupils** measurement). In both cases, we are reducing the dimensionality of the problem, but the difference between the two is whether we are simply filtering out irrelevant dimensions (feature selection) or combining existing features in order to derive a new representative feature (feature extraction).

The goal of feature selection is to select the subset of features or dimensions of your data that optimizes the accuracy of your model. Let's take a look at the naive approach to solving this problem: an exhaustive, brute force search of all possible subsets of dimensions. This approach is not viable in real-world applications, but it serves to frame the problem for us. If we take the e-commerce store example, our goal is to find some subset of dimensions or features that gives us the best results from our model. We know we have 50 features to choose from, but we don't know how many are in the optimum set of features. Solving this problem by brute force, we would first pick only one feature at a time, and train and evaluate our model for each feature.

For instance, we would use only `time on site` as a data point, train the model on that data point, evaluate the model, and record the accuracy of the model. Then we move on to `total past purchase amount`, train the model, evaluate the model, and record results. We do this 48 more times for the remaining features and record the performance of each. Then we have to consider combinations of two features at a time, for instance by training and evaluating the model on `time on site` and `total past purchase amount`, and then training and evaluating on `time on site` and `last purchase date`, and so on. There are 1,225 unique pairs of features out of our set of 50, and we must repeat the procedure for each pair. Then we must consider groups of three features at a time, of which there are 19,600 combinations. Then we must consider groups of four features, of which there are 230,300 unique combinations. There are 2,118,760 combinations of five features, and nearly 16 million combinations of six features available to us, and so on. Obviously this exhaustive search for the optimal set of features to use cannot be done in a reasonable amount of time: we'd have to train our model billions of times just to find out what the best subset of features to use is! We must find a better approach.

 In general, feature selection techniques are split into three categories: filter methods, wrapper methods, and embedded methods. Each category has a number of techniques, and the technique you select will depend on the data, the context, and the algorithm of your specific situation.

Filter methods are the easiest to implement and typically have the best performance. Filter methods for feature selection analyze a single feature at a time and attempt to determine that feature's relevance to the data. Filter methods typically do not have any relation to the ML algorithm you use afterwards, and are more typically statistical methods that analyze the feature itself.

For instance, you may use the Pearson correlation coefficient to determine if a feature has a linear relationship with the output variable, and remove features with a correlation very close to zero. This family of approaches will be very fast in terms of computational time, but has the disadvantage of not being able to identify features that are cross-correlated with one another, and, depending on the filter algorithm you use, may not be able to identify nonlinear or complex relationships.

Wrapper methods are similar to the brute force approach described earlier, however with the goal of avoiding a full exhaustive search of every combination of features as we did previously. For instance, you may use a genetic algorithm to select subsets of features, train and evaluate the model, and then use the evaluation of the model as evolutionary pressure to find the next subset of features to test.

The genetic algorithm approach may not find the perfect subset of features, but will likely discover a very good subset of features to use. Depending on the actual machine learning model you use and the size of the dataset, this approach may still take a long time, but it will not take an intractably long amount of time like the exhaustive search would. The advantage of wrapper methods is that they interact with the actual model you're training and therefore serve to directly optimize your model, rather than simply attempting to independently statistically filter out individual features. The major disadvantage of these methods is the computational time it takes to achieve the desired results.

There is also a family of methods called **embedded methods**, however this family of techniques relies on algorithms that have their own feature selection algorithm built in and are therefore quite specialized; we will not discuss them here.

Feature extraction techniques focus on combining existing features into new, derived features that better represent your data while also eliminating extra or redundant dimensionality. Imagine that your e-commerce shopper data includes both `time on site` and `total pixel scrolling distance while browsing` as dimensions. Also imagine that both of these dimensions do strongly correlate to the amount of money a shopper spends on the site. Naturally, these two features are related to each other: the more time a user spends on the site, the more likely they are to have scrolled a farther distance. Using only feature selection techniques, such as the Pearson correlation analysis, you would find that you should keep both `time on site` and `total distance scrolled` as features. The feature selection technique, which analyzes these features independently, has determined that both are relevant to your problem, but has not understood that the two features are actually highly related to each other and therefore redundant.

A more sophisticated feature extraction technique, such as **Principal Component Analysis (PCA)**, would be able to identify that time on site and scroll distance can actually be combined into a single, new feature (let's call it `site engagement`) that encapsulates the data represented by what used to be two separate features. In this case we have *extracted* a new feature from the time on site and scrolling distance measurements, and we are using that single feature instead of the two original features separately. This differs from feature selection; in feature selection we are simply choosing which of the original features to use when training our model, however in feature extraction we are creating brand new features from related combinations of original features. Both feature selection and feature extraction therefore reduce the dimensionality of our data, but do so in different ways.

Pearson correlation example

Let's return to our example of shoppers on the e-commerce store and consider how we might use the Pearson correlation coefficient to select data features. Consider the following example data, which records purchase amounts for shoppers given their time spent on site and the amount of money they had spent on purchases previously:

Purchase Amount	Time on Site (seconds)	Past Purchase Amount
$10.00	53	$7.00
$14.00	220	$12.00
$18.00	252	$22.00
$20.00	571	$17.00
$22.00	397	$21.00
$34.00	220	$23.00
$38.00	776	$29.00
$50.00	462	$74.00
$52.00	354	$63.00
$56.00	23	$61.00

Of course, in a real application of this problem you may have thousands or hundreds of thousands of rows, and dozens of columns, each representing a different dimension of data.

Let's now select features for this data manually. The `purchase amount` column is our output data, or the data that we want our algorithm to predict given other features. In this exercise, we can choose to train the model using both time on site and previous purchase amount, time on site alone, or previous purchase amount alone.

When using a filter method for feature selection we consider one feature at a time, so we must look at time on site's relation to purchase amount independently of past purchase amount's relation to purchase amount. One manual approach to this problem would be to chart each of our two candidate features against the `Purchase Amount` column, and calculate a correlation coefficient to determine how strongly each feature is related to the purchase amount data.

First, we'll chart time on site versus purchase amount, and use our spreadsheet tool to calculate the Pearson correlation coefficient:

Even a simple visual inspection of the data hints to the fact that there is only a small relationship—if any at all—between time on site and purchase amount. Calculating the Pearson correlation coefficient yields a correlation of about +0.1, a very weak, essentially insignificant correlation between the two sets of data.

However, if we chart the past purchase amount versus current purchase amount, we see a very different relationship:

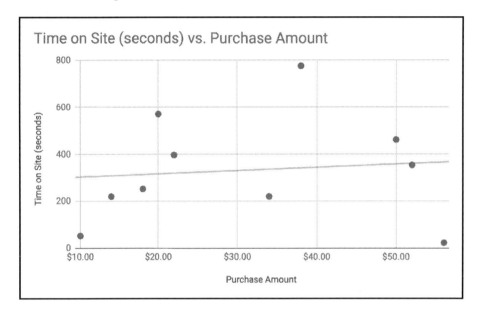

In this case, our visual inspection tells us that there is a linear but somewhat noisy relationship between the past purchase amount and the current purchase amount. Calculating the correlation coefficient gives us a correlation value of +0.9, quite a strong linear relationship!

This type of analysis tells us that we can ignore the time on site data when training our model, as there seems to be little to no statistical significance in that information. By ignoring time on site data, we can reduce the number of dimensions we need to train our model on by one, allowing our model to better generalize data and also improve performance.

If we had 48 other numerical dimensions to consider, we could simply calculate the correlation coefficient for each of them and discard each dimension whose correlation falls beneath some threshold. Not every feature can be analyzed using correlation coefficients, however, so you can only apply the Pearson algorithm to those features where such a statistical analysis makes sense; it would not make sense to use Pearson correlation to analyze a feature that lists *recently browsed product category*, for instance. You can, and should, use other types of feature selection filters for different dimensions representing different types of data. Over time, you will develop a toolkit of analysis techniques that can apply to different types of data.

Unfortunately, a thorough explanation of all the possible feature extraction and feature selection algorithms and tools is not possible here; you will have to research various techniques and determine which ones fit the shape and style of your features and data.

Some algorithms to consider for filter techniques are the Pearson and Spearman correlation coefficients, the chi-squared test, and information gain algorithms such as the Kullback–Leibler divergence.

Approaches to consider for wrapper techniques are optimization techniques such as genetic algorithms, tree-search algorithms such as best-first search, stochastic techniques such as random hill-climb algorithms, and heuristic techniques such as recursive feature elimination and simulated annealing. All of these techniques aim to select the best set of features that optimize the output of your model, so any optimization technique can be a candidate, however, genetic algorithms are quite effective and popular.

Feature extraction has many algorithms to consider, and generally focuses on cross-correlation of features in order to determine new features that minimize some error function; that is, how can two or more features be combined such that a minimum amount of data is lost. Relevant algorithms include PCA, partial least squares, and autoencoding. In NLP, latent semantic analysis is popular. Image processing has many specialized feature extraction algorithms, such as edge detection, corner detection, and thresholding, and further specializations based on problem domain such as face identification or motion detection.

Cleaning and preparing data

Feature selection is not the only consideration required when preprocessing your data. There are many other things that you may need to do to prepare your data for the algorithm that will ultimately analyze the data. Perhaps there are measurement errors that create significant outliers. There can also be instrumentation noise in the data that needs to be smoothed out. Your data may have missing values for some features. These are all issues that can either be ignored or addressed, depending, as always, on the context, the data, and the algorithm involved.

Additionally, the algorithm you use may require the data to be normalized to some range of values. Or perhaps your data is in a different format that the algorithm cannot use, as is often the case with neural networks which expect you to provide a vector of values, but you have JSON objects that come from a database. Sometimes you need to analyze only a specific subset of data from a larger source. If you're working with images you may need to resize, scale, pad, crop, or reduce the image to grayscale.

These tasks all fall into the realm of data preprocessing. Let's take a look at some specific scenarios and discuss possible approaches for each.

Handling missing data

In many cases, several data points may have values missing from certain features. If you're looking at Yes/No responses to survey questions, several participants may have accidentally or purposefully skipped a given question. If you're looking at time series data, your measurement tool may have had an error for a given period or measurement. If you're looking at e-commerce shopping habits, some features may not be relevant to a user, for instance `last login date` for users that shop as an anonymous guest. The individual situation and scenario, as well as your algorithm's tolerance for missing data, determines the approach you must take to remediate missing data.

Missing categorical data

In the case of categorical data, such as Yes/No survey questions that may not have been responded to, or an image that has not yet been labeled with its category, often the best approach is to create a new category called *undefined*, *N/A*, *unknown*, or *similar*. Alternatively, you may be able to select a reasonable default category to use for these missing values, perhaps choosing the most frequent category from the set, or choosing a category that represents the data point's logical parent. If you're analyzing photographs uploaded by users and are missing the category tag for a given photograph, you may instead use the *user's* stated category in place of the photo's individual category. That is, if a user is tagged as a fashion photographer, you may use the *fashion* category for the photo, even though the user has also uploaded a number of *travel* photographs. This approach will add noise in the form of miscategorized data points to the system, but may in fact have a positive overall effect of forcing the algorithm to generalize its model; the model may eventually learn that fashion and travel photography are similar.

Using an *undefined* or *N/A* category is also a preferred approach, as the fact that a data point has no category may be significant in and of itself—*No category* can itself be a valid category. The size of the dataset, the algorithm used, and the relative size of the *N/A* category within the dataset will affect whether this is a reasonable approach to take. In a classification scenario, for instance, two effects are possible. If the uncategorized items *do* form a pattern (for instance, *fashion* photos are uncategorized more often than other photos), you may find that your classifier incorrectly learns that fashion photos should be categorized as N/A! In this scenario, it may be better to ignore uncategorized data points entirely.

However, if the uncategorized photos are comprised of photos from various categories equally, your classifier may end up identifying difficult-to-classify photos as N/A, which could actually be a desired effect. In this scenario, you can consider N/A as a class of its own, being comprised of difficult, broken, or unresolvable photos.

Missing numerical data

Missing values for numerical data is trickier to handle than categorical data, as there is often no reasonable default for missing numerical values. Depending on the dataset, you may be able to use zeros as replacements, however in some cases using the mean or median value of that feature is more appropriate. In other scenarios, and depending on the algorithm used, it may be useful to fill in missing values with a very large value: if that data point needs to have an error calculation performed on it, using a large value will mark the data point with a large error, and discourage the algorithm from considering that point.

In other cases, you can use a linear interpolation to fill in missing data points. This makes sense in some time series applications. If your algorithm expects 31 data points representing the growth of some metric, and you're missing one value for day 12, you can use the average of day 11's and day 13's values to serve as an estimate for day 12's value.

Often the correct approach is to ignore and filter out data points with missing values, however, you must consider the effects of such an action. If the data points with missing values strongly represent a specific category of data, you may end up creating a strong selection bias as a side effect, as your analysis would have ignored a significant group. You must balance this type of side effect with the possible side effects caused by the other approaches: will zeroing out missing values significantly skew your distribution? Will using the mean or median as replacements taint the rest of the analysis? These questions can only be answered on a case-by-case basis.

Handling noise

Noise in data can come from many sources, but is not often a significant issue as most machine learning techniques are resilient to noisy datasets. Noise can come from environmental factors (for instance, the air conditioner compressor turning on randomly and causing signal noise in a nearby sensor), it can come from transcription errors (somebody recorded the wrong data point, selected the wrong option in a survey, or an OCR algorithm read a 3 as an 8), or it can be inherent to the data itself (such as fluctuations in temperature recordings, which will follow a seasonal pattern but have a noisy daily pattern).

Noise in categorical data can also be caused by category labels that aren't normalized, such as images that are tagged `fashion` or `fashions` when the category is supposed to be `Fashion`. In those scenarios, the best approach is to simply normalize the category label, perhaps by forcing all category labels to be made singular and fully lowercase—this will combine the `Fashion`, `fashion`, and `fashions` categories into one single `fashion` category.

Noise in time series data can be smoothed by taking a moving average of multiple values; however, first you should evaluate if smoothing the data is important to your algorithm and results in the first place. Often, the algorithm will still perform well enough for practical applications if there is a small amount of noise, and especially if the noise is random rather than systemic.

Consider the following example of daily measurements of some sensor:

Day	Value
1	0.1381426172
2	0.5678176776
3	0.3564009968
4	1.239499423
5	1.267606181
6	1.440843361
7	0.3322843208
8	0.4329166745
9	0.5499234277
10	-0.4016070826
11	0.06216906816
12	-0.9689103112
13	-1.170421963
14	-0.784125647
15	-1.224217169
16	-0.4689120937
17	-0.7458561671
18	-0.6746415566
19	-0.0429460593
20	0.06757010626
21	0.480806698

22	0.2019759014
23	0.7857692899
24	0.725414402
25	1.188534085
26	0.458488458
27	0.3017212831
28	0.5249332545
29	0.3333153146
30	-0.3517342423
31	-0.721682062

Graphing this data shows a noisy but periodic pattern:

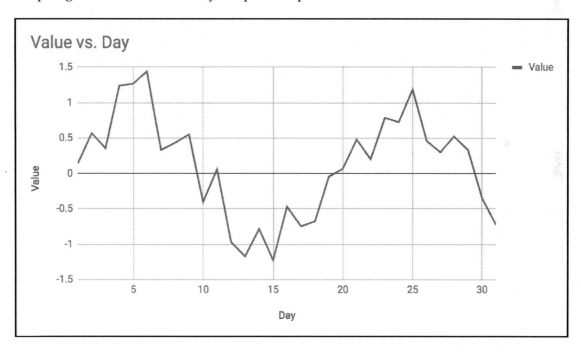

This may be acceptable in many scenarios, but other applications may require smoother data.

Also, note that several of the data points exceed +1 and -1, which may be of significance especially if your algorithm is expecting data between the -1 and +1 range.

We can apply a 5-Day Moving Average to the data to generate a smoother curve. To perform a 5-Day Moving Average, start with day 3, sum the values for days 1 to 5, and divide by 5. The result becomes the moving average for day 3.

Note that in this approach, we lose days 1 and 2, and also days 30 and 31, because we cannot look two days before day 1 nor can we look two days after day 31. However, if you require values for those days, you may use the raw values for days 1, 2, 30, and 31, or you may use 3-Day Moving Averages for days 2 and 30 in addition to single values for days 1 and 31. If you have more historical data, you can use data from the previous month calculating the 5-Day Moving Average for days 1 and 2 (calculate day 1 by using the previous month's last two days). The approach to how you handle this moving average will depend on the data available to you and the importance of having 5-day averages for each data point versus combining 5-day averages with 3-day and 1-day averages at the boundaries.

If we calculate the 5-Day Moving Average for our month, the data becomes the following:

Day	Value	5-Day Moving Average
1	0.1381426172	
2	0.5678176776	
3	0.3564009968	0.7138933792
4	1.239499423	0.974433528
5	1.267606181	0.9273268566
6	1.440843361	0.9426299922
7	0.3322843208	0.8047147931
8	0.4329166745	0.4708721403
9	0.5499234277	0.1951372817
10	-0.4016070826	-0.06510164468
11	0.06216906816	-0.3857693722
12	-0.9689103112	-0.6525791871
13	-1.170421963	-0.8171012043
14	-0.784125647	-0.9233174367

15	-1.224217169	-0.8787066079
16	-0.4689120937	-0.7795505266
17	-0.7458561671	-0.631314609
18	-0.6746415566	-0.3729571541
19	-0.0429460593	-0.1830133958
20	0.06757010626	0.006553017948
21	0.480806698	0.2986351872
22	0.2019759014	0.4523072795
23	0.7857692899	0.6765000752
24	0.725414402	0.6720364272
25	1.188534085	0.6919855036
26	0.458488458	0.6398182965
27	0.3017212831	0.561398479
28	0.5249332545	0.2533448136
29	0.3333153146	0.0173107096
30	-0.3517342423	
31	-0.721682062	

In some cases, the moving average differs from the day's data point by a significant margin. On day 3, for instance, the moving average is double that of the day's measurement.

This approach would not be appropriate in instances where you need to consider a given day's measurement in isolation, however, when we graph the moving average against the daily data points, we can see the value of this approach:

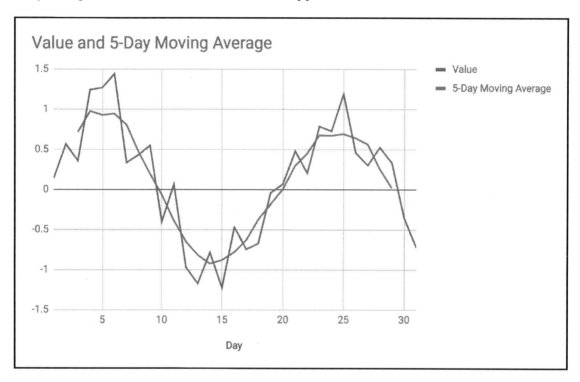

We can see that the moving average is much smoother than the daily measurements, and that the moving average better represents the periodic, sinusoidal nature of our data. An added bonus for us is that the moving average data no longer contains points that lie outside our [-1, +1] range; because the noise in this data was random, the random fluctuations have largely canceled each other out and brought our data back into range.

Increasing the window of the moving average will result in broader and broader averages, reducing resolution; if we were to take a *31-Day Moving Average,* we would simply have the average measurement for the entire month. If your application simply needs to smooth out data rather than reduce data to lower resolutions, you should start by applying the smallest moving average window that serves to clean the data enough, for instance, a 3-point moving average.

If you're dealing with measurements that are not time series, then a moving average approach may not be appropriate. For instance, if you're measuring the value of a sensor at arbitrary and random times where the time of measurement is not recorded, a moving average would not be appropriate because the dimension to average over is unknown (that is, we do not know the time period that the average moves over).

If you still need to eliminate noise from your data, you can try *binning* the measurements by creating a histogram of the data. This approach changes the nature of the data itself and does not apply to every situation, however, it can serve to obfuscate individual measurement fluctuations while still representing the relative frequency of different measurements.

Handling outliers

Your data will often have outlying values, or data points that are far away from the expected value for your dataset. Sometimes, outliers are caused by noise or errors (somebody recording a height of 7'3" rather than 6'3"), but other times, outliers are legitimate data points (one celebrity with a Twitter reach of 10 million followers joining your service where most of the users have 10,000 to 100,000 followers). In either case, you'll first want to identify outliers so that you can determine what to do with them.

One approach to identifying outliers is to calculate the mean and standard deviation of your dataset, and determine how many standard deviations away from the mean each data point is. The standard deviation of a dataset represents the overall variance or dispersion of the data. Consider the following data which represents the number of Twitter followers of accounts that you're analyzing:

Followers
1075
1879
3794
4111
4243
4885
7617
8555
8755
19422

31914	
36732	
39570	
1230324	

As you can see, the last value is much larger than the other values in the set. However, this discrepancy may not be so obvious if you're analyzing millions of records with dozens of features each. To automate our outlier identification we should first calculate the mean average of all our users, which in this case is an average of **100,205** followers. Then, we should calculate the standard deviation of the dataset, which for this data is **325,523** followers. Finally, we can inspect each data point by determining how many standard deviations away from the mean that data point is: find the absolute difference between the data point and the mean, and then divide by the standard deviation:

Followers	Deviation
1075	0.3045078726
1879	0.3020381533
3794	0.2961556752
4111	0.2951819177
4243	0.2947764414
4885	0.2928043522
7617	0.2844122215
8555	0.2815308824
8755	0.2809165243
19422	0.248149739
31914	0.2097769366
36732	0.1949770517
39570	0.1862593113
1230324	3.471487079

The approach has yielded good results: all data points except one are found within one standard deviation of the mean, and our outlier is far away from the average with a distance of nearly 3.5 deviations. In general, you can consider data points more than two or three standard deviations away from the mean to be outliers.

If your dataset represents a normal distribution, then you can use the **68-95-99.7** rule: 68% of data points are expected to be within one standard deviation, 95% are expected to be within two deviations, and 99.7% of data points are expected to be within three standard deviations. In a normal distribution, therefore, only 0.3% of data is expected to be farther than three standard deviations from the mean.

 Note that the preceding data presented is not a normal distribution, and much of your data will not follow normal distributions either, but the concept of standard deviation may still apply (the ratios of data points expected per standard deviation will differ based on the distribution).

Now that an outlier is identified, a determination must be made as to how to handle the outlying data point. In some cases, it's better to keep the outliers in your dataset and continue processing as usual; outliers that are based in real data are often important data points that can't be ignored, because they represent uncommon but possible values for your data.

For instance, if you're monitoring a server's CPU load average and find an average value of 2.0 with a standard deviation of 1.0, you would not want to ignore data points with load averages of 10.0—those data points still represent load averages that your CPU actually experienced, and for many types of analysis it would be self-defeating to ignore that data, even though those points are far away from the mean. Those points should be considered and accounted for in your analysis. However, in our Twitter followers example we may want to ignore the outlier, especially if our analysis is to determine behavioral patterns of Twitter users' audiences—our outlier most likely exhibits a completely separate class of behavioral patterns that may simply confuse our analysis.

There is another approach to handling outliers that works well when considering data that's expected to be linear, polynomial, exponential, or periodic—the types of datasets where a regression can be performed. Consider data that is expected to be linear, like the following:

Observation	Value
1	1
2	2
3	3

4	4
5	5
6	6
7	22
8	8
9	9
10	10

When performing a linear regression on this data, we can see that the outlying data point skews the regression upwards:

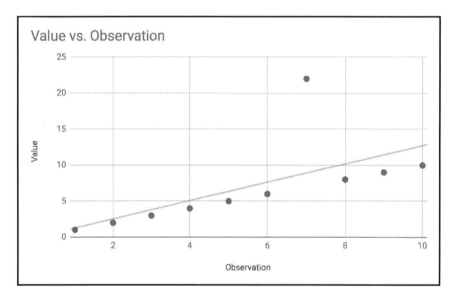

For this small set of data points the error in the regression may not be significant, but if you're using the regression to extrapolate future values, for instance, for observation number 30, the predicted value will be far from the actual value as the small error introduced by the outlier compounds the further you extrapolate values. In this case, we would want to remove the outlier before performing the regression so that the regression's extrapolation is more accurate.

In order to identify the outlier, we can perform a linear regression as we have before, and then calculate the squared error from the trendline for each point. If the data point exceeds an error of, for instance, 25%, we can consider that point an outlier and remove it before performing the regression a second time. Once we've removed the outlier and re-performed the regression, the trendline fits the data much better:

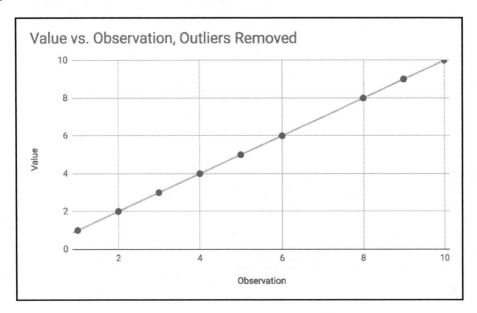

Transforming and normalizing data

The most common preprocessing task is to transform and/or normalize data into a representation that can be used by your algorithm. For instance, you may receive JSON objects from an API endpoint that you need to transform into vectors used by your algorithm. Consider the following JSON data:

```
const users = [
    {
        "name": "Andrew",
        "followers": 27304,
        "posts": 34,
        "images": 38,
        "engagements": 2343,
        "is_verified": false
    },
    {
```

```
        "name": "Bailey",
        "followers": 32102,
        "posts": 54,
        "images": 102,
        "engagements": 9488,
        "is_verified": true
    },
    {
        "name": "Caroline",
        "followers": 19932,
        "posts": 12,
        "images": 0,
        "engagements": 19,
        "is_verified": false
    }
];
```

Your neural network that processes the data expects input data in vector form, like so:

```
[followers, posts, images, engagements, is_verified]
```

In JavaScript, the easiest way to transform our JSON data in this situation is to use the built-in `Array.map` function. The following code will generate an array of vectors (an array of arrays). This form of transformation will be very common throughout this book:

```
const vectors = users.map(user => [
    user.followers,
    user.posts,
    user.images,
    user.engagements,
    user.is_verified ? 1 : 0
]);
```

Note that we are using the shortest form of ES6 arrow functions, which doesn't require parentheses around the parameters nor an explicit return statement, since we return our array of features directly. An equivalent ES5 example would look like the following:

```
var vectors = users.map(function(user) {
    return [
        user.followers,
        user.posts,
        user.images,
        user.engagements,
        user.is_verified ? 1 : 0
    ];
});
```

Also note that the `is_verified` field was converted to an integer using the ternary operator, `user.is_verified ? 1 : 0`. Neural networks can only work with numeric values, and so we must represent the Boolean value as an integer.

 We will discuss techniques for using natural language with neural networks in a later chapter.

Another common data transformation is to normalize data values into a given range, for instance between -1 and +1. Many algorithms depend on data values falling within this range, however, most real-world data does not. Let's revisit our noisy daily sensor data from earlier in the chapter, and let's assume that we have access to this data in a simple JavaScript array called **measurements** (detail-oriented readers will notice I changed the value of day 15 as compared with the earlier example):

Day	Value
1	0.1381426172
2	0.5678176776
3	0.3564009968
4	1.239499423
5	1.267606181
6	1.440843361
7	0.3322843208
8	0.4329166745
9	0.5499234277
10	-0.4016070826
11	0.06216906816
12	-0.9689103112
13	-1.170421963
14	-0.784125647
15	-1.524217169
16	-0.4689120937
17	-0.7458561671
18	-0.6746415566
19	-0.0429460593
20	0.06757010626

21	0.480806698
22	0.2019759014
23	0.7857692899
24	0.725414402
25	1.188534085
26	0.458488458
27	0.3017212831
28	0.5249332545
29	0.3333153146
30	-0.3517342423
31	-0.721682062

If we wish to normalize this data to the range [-1, +1], we must first discover the largest *absolute value* of all numbers in the set, which in this case is day 15's value of -1.52. If we were to simply use JavaScript's Math.max on this data, we would find the maximum value on the number line, which is day 6's value of 1.44—however, day 15 is more negative than day 6 is positive.

Finding the maximum absolute value in a JavaScript array can be accomplished with the following:

```
const absolute_max = Math.max.apply(null, measurements.map(Math.abs));
```

The value of absolute_max will be +1.524217169—the number became positive when we called Math.abs using measurements.map. It is important that the absolute maximum value remains positive, because in the next step we will divide by the maximum and want to preserve the signs of all data points.

Given the absolute maximum value, we can normalize our data points like so:

```
const normalized = measurements.map(value => value / absolute_max);
```

By dividing each number by the maximum value in the set, we ensure that all values lie in the range [-1, +1]. The maximum value will be (in this case) -1, and all other numbers in the set will be closer to 0 than the maximum will. After normalizing, our data now looks like this:

Day	Value	Normalized
1	0.1381426172	0.09063184696
2	0.5678176776	0.3725306927
3	0.3564009968	0.2338256018
4	1.239499423	0.8132039508
5	1.267606181	0.8316440777
6	1.440843361	0.9453005718
7	0.3322843208	0.218003266
8	0.4329166745	0.284025586
9	0.5499234277	0.3607907319
10	-0.4016070826	-0.2634841615
11	0.06216906816	0.04078753963
12	-0.9689103112	-0.6356773373
13	-1.170421963	-0.7678839913
14	-0.784125647	-0.5144448332
15	-1.524217169	-1
16	-0.4689120937	-0.3076412623
17	-0.7458561671	-0.4893372037
18	-0.6746415566	-0.4426151145
19	-0.0429460593	-0.02817581391
20	0.06757010626	0.04433102293
21	0.480806698	0.3154450087
22	0.2019759014	0.1325112363
23	0.7857692899	0.5155231854
24	0.725414402	0.4759258831
25	1.188534085	0.7797668924
26	0.458488458	0.3008025808
27	0.3017212831	0.1979516366
28	0.5249332545	0.3443953167
29	0.3333153146	0.2186796747

| 30 | -0.3517342423 | -0.2307638633 |
| 31 | -0.721682062 | -0.4734771901 |

There are no data points outside of the [-1, +1] range, and you can also see that day 15, with the maximum absolute value of the data, has been normalized as -1. Graphing the data shows the relationship between the original and normalized values:

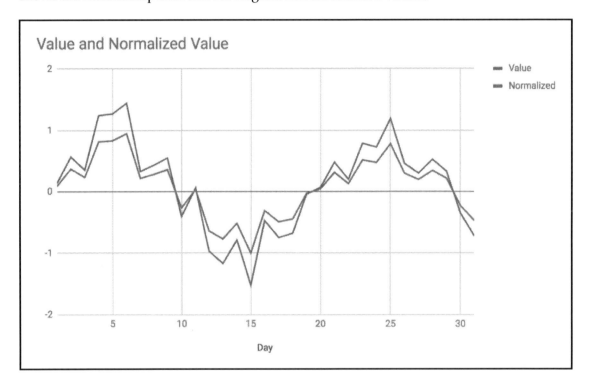

The shape of the data has been preserved, and the chart has simply been scaled by a constant factor. This data is now ready to use in algorithms that require normalized ranges, such as PCA, for instance.

Your data is likely much more complex than these preceding examples. Perhaps your JSON data is composed of complex objects with nested entities and arrays. You may need to run an analysis on only those items which have specific sub-elements, or you may need to generate dynamic subsets of data based on some user-provided query or filter.

For complex situations and datasets, you may want some help from a third-party library such as `DataCollection.js`, which is a library that adds SQL and NoSQL style query functionality to JavaScript arrays. Imagine that our preceding JSON data of **users** also contained an object called **locale** which gives the user's country and language:

```
const users = [
    {
        "name": "Andrew",
        "followers": 27304,
        "posts": 34,
        "images": 38,
        "engagements": 2343,
        "is_verified": false,
        "locale": {
            "country":"US",
            "language":"en_US"
        }
    },
    ...
];
```

To find only users whose language is `en_US`, you could perform the following query using `DataCollection.js`:

```
const collection = new DataCollection(users);
    const english_lang_users =
collection.query().filter({locale__language__is: "en_US"}).values();
```

Of course, you can accomplish the aforementioned in pure JavaScript easily:

```
const english_lang_users = users.filter(user => user.locale.language ===
'en_US');
```

However, the pure JavaScript version needs some tedious modifications to be resilient against undefined or null `locale` objects, and of course more complicated filters become ever more tedious to write in pure JavaScript. Most of the time, we will use pure JavaScript for the examples in this book, however, our examples will be contrived and much cleaner than real-world use cases; use a tool such as `DataCollection.js`, if you feel you need it.

Summary

In this chapter, we have discussed data preprocessing, or the art of delivering the most useful possible data to our machine learning algorithms. We discussed the importance of appropriate feature selection and the relevance of feature selection, both to overfitting and to the curse of dimensionality. We looked at correlation coefficients as a technique to help us determine the appropriate features to select, and also discussed more sophisticated wrapper methods for feature selection, such as using a genetic algorithm to determine the optimal set of features to choose. We then discussed the more advanced topic of feature extraction, which is a category of algorithms that can be used to combine multiple features into new individual features, further reducing the dimensionality of the data.

We then looked at some common scenarios you might face when dealing with real-world datasets, such as missing values, outliers, and measurement noise. We discussed various techniques you can use to correct for those issues. We also discussed common data transformations and normalizations you may need to perform, such as normalizing values to a range or vectorizing objects.

In the next chapter, we will look at machine learning in broad strokes and begin to introduce specific algorithms and their applications.

3
Tour of Machine Learning Algorithms

In this chapter, we're going to explore the different ways to categorize the types of tasks that **machine learning** (**ML**) can accomplish, and categorize the ML algorithms themselves. There are many different ways to organize the ML landscape; we can categorize algorithms by the type of training data we give them, we can categorize by the type of output we expect from the algorithms, we can categorize algorithms by their specific methods and tactics, we can categorize them by the format of the data they work with, and so on.

As we discuss the different types and categories of ML tasks and algorithms throughout this chapter, we'll also introduce many of the algorithms that you'll encounter throughout this book. Only the high-level concepts of algorithms will be discussed in this chapter, allowing us to go into detail in later chapters. The topics that we will be covering in this chapter are as follows:

- Introduction to machine learning
- Types of learning—unsupervised learning, supervised learning, and reinforcement learning
- Categories of algorithms—clustering, classification, regression, dimensionality reduction, optimization, natural language processing, and image processing

At the end of this chapter, you should have an understanding of supervised learning versus unsupervised learning, and should understand the overall landscape of the algorithms that we'll apply throughout this book.

Introduction to machine learning

In general, ML is the name we give to the practice of making computers learn without explicitly programming insights into the algorithm. The converse practice—that is, programming an algorithm with a set of instructions that it can apply to datasets—is often called **heuristics**. This is our first classification of algorithms: machine learning versus heuristic algorithms. If you are managing a firewall and are manually maintaining a blacklist of IP address ranges to block, you can be said to have developed a heuristic for your firewall. On the other hand, if you develop an algorithm that analyzes patterns in web traffic, infers from those patterns, and automatically maintains your blacklist, you can be said to have developed an ML approach to firewalls.

We can, of course, further subcategorize our ML firewall approach. If your algorithm is designed with no *a priori* knowledge (knowledge beforehand), that is, if the algorithm *starts from scratch*, then it can be called an **unsupervised learning** algorithm. On the other hand, if you train the algorithm by showing it examples of requests from sources that should be blocked and expect it to learn by example, then the algorithm can be called a **supervised learning** algorithm.

The specific algorithm you implement may also fall into yet another subcategory. Your algorithm may rely on *clustering* similar requests in order to determine which cluster a given request might belong to, or your algorithm may use Bayesian statistics to determine the probability that a request should be *classified* good or bad, or your algorithm may use a combination of techniques such as clustering, classification, and heuristics! Like many other taxonomical systems, there is often ambiguity in classifying special cases, but for the most part, algorithms can be divided into different categories.

Types of learning

All ML algorithms consume data as an input and are expected to generate insights, predictions, classifications, or analyses as an output. Some algorithms have an additional *training* step, where the algorithm is trained on some data, tested to make sure that they have learned from the training data, and at a future date given a new data point or set of data for which you desire insights.

All ML algorithms that use training data expect the data to be *labeled*, or somehow marked with the desired result for that data. For instance, when building a spam filter, you must first teach or train the algorithm on what spam looks like as compared to what normal messages (called **ham**) look like. You must first train the spam filter on a number of messages, each labeled either *spam* or *ham*, so that the algorithm can learn to distinguish between the two. Once the algorithm is trained, you can present it with a new, never-before-seen message, and expect it to guess whether that message is ham or spam. In this example, the set of messages you train the algorithm with is called the **training data** or **training set**, the labels in use are *spam* and *ham*, and the guesswork that the algorithm performs is called **inference**. This practice of training an algorithm on a set of prelabeled training data is called **supervised learning**.

Other algorithms do not require training, or can inspect a dataset without any labels and develop insights directly from the data. This is called **unsupervised learning**, and this classification is marked by the lack of labels on the data. If you work in a scientific laboratory and are developing an image processing algorithm to inspect pictures of bacterial cultures in Petri dishes, with the goal of the algorithm telling you how many distinct bacterial colonies are seen in the photograph, you have developed an unsupervised learning algorithm. In this case, you do not need to train the algorithm with training data that has the number of colonies prelabeled; the algorithm is expected to work from scratch to find patterns and structures in the data. The inputs and outputs are similar to the supervised learning example, in that you give the data to the algorithm and expect to receive insights as output, but these inputs and outputs are different in that there is no training step or *a priori* knowledge required by the algorithm.

There are further classifications that fall within a spectrum between supervised and unsupervised learning. For instance, in *semi-supervised* learning, an algorithm receives a prelabeled training set, but not every label is represented by the training data. In this case, the algorithm is expected to fit examples to the trained labels where applicable, but also expected to generate new labels when appropriate.

Another mode of learning is **reinforcement learning**. Reinforcement learning is similar to both supervised learning and unsupervised learning in various ways. In reinforcement learning, the training data does not have explicit labels, but the results that the algorithm generates may be associated with a certain penalty or reward; the goal of the algorithm is to eventually optimize its results such that the penalty is minimized. Reinforcement learning is often used in conjunction with supervised learning. An algorithm may be initially trained on some labeled training data, but then is expected to update its model based on feedback about the decisions it has made.

For the most part, you will find that supervised and unsupervised learning are the two major categories of algorithms.

Unsupervised learning

In unsupervised learning, the goal is to infer structure or patterns from data without needing any prior labeling of the data. Because the data is unlabeled, there is typically no way to evaluate the accuracy of the learning algorithm, a major distinction from supervised learning. Unsupervised learning algorithms typically are not given any *a priori* knowledge of the data, except perhaps indirectly by the tuning parameters given to the algorithm itself.

Unsupervised learning is commonly used for problems that might be solvable by eye if the data had very few dimensions, but the large dimensionality of the data makes this impossible or very difficult for a human to infer. Unsupervised learning can also be used for lower-dimension problems that may be solved intuitively by a human, but where there is a lot of data to be processed, it is unreasonable to do manually.

Imagine that you're writing an algorithm that looks at satellite imagery data and the task is to identify buildings and cluster them into geographically-separated neighborhoods. If you have just one image, or a handful of images, this is easy to accomplish by hand. A researcher would mark all the buildings on a photo and visually inspect the photo to determine clusters of buildings. The researcher then records the latitude and longitude of the neighborhood's center and puts the results in a spreadsheet. Great, the head scientist says, only three million more images to go! This is an example of a low-dimensional problem (there are only two dimensions, *latitude* and *longitude*, to consider) that is made implausible by the sheer volume of the task. Clearly a more sophisticated solution is required.

To develop an unsupervised learning approach to this problem, a researcher might divide the problem into two stages: **preprocessing** and **analysis**. In the preprocessing step, each image should be run through an algorithm that detects buildings in the photograph and returns their latitude/longitude coordinates. This preprocessing step can be managed in several ways: one approach would be to send the images to a team of interns to be manually marked; another approach could be a non-machine learning edge detection algorithm that looks for rectangular shapes; and a third approach could be a **Convolutional Neural Network (CNN)** that is trained to identify images of buildings.

Once the preprocessing has been done and a list of building coordinates is on hand, the coordinates can then be run through an unsupervised clustering algorithm, such as the k-means algorithm, which we'll explore later. The unsupervised algorithm does not need to know what a *building* is, it doesn't need to know about any existing neighborhoods or clusters of buildings, and doesn't need any other *a priori* knowledge of the problem. The algorithm is simply able to read a list of millions or billions of latitude/longitude coordinates, and group them into geographically-centered clusters.

Because unsupervised algorithms cannot judge the accuracy of their results, there is no guarantee that this algorithm will generate neighborhoods that match up with census data or that the algorithm's concept of *neighborhood* will be semantically correct. It's possible that a single town or neighborhood may be considered two separate neighborhoods if, for instance, a wide highway divides two halves of the town. It's also possible that the algorithm may combine two neighborhoods that are considered by their residents to be distinct into one single cluster, if there is no clear separation between the two neighborhoods.

In many cases, this type of semantic error is acceptable; the benefit of this approach to the problem is that it can process millions or billions of data points quickly and provides at least a logical sense of clustering. The results of the unsupervised clustering can be further postprocessed, either by another algorithm or reviewed by hand, to add semantic information to the results.

Unsupervised algorithms can also find patterns in high-dimensional datasets that humans are unable to visualize intuitively. In the building clustering problem, it's easy for a researcher to visually inspect the two-dimensional map and identify clusters by eye. Imagine now that you have a set of data points, each existing in a 100-dimensional space (that is, data that has 100 distinct features). If the amount of data you possess is non-trivial, for example, more than 100 or 1,000 data points, it may be nearly impossible for a human to interpret the data, because the relationships between the features are too difficult to visualize in a 100-dimensional space.

As a contrived example of the preceding problem, imagine you're a psychologist and your task is to interpret a thousand surveys given to participants that ask 100 different questions, each on a 1-10 scale. Each question is designed to rate a different aspect of the participant's personality. Your goal in interpreting this data is to determine how many distinct personality types are represented by the respondents.

Processing only 1,000 data points by hand is certainly achievable, and common practice in many fields. In this case, however, the high dimensionality of the data makes it very difficult to discover patterns. Two respondents may have answered some questions very similarly, but answered other questions differently; are these two respondents similar enough to be considered of the same personality type? And how similar is that personality type to any other given personality type? The same algorithm we used previously to detect clusters of buildings can be applied to this problem in order to detect clusters of respondents and their personality types (my apologies to any actual psychologists reading this; I know I have grossly oversimplified the problem!).

In this case, the unsupervised clustering algorithm does not have any difficultly with *visualizing* the 100 dimensions involved, and will perform similarly to the two-dimensional neighborhood clustering problem. The same caveats apply, as well: there is no guarantee that the clusters the algorithm detects will be psychologically correct, nor that the questions themselves were designed correctly to appropriately capture all the distinct personality types. The only promise this algorithm makes is that it will identify clusters of similar data points.

In `Chapter 2`, *Data Exploration*, we discussed the importance of preprocessing data before giving it to a ML algorithm. We are now beginning to understand the importance of postprocessing and interpreting results, especially when looking at unsupervised algorithms. Because unsupervised algorithms can only judge their overall statistical distribution (that is, the average distance from any point to its cluster center in this case), rather than their semantic error (that is, how many data points are actually **correct**), the algorithm cannot make any claims as to its semantic correctness. Looking at metrics such as root-mean-squared error or standard deviation may give you a hint as to how the algorithm performed, but this cannot be used as a judgment of the algorithm's accuracy, and can only be used to describe the statistical properties of the dataset. Looking at these metrics won't tell you if the results are correct, and will only tell you how clustered or unclustered the data is (some neighborhoods are sparse, other neighborhoods are dense, and so on).

So far we have considered unsupervised learning in the context of clustering algorithms, which is indeed a major family of unsupervised learning algorithms, but there are also many others. For instance, our discussion of outlier detection from `Chapter 2`, *Data Exploration*, would fall under the category of unsupervised learning; we are looking at unlabeled data with no *a priori* knowledge, and attempting to glean insights from that data.

Another example of a popular unsupervised learning technique is **Principal Component Analysis (PCA)**, which we briefly introduced in `Chapter 2`, *Data Exploration*. PCA is an unsupervised learning algorithm commonly used during preprocessing for feature detection and dimensionality reduction, and this algorithm fits the use case of interpreting high dimensional data. Unlike clustering algorithms, which aim to tell you how many logical clusters of data points exist in a dataset, PCA aims to tell you which features or dimensions of a dataset can be neatly combined into statistically significant derived features. In some sense, PCA can be thought of as the clustering of features or dimensions, rather than the clustering of data points.

An algorithm such as PCA does not necessarily need to be used exclusively for preprocessing, and can in fact be used as the primary ML algorithm from which you want to gain insight.

Let's return to our psychological survey example. Rather than clustering survey respondents, we might want to analyze the questions themselves with a PCA. The results of the algorithm would tell you which survey questions are most significantly correlated to one another, and this insight can help you rewrite the actual survey questions so that they better target the personality traits that you wish to study. Additionally, the dimensionality reduction that PCA provides can help a researcher visualize the relationship between the questions, respondents, and results. The algorithm will convert your 100-dimensional, highly interconnected feature space that's impossible to visualize into distinct, lower-dimensional spaces that can actually be graphed and visually inspected.

As with all unsupervised learning algorithms, there is no guarantee that the principal component algorithm will be semantically correct, there is only a guarantee that the algorithm will be able to statistically determine the relationships between features. This means that some results may seem nonsensical or unintuitive; the algorithm might combine questions that don't seem to make intuitive sense when combined. In a situation like this, it's up to the researcher to postprocess and interpret the results of the analysis, potentially modifying the questions or changing their approach for the next round of surveys.

There are many other examples of unsupervised learning algorithms, including the autoencoder neural network, which we will discuss in a later chapter. The most important feature of an unsupervised learning algorithm is the lack of labels in its input data, which results in the inability to determine the semantic correctness of its results. Do not make the mistake of dismissing unsupervised learning algorithms as being *lesser* than other algorithms, however, as they are very important in data preprocessing and many other types of data exploration tasks. Just as a wrench is no more and no less valuable than a screwdriver, each tool has its place and purpose in the world of ML.

Supervised learning

Like unsupervised learning, the goal of a supervised learning algorithm is to interpret input data and generate insights as its output. Unlike unsupervised learning, supervised learning algorithms are first trained on labeled training examples. The training examples are used by the algorithm to build a *model*, or an internal representation of the relationships between the data's properties and its label, and the model is then applied to new, unlabeled data points that you wish to glean insight from.

Supervised learning is often more exciting to ML students, as this category of algorithms aims to provide semantically correct results. When a supervised learning algorithm works well, the results almost seem magical! You can train an algorithm on 1,000 prelabeled data points and then use that model to process millions of future data points, with some expectation of semantic accuracy in the results.

Because supervised learning algorithms aim to be semantically correct, we must first discuss how this correctness is measured. First, we must introduce the concepts of *true positives*, *false positives*, *true negatives*, and *false negatives*, then we will introduce the concepts of accuracy, precision, and recall.

Measuring accuracy

Imagine you are developing a spam filter for a commenting system you've developed for your blog. Spam filters are a type of supervised learning algorithm, as the algorithm must first be told what constitutes spam versus ham. You train your spam system on many examples of ham and spam messages, and then release it into production and allow it to classify all new comments, automatically blocking spam messages and letting genuine ham messages go through.

Let us consider a *positive* to be a comment that the algorithm identifies as spam (we're calling this *positive* because we're calling the algorithm a spam filter; this is only a semantic distinction, as we could call the filter a *ham filter* and instead use *positive* to denote suspected ham messages). Let's consider a *negative* to be a comment identified as a genuine (ham) comment.

If your algorithm categorizes a comment as spam (positive), and does so semantically correctly (that is, when you read the message, you also determine that it is spam), the algorithm has generated a *true positive*, or a positive result that is truly and correctly a positive result. If, on the other hand, a genuine comment incorrectly gets identified as spam and blocked, that is considered a *false positive*, or a positive result that is not actually positive. Similarly, a genuine ham message that is identified as ham is a *true negative*, and a spam comment that is identified as ham and let through is considered a *false negative*. It is unreasonable to expect an algorithm to provide 100% correct results, so there will always be some amount of false positives and false negatives in practice.

If we take our four classifications of result accuracy, we can count the number of instances of each classification and determine a rate for each: we can easily calculate the false positive rate, the true positive rate, the false negative rate, and the true negative rate. However, these four rates may be clumsy to discuss if we treat them independently, so we can also combine these rates into other categories.

For instance, the *recall*, or *sensitivity*, of an algorithm is its true positive rate, or the percentage of times that a positive classification is a true positive. In our spam example, the recall therefore refers to the percentage of spam messages correctly identified out of all actual spam messages. This can be calculated as either *true positives divided by actual positives*, or alternatively *true positives divided by true positives plus false negatives* (recall that false negatives are comments that are actually spam, but incorrectly identified as ham). Recall, in this case, refers to the algorithm's ability to correctly detect a spam comment, or put simply, *of all the actual spam messages there are, how many did we identify?*

Specificity is similar to recall, except that it represents the algorithm's true negative rate. Specificity asks the question *of all actual ham messages, how many did we correctly identify?*

Precision, on the other hand, is defined as the number of true positives divided by the sum of true positives and false positives. In terms of our spam example, precision answers the question *of all the messages we think are spam, how many guesses did we get correctly?* The distinction between the two metrics lies in whether we are considering all *actual* spam messages, or considering messages we *think* are spam.

Accuracy is distinct from both precision and recall, and focuses on overall correct results. It is defined as the rate of true positives and true negatives divided by the total number of trials (that is, how many guesses were correct overall). A common mistake that students of ML often make is to focus on accuracy alone, because it is intuitively easier to understand, but accuracy often is not sufficient when evaluating the performance of an algorithm.

To demonstrate this, we must consider the impact of the performance of our spam filter on our real-world results. In some cases, you want a spam filter that never ever lets a single spam message through, even if that means incorrectly blocking some ham messages. In other cases, it's better to make sure that all ham messages are allowed, even if a few spam messages evade your filter. It's possible for two different spam filters to have the same exact *accuracy*, but totally different characteristics of precision and recall. For this reason, accuracy (while very useful) cannot always be the only performance metric you consider.

Because the previous mathematical definitions may be a little difficult to internalize, let's put numbers to the example. Consider 100 messages, 70 of which are genuinely ham and 30 of which are genuinely spam:

	30 Actual Spam (Positive)	70 Actual Ham (Negative)
26 Guessed Spam	22 (True Positive)	4 (False Positive)
74 Guessed Ham	8 (False Negative)	66 (True Negative)

To calculate the accuracy of the algorithm, we add up the correct guesses: 22 true positives and 66 true negatives, which equals 88 correct guesses in total. Our accuracy is therefore 88%.

As an aside: 88% accuracy would be considered very good for advanced algorithms on difficult problems, but a little poor for a spam filter.

The recall or sensitivity of the algorithm is the *true positive rate*, or the number of times we guessed correctly when looking at examples that are *actually* spam. This means that we only consider the left hand column in the preceding table. The recall of the algorithm is the number of true positives among the actual positives, that is, the number of true positives divided by the true positives plus the false negatives. In this case, we have 22 true positives and 30 actual spam messages, so the recall of our algorithm is 22/30, or 73%.

The precision of the algorithm relates not to the messages that are *actually* spam, but instead to the messages that we *guessed* are spam. In this case, we only consider the top row, or the true positives divided by the sum of true positives and false positives; that is, the true positives divided by the guessed positives. In our case, there are 22 true positives and 26 total guessed positives, so our precision is 22/26, or 84%.

Note that this algorithm is more precise than it is sensitive. This means that its spam guesses are 84% correct *when it guesses spam*, but the algorithm also has a tendency to lean towards guessing ham, and misses a good number of actual spam messages. Also note that the total accuracy is 88%, but both its precision and recall are lower than that figure.

Another way to think about these performance metrics intuitively is as follows: precision is the algorithm's ability to guess correctly when it guesses positive, but recall is the algorithm's ability to remember what a spam message looks like. High precision and low recall would mean that an algorithm is very selective when guessing that a message is spam; the algorithm really needs to be convinced that a message is spam before identifying it as spam.

The algorithm is very *precise* about saying that a message is spam.

It, therefore, might favor letting ham messages through at the cost of accidentally letting some spam through. A low-precision, high-recall algorithm, on the other hand, will tend to more aggressively identify messages as spam, however, it will also incorrectly block a number of ham messages (the algorithm better *recalls* what spam looks like, it is more *sensitive* to spam, therefore it thinks more messages are spam and will act accordingly).

Of course, some algorithms can have high accuracy, precision, and recall—but more realistically, the way you train your algorithms will involve trade-offs between precision and recall, and you must balance these trade-offs against the desired goals of your system.

Supervised learning algorithms

Now that we have developed an understanding of accuracy, precision, and recall, we can continue with the topic at hand: supervised learning algorithms. The key distinction between supervised and unsupervised learning algorithms is the presence of prelabeled data, typically introduced during the training phase of the algorithm. A supervised learning algorithm should be able to learn from labeled training data and then analyze a new, unlabeled data point and guess that data's label.

Supervised learning algorithms further divide into two subcategories: **classification** and **regression**. Classification algorithms aim to predict the label of an unseen data point, based on the generalized patterns that it has learned from the training data, as described previously. Regression algorithms aim to predict the value of a new point, again based on the generalized patterns that it has learned during training. While classification and regression feel different in practice, the preceding description betrays how similar the two categories actually are; the major distinction between the two is that regression algorithms typically work with continuous data, for instance, time-series or coordinate data. For the rest of this section, however, we will discuss only classification tasks.

Because the algorithm builds a model from labeled data, it is expected that the algorithm can generate *semantically* correct results, as opposed to the *statistically* correct results that unsupervised algorithms generate. A semantically correct result is a result that would hold up to external scrutiny, using the same techniques by which the training data was labeled. In a spam filter, a semantically correct result is a guess that the algorithm makes that a human would agree with.

The ability to generate semantically correct results is enabled by the prelabeled training data. The training data itself represents the semantics of the problem, and is how the algorithm learns to generate its semantically correct results. Notice that this entire discussion—and the entire discussion of accuracy, precision, and recall—hinges on the ability to introduce externally validated information to the model. You can only know if an individual guess is correct if an external entity independently validates the result, and you can only teach an algorithm to make semantically correct guesses if an external entity has provided enough data points with their correct labels to train the algorithm on. You can think of the training data for a supervised learning algorithm as the source of truth from which all guesses originate.

While supervised learning algorithms may indeed seem like magic when they're working well, there are many potential pitfalls. Because the training data is of crucial importance to the algorithm, your results will only be as good as your training data and your training methods. Some noise in training data can often be tolerated, but if there is a source of systemic error in the training data, you will also have systemic errors in your results. These may be difficult to detect, since the validation of a model typically uses a subset of the training data that you set aside—the same data that has the systemic error is used to validate the model, so you will think that the model is running well!

Another potential pitfall is not having enough training data. If the problem you're solving is highly-dimensional, you will need a correspondingly large amount of training data; the training data must be sufficient to actually present all of the various patterns to the machine learning algorithm. You wouldn't expect to train a spam filter on only 10 emails and also expect great results.

These factors often present a sort of startup cost to supervised learning. Some amount of investment needs to be made in procuring or generating an appropriate amount of and in the distribution of training examples. The training data typically, though not always, needs to be generated by human knowledge and evaluation. This can be costly, especially in the case of image processing and object detection, which generally need many labeled training examples. In a world where ML algorithms are becoming ever more accessible, the true competition lies in having the best data to work with.

In the case of our spam filter, the need for training data means that you cannot simply write and launch the spam filter. You'll also need to spend some time manually recording which emails are spam and ham (or have your users report this). Before deploying your spam filter, you should make sure that you have enough training data to both train and validate the algorithm with, and that could mean having to wait until you have hundreds or thousands of examples of spam messages flagged by a human.

Assuming you have an appropriate amount of high-quality training data, it's also possible to mismanage the training process and cause bad results with good data. ML novices often believe that more training is categorically better, but this is not the case.

There are two new concepts to introduce at this point: **bias** and **variance**. When training a ML model, your hope is that the model will learn the *general* attributes of the training data and be able to extrapolate from there. If an algorithm has made significant incorrect assumptions about the structure of the data, it can be said to be highly biased and therefore *underfitted*. On the other hand, a model can demonstrate high variance, or a high sensitivity to small differences in training data. This is called **overfitting**, and can be thought of as the algorithm learning to identify individual examples, or the specific noise in individual examples, rather than the general trend of the data.

Overtraining models can easily lead to overfitting. Imagine that you use the same keyboard every day for 10 years, but the keyboard is actually a strange model with an odd layout and lots of quirks. It's to be expected that you'd become very good at typing on such a keyboard after so much time. Then, unexpectedly, the keyboard breaks and you get a new standard keyboard only to find that you have no idea how to type on it! The muscle memory that you've trained over a decade of typing is used to the period key being *just so*, the letter *o* being shifted off a little further to the right, and so on. When using the new keyboard, you find that you can't type a single word without a typo. A decade of overtraining on a bad keyboard has only taught you how to type *on that keyboard*, and you haven't been able to generalize your skill to other keyboards. Overfitting a model is the same concept: your algorithm gets very good at identifying your training data *and nothing else*.

For this reason, training a model is not as simple as plugging in training data and letting the algorithm train for an arbitrary amount of time. One crucial step in the process is to divide your training data into two parts: one set for training the algorithm, and another part used *only* to validate the results of your model. You should not train the algorithm on your validation data, because you run the risk of training the model on how to identify your validation data, rather than training it and then using the validation data to independently verify the accuracy of your algorithm. The need for a validation set increases the cost of generating training data. If you determine that you need 1,000 examples to train your algorithm on, you may actually need to generate 1,500 examples in total in order to have a reasonable validation set.

Validation data is not just used to test the overall accuracy of the algorithm. You also often use validation data to determine when to *stop* training. During the training process, you should periodically test the algorithm with your validation data. Over time you will find that the accuracy of the validation will increase, as expected, and then at a certain point the validation accuracy may actually *decrease.* This change in direction is the point at which your model has begun overfitting your training data. The algorithm will always continue to get more accurate when you present it with an example from your training set (those are the examples it's learning directly), but once the model begins to overfit the training data, it'll begin to lose the ability to generalize and therefore perform worse—not better—with data it has not been trained on. For this reason, maintaining an independent set of validation data is crucial. If you ever train an algorithm and it has 100% accuracy when testing its own training data, the odds are you've overfitted the data and it will likely perform very poorly on unseen data. The algorithm has gone past learning the general trends in the data and is starting to memorize specific examples, including the various bits of noise in the data.

Aside from maintaining a validation set, proper preprocessing of your data will also combat overfitting. The various noise reduction, feature selection, feature extraction, and dimensionality reduction techniques we discussed in Chapter 2, *Data Exploration*, will all serve to help generalize your model and avoid overfitting.

Finally, because the semantic correctness of your algorithm's inferences can only be determined by an external source, it's often impossible to know whether a guess is actually correct (unless you receive user feedback on a specific guess). At best, you can only infer from the precision, recall, and accuracy values you've calculated during your training and validation stage what the overall effectiveness of the algorithm is. Fortunately, many supervised learning algorithms present their results in a probabilistic manner (for example, *I think there's a 92% chance this is spam*), so you can have some indication of the algorithm's confidence in an inference, however, when you combine this confidence level with the precision and recall of the model and the fact that your training data may have systemic errors, even the confidence level that comes with an inference is questionable.

Despite these potential pitfalls, supervised learning is a very powerful technique. The ability to extrapolate from only a few thousand training examples in a complex problem domain and quickly make inferences on millions of unseen data points is both impressive and highly valuable.

As with unsupervised learning, there are many types of supervised learning algorithms, each with their own strengths and weaknesses. Neural networks, Bayesian classifiers, k-nearest neighbor, decision trees, and random forests are all examples of supervised learning techniques.

Reinforcement learning

While supervised and unsupervised learning are the two primary subclassifications of machine learning algorithms, they are in fact part of a spectrum and there are other modes of learning. The next most significant learning mode in the context of this book is reinforcement learning, which in some ways can be considered a hybrid of supervised and unsupervised learning; however, most would categorize reinforcement learning as an unsupervised learning algorithm. This is one of those cases where the taxonomy becomes a little vague!

In unsupervised learning, almost nothing is known about the data to be processed and the algorithm must infer patterns from a blank slate. In supervised learning, significant resources are dedicated to training the algorithm on known examples. In reinforcement learning, *something* is known (or can be known) about the data, but the knowledge of the data is not an explicit labeling or a categorization. Instead, the *something* that is known (or can be known) is the result of an action based on a decision made with the data. Reinforcement learning is considered by many to be an unsupervised learning algorithm, because the algorithm *starts from scratch*, however reinforcement also *closes the loop* and continually retrains itself based on its own actions, which has some similarities to training in supervised learning.

To use an absurd and contrived example, imagine that you're writing an algorithm that is supposed to replace the function of government. The algorithm will receive as its input the current state of affairs of the country and must, as an output, develop new policies and laws in order to optimize the country in many dimensions: citizen happiness, economic health, low crime, and so on. The reinforcement learning approach to this problem starts from scratch, knowing nothing about how its laws and policies will affect the country. The algorithm then implements a law or set of laws; because it has just started, the law it implements will be completely arbitrary. After the law has taken some time to go into effect and make its impact on society, the algorithm will once again read the state of affairs of the country and may discover that it has turned the country into a chaotic wasteland. The algorithm learns from this feedback, adjusts itself, and implements a new set of laws. Over time, and using the initial laws it implements as experiments, the algorithm will come to understand the cause and effect of its policies and begin to optimize. Given enough time, this approach may develop a near-perfect society—if it doesn't accidentally destroy the society with its initial failed experiments.

Reinforcement learning techniques are distinct from supervised and unsupervised algorithms in that they directly interact with their environment and monitor the effects of their decisions in order to update their models. Rather than aiming to detect patterns or to classify data, most reinforcement learning aims to optimize some cost or reward within an environment. The environment in question can either be a real-world environment, as is often the case in the field of control systems, or it can be a virtual environment, as is the case with genetic algorithms. In either case, the algorithm must have some way of characterizing an overall *cost/penalty* or *reward*, and will work to optimize that value. Reinforcement learning is an important optimization technique, especially in highly dimensional problem spaces, since a brute-force trial-and-error approach is often impossible to achieve in a reasonable amount of time.

Examples of reinforcement learning algorithms include genetic algorithms, which we will discuss in depth in a later chapter, Monte Carlo methods, and gradient descent (which we will discuss alongside neural networks).

Categories of algorithms

We've categorized ML algorithms by their learning mode, but that's not the only way to categorize algorithms. Another approach is to categorize them by their task or function. In this section we will briefly present the basic functions of ML algorithms and name some example algorithms.

Clustering

Clustering algorithms aim to identify groups of data points that are similar to one another. The definition of *similar* depends on the type of data, the problem domain, and the algorithm used. The easiest way to intuitively understand clustering algorithms is to visualize points on an x/y grid. A clustering algorithm's aim is typically to draw circles around groups of similar points; each set of circled points is taken to be a cluster. The clusters are generally not known beforehand, so clustering algorithms are generally classified as unsupervised learning problems.

Some examples of clustering algorithms include:

- k-means, and variants such as k-medians
- Gaussian mixture models
- Mean-shift

Classification

Classification is a very broad (and very popular) category of supervised learning algorithms, with the goal of trying to identify a data point as belonging to some classification (spam or ham; male or female; animal, mineral or vegetable, and so on). A multitude of algorithms for classification exists, including:

- k-nearest neighbor
- Logistic regression
- Naive Bayes classifier
- Support Vector Machines
- (Most) neural networks
- Decision trees
- Random forests

Regression

Regression algorithms aim to determine and characterize the relationship between variables. In the most simple case of two-dimensional linear regression, the algorithm's goal is to determine the line that can be drawn most closely through a set of points, however, higher-degree and higher-dimensional regressions can generate significant insights and make predictions concerning complex data. Because these algorithms necessarily require known data points, they are considered to be supervised learning algorithms. Some examples:

- Linear regression
- Polynomial regression
- Bayesian linear regression
- Least absolute deviation

Dimensionality reduction

Dimensionality reduction is a family of techniques whose purpose is to convert data with a high number of dimensions into data with a lower number of dimensions. Used as a general term, this can mean either discarding dimensions entirely (such as feature selection), or to create new individual dimensions that simultaneously represent multiple original dimensions, with some loss of resolution (such as feature extraction).

Some algorithms that can be used for dimensionality reduction include:

- Various types of regressions
- PCA
- Image transformations (for example, converting an image to grayscale)
- Stemming and lemmatization (in natural language processing)

Optimization

Optimization algorithms have the goal of selecting a set of parameters, or the values for a set of parameters, such that the cost or error of a system is minimized (alternatively, such that the reward of a system is maximized). Feature selection and feature extraction is actually a form of optimization; you are modifying parameters with the purpose of reducing dimensionality while preserving important data. In the most basic optimization technique, a brute-force search, you simply try every possible combination of parameters and select the combination with the best results. In practice, most problems are complex enough that a brute-force search may take an unreasonable amount of time (that is, millions of years on a modern computer). Some optimization techniques include:

- A brute force search (also known as an *exhaustive search*)
- Gradient descent
- Simulated annealing
- Genetic algorithms

Natural language processing

Natural language processing (**NLP**) is an entire field on its own and contains many techniques that are not considered in machine learning. However, NLP is often used in concert with ML algorithms, as the two fields combined are necessary to achieve generalized artificial intelligence. Many ML classification algorithms operate on text rather than numbers (such as our spam filter), and in those situations, we rely on techniques from the field of NLP: stemming, in particular, is a quick and easy dimensionality reduction technique for text classifiers. Some NLP techniques relevant to ML include:

- Tokenization
- String distance
- Stemming or lemmatization
- TF-IDF

Image processing

Like NLP, image processing is its own field of study that has overlapped with ML but is not fully encompassed by ML. As with NLP, we may often use image processing techniques to reduce dimensionality before applying an ML algorithm to an image. Some image processing techniques relevant to machine learning include:

- Edge detection
- Scale invariant transformations
- Color space transformations
- Object detection
- Recurrent neural networks

Summary

In this chapter, we've discussed the various ways we can categorize machine learning techniques. In particular, we discussed the difference between unsupervised learning, supervised learning, and reinforcement learning, presenting various examples of each.

We also discussed different ways to judge the accuracy of machine learning algorithms, in particular, the concepts of accuracy, precision, and recall as applied to supervised learning techniques. We also discussed the importance of the training step in supervised learning algorithms, and illustrated the concepts of bias, variance, generalization, and overfitting.

Finally, we looked at how machine learning algorithms can be categorized not by learning mode but instead by task or technique, and presented a number of algorithms that fit into the categories of clustering, classification, regression, dimensionality reduction, natural language processing, and image processing.

In the next chapter, we'll get our hands dirty and take a deep dive into clustering algorithms.

4
Grouping with Clustering Algorithms

A common and introductory unsupervised learning problem is that of *clustering*. Often, you have large datasets that you wish to organize into smaller groups, or wish to break up into logically similar groups. For instance, you can try to divide census data of household incomes into three groups: low, high, and super rich. If you feed the household income data into a clustering algorithm, you would expect to see three data points as a result, with each corresponding to the average value of your three categories. Even this one-dimensional problem of clustering household incomes may be difficult to do by hand, because you might not know where one group should end and the other should begin. You could use governmental definitions of income brackets, but there's no guarantee that those brackets are geometrically balanced; they were invented by policymakers and may not accurately represent the data.

A *cluster* is a group of logically similar data points. They can be users with similar behavior, citizens with similar income ranges, pixels with similar colors, and so on. The k-means algorithm is numerical and geometric, so the clusters it identifies will all be numerically similar, with data points that are geometrically close to one another. Fortunately, most data can be represented numerically, so the k-means algorithm is useful for many different problem domains.

The k-means algorithm is a powerful, fast, and popular clustering algorithm for numerical data. The name k-means is comprised of two parts: *k*, which represents the number of clusters that we want the algorithm to find, and ***means,*** which is the method of determining where those cluster centers are (you could, for instance, also use k-medians or k-modes). Translated into plain English, we might ask the algorithm to find us three cluster centers that are the mean values of the points they represent. In that case, $k = 3$ and we can tell our bosses that we did a k-means analysis with $k = 3$ when filing our report.

The k-means algorithm is an iterative algorithm, which means it runs a loop and continually updates its model until the model reaches steady state, at which point it will return its results. Put into narrative form, the k-means algorithm works like this: plot the data that you wish to analyze, and pick a value for k. You must know the value of k beforehand, or at least have an idea of what it should be (though we'll also explore a way around this later in the chapter). Randomly create k points (if $k = 5$, create five points) and add them to your plot; these points are called the **centroids**, as they will ultimately represent the geometric centers of the clusters. For each data point in the plot, find the centroid closest to that point and connect or assign it to the point. Once all the assignments have been made, look at each centroid in turn and update its position to the mean position of all the points assigned to it. Repeat the assign-then-update procedure until the centroids stop moving; these final positions of the centroids are the output of the algorithm, and can be considered your cluster centers. If the narrative is hard to follow, don't worry, we'll dig into it more deeply as we build this algorithm from scratch.

In this chapter, we'll first discuss the concepts of average and distance and how they apply to the k-means algorithm. Then we'll describe the algorithm itself and build a JavaScript class from scratch to implement the k-means algorithm. We'll test our k-means solver with a couple of simple datasets, and then discuss what to do when you don't know the value of k beforehand. We'll build another tool that automates the discovery of the value k. We'll also discuss what the concept of *error* means for k-means applications, and how to design an error algorithm that helps us achieve our goals. The following are the topics that will be covered in this chapter:

- Average and distance
- Writing the k-means algorithm
- Example 1—k-means on simple 2D data
- Example 2—3D data
- K-means where k is unknown

Average and distance

The k-means algorithm relies on two concepts in order to operate: average and distance. In order to tell you where the center of a cluster is, the algorithm will calculate an average value for these points. In this case, we will use the arithmetic mean, or the sum of values divided by the number of values, to represent our average. In ES5/classic JavaScript (I'm also being purposefully explicit in this example, for any readers who are not familiar with calculating the mean), we might write a function like this:

```
/**
 * @param {Array.<number>} numbers
 * @return {float}
 */
function mean(numbers) {
    var sum = 0, length = numbers.length;

    if (length === 0) {
        /**
         * Mathematically, the mean of an empty set is undefined,
         * so we could return early here. We could also allow the function
         * to attempt dividing 0/0, would would return NaN in JavaScript but
         * fail in some other languages (so probably a bad habit to encourage).
         * Ultimately, I would like this function to not return mixed types,
         * so instead let's throw an error.
         */
        throw new Error('Cannot calculate mean of empty set');
    }

    for (var i = 0; i < length; i++) {
        sum += numbers[i];
    }

    return sum / length;
}
```

In ES6, we can abuse our shorthand privileges and write the following:

```
const mean = numbers => numbers.reduce((sum, val) => sum + val, 0) /
numbers.length;
```

This is a handy ES6 one-liner to keep in your back pocket, however, it assumes all values are already numeric and defined, and it will return NaN if you give it an empty array. If the shorthand is confusing, we can break it up like so:

```
const sum = (numbers) => numbers.reduce((sum, val) => sum + val, 0);
const mean = (numbers) => sum(numbers) / numbers.length;
```

Keep in mind we can use any type of average, including the median and mode. In fact, it's sometimes preferable to use k-medians over k-means. The median does a better job of muting outliers than the mean does. You should therefore always ask yourself which average you actually need. If you want a representation of total resources consumed, for instance, you might use the arithmetic mean. If you suspect outliers are caused by faulty measurements and should be ignored, k-medians could suit you better.

We will also need a concept of distance in this algorithm. It can be any distance measure, however, for numeric data you will mostly use the typical Euclidean distance—the standard distance measure you'd learn in high school—which in ES5 JavaScript looks like this for two dimensions:

```
/**
 * Calculates only the 2-dimensional distance between two points a and b.
 * Each point should be an array with length = 2, and both elements defined
and numeric.
 * @param {Array.number} a
 * @param {Array.number} b
 * @return {float}
 */
function distance2d(a, b) {
    // Difference between b[0] and a[0]
    var diff_0 = b[0] - a[0];
    // Difference between b[1] and a[1]
    var diff_1 = b[1] - a[1];

    return Math.sqrt(diff_0*diff_0 + diff_1*diff_1);
}
```

We must support many more than two dimensions, however, so we can generalize to the following:

```
/**
 * Calculates the N-dimensional distance between two points a and b.
 * Each point should be an array with equal length, and all elements
defined and numeric.
 * @param {Array.number} a
 * @param {Array.number} b
 * @return {float}
```

```
    */
function distance(a, b) {

    var length = a.length,
        sumOfSquares = 0;

    if (length !== b.length) {
        throw new Error('Points a and b must be the same length');
    }

    for (var i = 0; i < length; i++) {
        var diff = b[i] - a[i];
        sumOfSquares += diff*diff;
    }

    return Math.sqrt(sumOfSquares);
}
```

We can write an ES6 one-liner for this, but it won't be as readable as the lengthier, explicit example:

```
const distance = (a, b) => Math.sqrt(
    a.map((aPoint, i) => b[i] - aPoint)
      .reduce((sumOfSquares, diff) => sumOfSquares + (diff*diff), 0)
);
```

Armed with these tools, we can start writing the k-means algorithm itself.

Writing the k-means algorithm

The k-means algorithm is relatively simple to implement, so in this chapter we'll write it from scratch. The algorithm requires only two pieces of information: the k in k-means (the number of clusters we wish to identify), and the data points to evaluate. There are additional parameters the algorithm can use, for example, the maximum number of iterations to allow, but they are not required. The only required output of the algorithm is k centroids, or a list of points that represent the centers of the clusters of data. If $k = 3$, then the algorithm must return three centroids as its output. The algorithm may also return other metrics, such as the total error, the total number of iterations required to reach steady state, and so on, but again these are optional.

A high-level description of the k-means algorithm is as follows:

1. Given the parameter *k* and the data to process, initialize *k* candidate centroids randomly
2. For each data point, determine which candidate centroid is closest to that point and *assign* the point to that centroid
3. For each centroid, update its position to be the mean position of all the points assigned to it
4. Repeat *Step 2* and *Step 3* until the centroids' positions reach steady state (that is, the centroids stop moving)

At the end of this process, you may return the positions of the centroids as the algorithm's output.

Setting up the environment

Let's take a moment to set up our development environment for this algorithm. The environment will be as described in Chapter 1, *Exploring the Potential of JavaScript*, however, we'll run through the entire process here.

First, create a new folder for this project. I've named the folder Ch4-kmeans. Create a subfolder called src inside Ch4-kmeans.

Next, add a file called package.json to the Ch4-kmeans folder. Add the following content to the file:

```
{
  "name": "Ch4-kmeans",
  "version": "1.0.0",
  "description": "ML in JS Example for Chapter 4 - kmeans",
  "main": "src/index.js",
  "author": "Burak Kanber",
  "license": "MIT",
  "scripts": {
    "build-web": "browserify src/index.js -o dist/index.js -t [ babelify --
presets [ env ] ]",
    "build-cli": "browserify src/index.js --node -o dist/index.js -t [
babelify --presets [ env ] ]",
    "start": "yarn build-cli && node dist/index.js"
  },
  "dependencies": {
    "babel-core": "^6.26.0",
    "babel-preset-env": "^1.6.1",
```

```
    "babelify": "^8.0.0",
    "browserify": "^15.1.0"
  }
}
```

After creating the `package.json` file, switch to your terminal program and (from the `Ch4-kmeans` folder) run the `yarn install` command.

Next, create three new files inside the `Ch4-kmeans/src` folder: `index.js`, `data.js`, and `kmeans.js`. We will write the actual k-means algorithm inside `kmeans.js`, we will load some example data into `data.js`, and we'll use `index.js` as our bootstrapping point to set up and run a number of examples.

At this point, you may want to stop and test that everything is working. Add a simple `console.log("Hello");` to `index.js` and then run the command `yarn start` from the command line. You should see the file compile and run, printing `Hello` to the screen before exiting. If you get errors or do not see the `Hello`, you may want to take a step back and double-check your environment. If everything is working, you can delete the `console.log("Hello");` from `index.js`.

Initializing the algorithm

In this section, we'll be working in the `kmeans.js` file. The first thing to do is to add our functions for mean and distance to the top of the file. Since these are generic functions that can be called **statistically**, we will not define them inside a class. Add the following to the top of the file:

```
/**
 * Calculate the mean of an array of numbers.
 * @param {Array.<number>} numbers
 * @return {number}
 */
const mean = numbers => numbers.reduce((sum, val) => sum + val, 0) /
numbers.length;

/**
 * Calculate the distance between two points.
 * Points must be given as arrays or objects with equivalent keys.
 * @param {Array.<number>} a
 * @param {Array.<number>} b
 * @return {number}
 */
const distance = (a, b) => Math.sqrt(
```

```
    a.map((aPoint, i) => b[i] - aPoint)
      .reduce((sumOfSquares, diff) => sumOfSquares + (diff*diff), 0)
);
```

Next, create and export a KMeans class. We will fill this in with many more methods throughout this chapter, but let's start with the following. Add this to the kmeans.js file beneath the code you just added:

```
class KMeans {

    /**
     * @param k
     * @param data
     */
    constructor(k, data) {
        this.k = k;
        this.data = data;
        this.reset();
    }

    /**
     * Resets the solver state; use this if you wish to run the
     * same solver instance again with the same data points
     * but different initial conditions.
     */
    reset() {
        this.error = null;
        this.iterations = 0;
        this.iterationLogs = [];
        this.centroids = this.initRandomCentroids();
        this.centroidAssignments = [];
    }
}

export default KMeans;
```

We've created a class called KMeans and are exporting it as the default export for this file. The preceding code also initializes some of the instance variables that the class will need, which we will describe shortly.

The constructor for the class takes two parameters, k and data, and stores both as instance variables. The k parameter represents the k in k-means, or the desired number of clusters as the algorithm's output. The data parameter is an array of data points that the algorithm will process.

At the end of the constructor, we call the `reset()` method, which is used to initialize (or reset) the solver's state. Specifically, the instance variables we initialize in the `reset` method are:

- `iterations`, which is a simple counter of how many iterations the solver has run, starting from 0
- `error`, which records the **root mean square error** (**RMSE**) of the points' distance to their centroids for the current iteration
- `centroidAssignments`, which is an array of data point index numbers that map to a centroid index number
- `centroids`, which will store the solver's candidates for the *k* centroids at the current iteration

Notice that in the `reset` method, we're making a call to `this.initRandomCentroids()`, which we have not yet defined. The k-means algorithm must start with a set of candidate centroids, so the purpose of that method is to generate the correct number of centroids randomly. Because the algorithm starts with a random state, it can be expected that multiple runs of the algorithm will return different results based on the initial conditions. This is actually a desired property of the k-means algorithm, because it is susceptible to finding local optima, and running the algorithm multiple times with different initial conditions may help you find the global optimum.

We have some prerequisites to satisfy before we can generate our random centroids. First, we must know the dimensionality of the data. Are we working with 2D data, 3D data, 10D data, or 1324D data? The random centroids we generate must have the same number of dimensions as the rest of the data points. This is an easy problem to solve; we assume that all the data points have the same number of dimensions, so we can just inspect the first data point we encounter. Add the following method to the `KMeans` class:

```
/**
 * Determines the number of dimensions in the dataset.
 * @return {number}
 */
getDimensionality() {
    const point = this.data[0];
    return point.length;
}
```

The other consideration we must make when generating random initial centroids is that the centroids should be close to the data that we're working with. For instance, if all your data points are points between (0, 0) and (10, 10), you would not want to generate a random centroid such as (1200, 740). Similarly, if your data points are all negative, you would not want to generate positive centroids, and so on.

Why should we care where the random centroids start? In this algorithm, points will be assigned to the centroid closest to it and gradually *pull* the centroid towards the cluster center. If the centroids are all to the right of the data points, then the centroids themselves will follow similar paths towards the data and may get all clumped together in one single cluster, converging to a local optimum. By making sure that the centroids are randomly distributed within the range of the data, we have a better chance of avoiding this type of local optimum.

Our approach to generating our centroid starting positions will be to determine the range of each dimension of the data, and then choose random values for our centroid's position within those ranges. For instance, imagine three two-dimensional data points in an x, y plane: (1, 3), (5, 8), and (3, 0). The range of the x dimension lies between 1 and 5, while the range of the y dimension lies between 0 and 8. Therefore, when creating a randomly initialized centroid, we will choose a random number between 1 and 5 for its x position, and a random number between 0 and 8 for its y position.

We can use JavaScript's `Math.min` and `Math.max` to determine the data ranges for each dimension. Add the following method to the `KMeans` class:

```
/**
 * For a given dimension in the dataset, determine the minimum
 * and maximum value. This is used during random initialization
 * to make sure the random centroids are in the same range as
 * the data.
 *
 * @param n
 * @returns {{min: *, max: *}}
 */
getRangeForDimension(n) {
    const values = this.data.map(point => point[n]);
    return {
        min: Math.min.apply(null, values),
        max: Math.max.apply(null, values)
    };
}
```

This method first collects all the values of the given dimension from the data points as an array and then returns an object containing that range's `min` and `max`. Returning to our preceding example of three data points ((1, 3), (5, 8), and (3, 0)), calling `getRangeForDimension(0)` would return {min: 1, max: 5}, and calling `getRangeForDimension(1)` would return {min: 0, max: 8}.

It will be useful for us to have an object of all dimensions and their ranges that we can cache while initializing centroids, so add the following method to the KMeans class as well:

```
/**
 * Get ranges for all dimensions.
 * @see getRangeForDimension
 * @returns {Array} Array whose indices are the dimension number and whose
 members are the output of getRangeForDimension
 */
getAllDimensionRanges() {
    const dimensionRanges = [];
    const dimensionality = this.getDimensionality();

    for (let dimension = 0; dimension < dimensionality; dimension++) {
        dimensionRanges[dimension] = this.getRangeForDimension(dimension);
    }

    return dimensionRanges;

}
```

This method simply looks at all dimensions and returns the `min` and `max` ranges for each, structured as objects in an array indexed by the dimension. This method is primarily a convenience, but we will use it shortly.

We can finally generate our randomly initialized centroids. We will need to create *k* centroids, and work dimension by dimension to choose a random point inside the range of each dimension. Add the following method to the KMeans class:

```
/**
 * Initializes random centroids, using the ranges of the data
 * to set minimum and maximum bounds for the centroids.
 * You may inspect the output of this method if you need to debug
 * random initialization, otherwise this is an internal method.
 * @see getAllDimensionRanges
 * @see getRangeForDimension
 * @returns {Array}
 */
initRandomCentroids() {
```

```
const dimensionality = this.getDimensionality();
const dimensionRanges = this.getAllDimensionRanges();
const centroids = [];

// We must create 'k' centroids.
for (let i = 0; i < this.k; i++) {

    // Since each dimension has its own range, create a placeholder at
first
    let point = [];

    /**
     * For each dimension in the data find the min/max range of that
dimension,
     * and choose a random value that lies within that range.
     */
    for (let dimension = 0; dimension < dimensionality; dimension++) {
        const {min, max} = dimensionRanges[dimension];
        point[dimension] = min + (Math.random()*(max-min));
    }

    centroids.push(point);

}

return centroids;

}
```

The preceding algorithm contains two loops; the outer loop creates k candidate centroids. Because the number of dimensions in the dataset is arbitrary, and because each dimension itself has an arbitrary range, we must then work dimension by dimension for each centroid in order to generate a random position. If your data is three-dimensional, the inner loop will consider dimensions 0, 1, and 2 separately, determining the min and max values for each dimension, choosing a random value in that range, and assigning that value to that specific dimension of the centroid point.

Testing random centroid generation

We've already written a significant amount of code, so now would be a good time to stop and test our work. We should also start setting up our data.js file that we'll use to hold some example data.

Open up the `data.js` file and add the following:

```
const example_randomCentroids = [
    [1, 3], [5, 8], [3, 0]
];

export default {
    example_randomCentroids
};
```

The values used are the same ones from our simple data point example written in the preceding block.

Now, switch to `index.js` and add the following code:

```
import KMeans from './kmeans.js';
import example_data from './data.js';

console.log("\nML in JS Chapter 4 k-means clustering examples.");
console.log("=================================================\n");

console.log("Testing centroid generation:");
console.log("=================================================\n");

const ex_randomCentroids_solver = new KMeans(2,
example_data.example_randomCentroids);

console.log("Randomly initialized centroids: ");
console.log(ex_randomCentroids_solver.centroids);
console.log("\n-------------------------------------------------\n\n");
```

First, we import the `KMeans` class and the `example_data` object from their respective files. We print some helpful output to the screen, and then initialize a `KMeans` solver instance for our simple data. We can check the randomly initialized centroids by inspecting the value of `ex_randomCentroids_solver.centroids`.

Once you've added this code, run `yarn start` from the command line, and you should see something similar to the following output. Note that because the centroid initialization is random, you will not see the same values that I see; however, what we're looking for is to make sure that the random centroids lie within the correct ranges. Specifically, we want our centroids to have x positions between 1 and 5, and y positions between 0 and 8. Run the code a number of times to make sure that the centroids have the correct position:

```
$ yarn start
yarn run v1.3.2
$ yarn build-cli && node dist/index.js
```

```
$ browserify src/index.js --node -o dist/index.js -t [ babelify --presets [
env ] ]

ML in JS Chapter 4 k-means clustering examples.
================================================

Testing centroid generation:
================================================

Randomly initialized centroids:
[ [ 4.038663181817283, 7.765675509733137 ],
  [ 1.976405159755187, 0.026837564634993427 ] ]
```

If you see something similar to the preceding block, that means everything is working well
so far and we're ready to continue implementing the algorithm.

Assigning points to centroids

The iteration loop that the k-means algorithm performs has two steps: assigning each point
to the centroid closest to it, and then updating the location of the centroids to be the mean
value of all the points assigned to that centroid. In this section, we'll implement the first
part of the algorithm: assigning points to centroids.

At a high level, our task is to consider each point in the dataset and determine which
centroid is closest to it. We also need to record the results of this assignment so that we can
later update the centroid's location based on the points assigned to it.

Add the following method to the body of the KMeans class:

```
/**
 * Given a point in the data to consider, determine the closest
 * centroid and assign the point to that centroid.
 * The return value of this method is a boolean which represents
 * whether the point's centroid assignment has changed;
 * this is used to determine the termination condition for the algorithm.
 * @param pointIndex
 * @returns {boolean} Did the point change its assignment?
 */
assignPointToCentroid(pointIndex) {

    const lastAssignedCentroid = this.centroidAssignments[pointIndex];
    const point = this.data[pointIndex];
    let minDistance = null;
    let assignedCentroid = null;
```

```
for (let i = 0; i < this.centroids.length; i++) {
    const centroid = this.centroids[i];
    const distanceToCentroid = distance(point, centroid);

    if (minDistance === null || distanceToCentroid < minDistance) {
        minDistance = distanceToCentroid;
        assignedCentroid = i;
    }

}

this.centroidAssignments[pointIndex] = assignedCentroid;

return lastAssignedCentroid !== assignedCentroid;
```

}

This method considers a single data point, given by its index, and considers each centroid in the system in turn. We also keep track of the last centroid this point has been assigned to in order to determine if the assignment has changed.

In the preceding code, we loop over all centroids and use our distance function to determine the distance between the point and the centroid. If the distance is less than the lowest distance we've seen so far, or if this is the first centroid we're considering for this point (minDistance will be null in that case), we record the distance and the index position of the centroid. After looping over all centroids, we will now know which centroid is closest to the point under consideration.

Finally, we record the assignment of the centroid to the point by setting it to the this.centroidAssignments array—in this array, the index is the index of the point, and the value is the index of the centroid. We return a Boolean from this method by comparing the last known centroid assignment to the new centroid assignment—it will return true if the assignment has changed, or false if not. We'll use this information to figure out when the algorithm has reached steady state.

The previous method considers only a single point, so we should also write a method to process the centroid assignments of all points. Additionally, the method we write should determine if *any* point has updated its centroid assignment. Add the following to the KMeans class:

```
/**
 * For all points in the data, call assignPointsToCentroids
 * and returns whether _any_ point's centroid assignment has
 * been updated.
 *
```

```
 * @see assignPointToCentroid
 * @returns {boolean} Was any point's centroid assignment updated?
 */
assignPointsToCentroids() {
    let didAnyPointsGetReassigned = false;
    for (let i = 0; i < this.data.length; i++) {
        const wasReassigned = this.assignPointToCentroid(i);
        if (wasReassigned) didAnyPointsGetReassigned = true;
    }
    return didAnyPointsGetReassigned;
}
```

This method defines a variable called `didAnyPointsGetReassigned`, initialized to `false`, and then loops over all points in the dataset to update their centroid assignments. If any point is assigned to a new centroid, the method will return `true`. If no assignments were changed, the method returns `false`. The return value from this method will become one of our termination conditions; if no points update after an iteration, we can consider the algorithm to have reached steady state and can terminate it.

Let's now address the second part of the k-means algorithm: updating centroid locations.

Updating centroid locations

In the previous section, we implemented the first part of the k-means algorithm: looking at all points in the dataset and assigning them to the centroid that's geographically closest. The next step in the algorithm is to look at all centroids and update their locations to the mean value of all the points assigned to them.

To make an analogy, you can imagine each point reaching out and grabbing the centroid closest to it. The points give the centroid a tug, trying to pull it closer to them. We've already implemented the *reach out and grab portion* of the algorithm, and now we'll implement the *pull the centroid closer* portion.

At a high level, our task is to loop over all the centroids, and for each, determine the mean position of all the points assigned to it. We'll then update the centroid's position to that mean value. Breaking this down further, we must first collect all the points assigned to a centroid, and then we have to calculate the average value of these points, always keeping in mind that points can have any number of dimensions.

Let's start with the easy task of collecting all the points assigned to a centroid. We already have a mapping of point indexes to centroid indexes in our `this.centroidAssignments` instance variable. Add the following code to the body of the KMeans class:

```
/**
 * Given a centroid to consider, returns an array
 * of all points assigned to that centroid.
 *
 * @param centroidIndex
 * @returns {Array}
 */
getPointsForCentroid(centroidIndex) {
    const points = [];
    for (let i = 0; i < this.data.length; i++) {
        const assignment = this.centroidAssignments[i];
        if (assignment === centroidIndex) {
            points.push(this.data[i]);
        }
    }
    return points;
}
```

The preceding method is quite standard: looping over all data points, we look up that point's centroid assignment, and if it is assigned to the centroid in question, we add the point to an output array.

We can now use this list of points to update the centroid's location. Our goal is to update the centroid's location to be the mean value of all the points we found previously. Because the data may be multi-dimensional, we must also consider each dimension independently.

Using our simple example of points (1, 3), (5, 8), and (3, 0), we would find a mean location of (3, 3.6667). To get this value, we first calculate the mean value of the x dimension ($(1 + 5 + 3) / 3 = 3$), and then calculate the mean value of the y dimension ($(3 + 8 + 0) / 3 = 11/3 = 3.6666...$). If we're working in more than two dimensions, we simply repeat the procedure for each dimension.

We can write this algorithm in JavaScript. Add the following to the body of the KMeans class:

```
/**
 * Given a centroid to consider, update its location to
 * the mean value of the positions of points assigned to it.
 * @see getPointsForCentroid
 * @param centroidIndex
 * @returns {Array}
 */
```

```
updateCentroidLocation(centroidIndex) {
    const thisCentroidPoints = this.getPointsForCentroid(centroidIndex);
    const dimensionality = this.getDimensionality();
    const newCentroid = [];
    for (let dimension = 0; dimension < dimensionality; dimension++) {
        newCentroid[dimension] = mean(thisCentroidPoints.map(point =>
point[dimension]));
    }
    this.centroids[centroidIndex] = newCentroid;
    return newCentroid;
}
```

The preceding method considers only one centroid at a time, specified by its index. We use the `getPointsForCentroid` method that we just added to get an array of points assigned to this centroid. We initialize a variable called `newCentroid` as an empty array; this will ultimately replace the current centroid.

Considering one dimension at a time, we collect the positions of the points *in that dimension only*, and then calculate the mean. We use JavaScript's `Array.map` to extract the positions for the correct dimension only, and then we use our `mean` function to calculate the average position in that dimension.

If we work this example by hand with the data points (1, 3), (5, 8), and (3, 0), we start by examining dimension 0, or the x dimension. The result of `thisCentroidPoints.map(point => point[dimension])` is the array `[1, 5, 3]` for dimension 0, and for dimension 1, the result is `[3, 8, 0]`. Each of these arrays is passed to the `mean` function, and the mean value is used in `newCentroid` for that dimension.

At the end of this method, we update our array of `this.centroids` with the newly calculated centroid position.

We will also write a convenience method to loop over all centroids and update their positions. Add the following to the body of the `KMeans` class:

```
/**
 * For all centroids, call updateCentroidLocation
 */
updateCentroidLocations() {
    for (let i = 0; i < this.centroids.length; i++) {
        this.updateCentroidLocation(i);
    }
}
```

Before finishing the algorithm and tying together all the pieces, we have one final prerequisite to satisfy. We're going to introduce the concept of *error* into the algorithm. Calculating the error is not required for the k-means algorithm to function, but you'll see later that this can be advantageous in certain situations.

Because this is an unsupervised learning algorithm, our concept of error does not relate to semantic error. Instead, we will use an error metric that represents the average distance of all points from their assigned centroids. We'll use the RMSE for this, which penalizes bigger distances more harshly, so our error metric will be a good indication of how tight the clustering is.

To perform this error calculation, we loop over all points and determine the distance of that point from its centroid. We square each distance before adding it to a running total (the *squared* in root-mean-squared), then divide the running total by the number of points (the *mean* in root-mean-squared), and finally take the square root of the whole thing (the *root* in root-mean-squared).

Add the following code to the body of the KMeans class:

```
/**
 * Calculates the total "error" for the current state
 * of centroid positions and assignments.
 * Here, error is defined as the root-mean-squared distance
 * of all points to their centroids.
 * @returns {Number}
 */
calculateError() {

    let sumDistanceSquared = 0;
    for (let i = 0; i < this.data.length; i++) {
        const centroidIndex = this.centroidAssignments[i];
        const centroid = this.centroids[centroidIndex];
        const point = this.data[i];
        const thisDistance = distance(point, centroid);
        sumDistanceSquared += thisDistance*thisDistance;
    }

    this.error = Math.sqrt(sumDistanceSquared / this.data.length);
    return this.error;
}
```

We're now ready to tie everything together and implement the main loop of the algorithm.

The main loop

All the supporting and foundational logic for the k-means algorithm is now implemented. The last thing to do is to tie it all together and implement the main loop of the algorithm. To run the algorithm, we should repeat the procedure of assigning points to centroids and then updating centroid locations until the centroids stop moving. We can also perform optional steps such as calculating the error and making sure that the algorithm does not exceed some maximum allowable number of iterations.

Add the following code to the body of the KMeans class:

```
/**
 * Run the k-means algorithm until either the solver reaches steady-state,
 * or the maxIterations allowed has been exceeded.
 *
 * The return value from this method is an object with properties:
 * {
 *   centroids {Array.<Object>},
 *   iteration {number},
 *   error {number},
 *   didReachSteadyState {Boolean}
 * }
 *
 * You are most likely interested in the centroids property of the output.
 *
 * @param {Number} maxIterations Default 1000
 * @returns {Object}
 */
solve(maxIterations = 1000) {

    while (this.iterations < maxIterations) {

        const didAssignmentsChange = this.assignPointsToCentroids();
        this.updateCentroidLocations();
        this.calculateError();

        this.iterationLogs[this.iterations] = {
            centroids: [...this.centroids],
            iteration: this.iterations,
            error: this.error,
            didReachSteadyState: !didAssignmentsChange
        };

        if (didAssignmentsChange === false) {
            break;
        }
```

```
        this.iterations++;

    }

    return this.iterationLogs[this.iterationLogs.length - 1];

}
```

We've written a `solve` method that also accepts a limit on the maximum number of iterations allowed, which we've defaulted to `1000`. We run the algorithm in a `while` loop, and for each iteration in the loop, we call `assignPointsToCentroids` (recording its output value, `didAssignmentsChange`), call `updateCentroidLocations`, and call `calculateError`.

In order to help debugging and maintain a history of what the algorithm has accomplished, we maintain an array of `this.iterationLogs`, and for each iteration we'll record the centroid locations, the iteration number, the calculated error, and whether or not the algorithm has reached steady state (which is the opposite of `didAssignmentsChange`). We use ES6's array spread operator on `this.centroids` when recording logs to avoid passing this array as a reference, otherwise the iteration logs would show the last state of centroids instead of its progress over time.

If the point/centroid assignments don't change from one iteration to the next, we consider the algorithm to have reached steady state and can return results. We accomplish this by using the `break` keyword to break from the `while` loop early. If the algorithm never reaches steady state, the `while` loop will continue until it has performed the maximum number of iterations allowed, and return the latest available result. The output for the `solve` method is simply the most recent iteration log, which contains all the information a user of this class would need to know.

Example 1 – k-means on simple 2D data

We've got our implementation of the k-means algorithm written and coded, so now it's time to see how it works. In our first example, we'll run our algorithm against a simple dataset of two-dimensional data. The data itself will be contrived so that the algorithm can easily find three distinct clusters.

First, modify the `data.js` file to add the following data, anywhere preceding the `export default` line:

```
const example_2d3k = [
    [1, 2], [2, 3], [2, 5], [1, 6], [4, 6],
    [3, 5], [2, 4], [4, 3], [5, 2], [6, 9],
    [4, 4], [3, 3], [8, 6], [7, 5], [9, 6],
    [9, 7], [8, 8], [7, 9], [11, 3], [11, 2],
    [9, 9], [7, 8], [6, 8], [12, 2], [14, 3],
    [15, 1], [15, 4], [14, 2], [13, 1], [16, 4]
];
```

Then, update the final export line to look like this:

```
export default {
    example_randomCentroids,
    example_2d3k
};
```

If we were to graph the preceding data points, we would see the following:

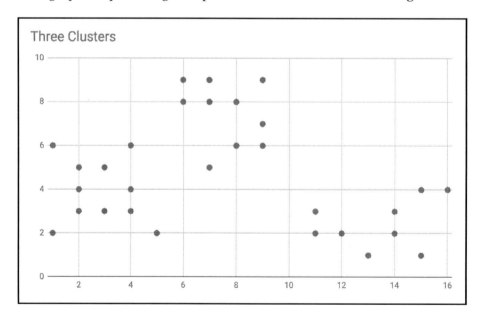

Visually, we can see that there are three neatly clustered groups of data points. When we run the algorithm, we will use $k = 3$ and expect that the centroids neatly position themselves to the centers of those three clusters. Let's try it out.

Open up `index.js` and add the following. You can either replace the code you added earlier (preserving the `import` statements), or simply add this at the bottom:

```
console.log("Solving example: 2d data with 3 clusters:");
console.log("=============================================\n");


console.log("Solution for 2d data with 3 clusters:");
console.log("-------------------------------------");
const ex_1_solver = new KMeans(3, example_data.example_2d3k);
const ex_1_centroids = ex_1_solver.solve();
console.log(ex_1_centroids);
console.log("");
```

After outputting some headers, we create a new `KMeans` instance called `ex_1_solver` and initialize it with k = 3 and the `example_data.example_2d3k` that we just added. We call the `solve` method, with no parameters (that is, the max allowed iterations will be 1,000), and capture the output in the variable `ex_1_centroids`. Finally, we print the results to the screen and add a newline—we'll add a few more tests and examples following this point.

 Note that the order of your centroids may be different to mine, since random initial conditions will differ.

You can now run `yarn start` and should see output that looks similar to this. Additionally, because of the random initialization, it's possible that some runs of the solver will get caught in local optima and you'll see different centroids. Run the program a few times in a row and see what happens. Here's what my output looks like:

```
Solving example: 2d data with 3 clusters:
=============================================

Solution for 2d data with 3 clusters:
-------------------------------------
 { centroids:
    [ [ 2.8181818181818183, 3.909090909090909 ],
      [ 13.444444444444445, 2.444444444444446 ],
      [ 7.6, 7.5 ] ],
   iteration: 1,
   error: 1.878739816915397,
   didReachSteadyState: true }
```

The output of the program tells us that the algorithm reached steady state after only two iterations (iteration 1 is the 2nd iteration, because we start counting from zero), and that our centroids are located at (2.8, 3.9), (13.4, 2.4), and (7.6, 7.5).

Let's graph these centroids along with the original data and see what it looks like:

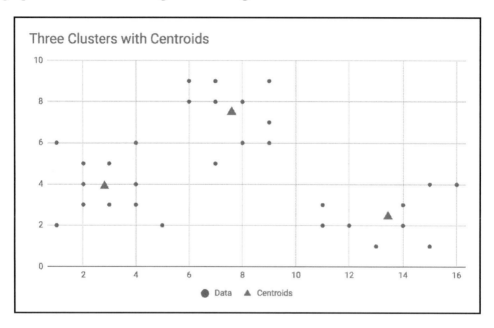

As you can see, k-means has done its job splendidly, reporting centroids exactly where we would expect them to be.

Let's take a deeper look into what this algorithm is doing, by printing the iterationLogs after the solution. Add the following code to the bottom of index.js:

```
console.log("Iteration log for 2d data with 3 clusters:");
console.log("----------------------------------------------");
ex_1_solver.iterationLogs.forEach(log => console.log(log));
console.log("");
```

Run yarn start again, and you should see output like the following. As always, based on initial conditions, your version may have required more or fewer iterations than mine so your output will differ, but you should see something like this:

```
Solving example: 2d data with 3 clusters:
===================================================================
```

```
Solution for 2d data with 3 clusters:
------------------------------------------------------------------------
{ centroids:
   [ [ 2.8181818181818183, 3.909090909090909 ],
     [ 13.444444444444445, 2.444444444444446 ],
     [ 7.6, 7.5 ] ],
  iteration: 4,
  error: 1.878739816915397,
  didReachSteadyState: true }

Iteration log for 2d data with 3 clusters:
------------------------------------------------------------------------
{ centroids: [ [ 2.7, 3.7 ], [ 9, 4.125 ], [ 10.75, 5.833333333333333 ] ],
  iteration: 0,
  error: 3.6193538404281806,
  didReachSteadyState: false }
{ centroids:
   [ [ 2.8181818181818183, 3.909090909090909 ],
     [ 9.714285714285714, 3.857142857142857 ],
     [ 10.75, 5.833333333333333 ] ],
  iteration: 1,
  error: 3.4964164297074007,
  didReachSteadyState: false }
{ centroids: [ [ 3.0833333333333335, 4.25 ], [ 11.375, 2.75 ], [ 10, 6.7 ]
],
  iteration: 2,
  error: 3.19709069137691,
  didReachSteadyState: false }
{ centroids:
   [ [ 2.8181818181818183, 3.909090909090909 ],
     [ 13.444444444444445, 2.444444444444446 ],
     [ 7.6, 7.5 ] ],
  iteration: 3,
  error: 1.878739816915397,
  didReachSteadyState: false }
{ centroids:
   [ [ 2.8181818181818183, 3.909090909090909 ],
     [ 13.444444444444445, 2.444444444444446 ],
     [ 7.6, 7.5 ] ],
  iteration: 4,
  error: 1.878739816915397,
  didReachSteadyState: true }
```

As you can see, the algorithm took five iterations to reach steady state, as opposed to only two iterations like it did earlier. This is normal and expected due to the differing random initial conditions between the two runs. Looking through the logs, you can see that the error reported by the algorithm goes down with time. Also, notice that the first centroid, (2.8, 3.9), reaches its final destination after the first iteration, while the other centroids take more time to catch up. This is because the first centroid was randomly initialized to a location very close to its final destination, starting at (2.7, 3.7) and finishing at (2.8, 3.9).

It is possible, though somewhat rare, to catch the algorithm caught in a local optimum on this dataset. Let's add the following code to the bottom of `index.js` to run the solver multiple times and see if it'll find a local optimum instead of a global optimum:

```
console.log("Test 2d data with 3 clusters five times:");
console.log("------------------------------------------");
for (let i = 0; i < 5; i++) {
    ex_1_solver.reset();
    const solution = ex_1_solver.solve();
    console.log(solution);
}
console.log("");
```

Run this with `yarn start` a few times until you see an unexpected result. In my case, I found the following solution (I'm omitting the other output of the preceding program):

```
Test 2d data with 3 clusters five times:
------------------------------------------------------------
{ centroids:
   [ [ 13.444444444444445, 2.444444444444446 ],
     [ 2.8181818181818183, 3.909090909090909 ],
     [ 7.6, 7.5 ] ],
  iteration: 2,
  error: 1.878739816915397,
  didReachSteadyState: true }
{ centroids:
   [ [ 2.8181818181818183, 3.909090909090909 ],
     [ 7.6, 7.5 ],
     [ 13.444444444444445, 2.444444444444446 ] ],
  iteration: 1,
  error: 1.878739816915397,
  didReachSteadyState: true }
{ centroids:
   [ [ 7.6, 7.5 ],
     [ 13.444444444444445, 2.444444444444446 ],
     [ 2.8181818181818183, 3.909090909090909 ] ],
  iteration: 3,
  error: 1.878739816915397,
```

```
  didReachSteadyState: true }
{ centroids:
   [ [ 11.333333333333334, 2.3333333333333335 ],
     [ 5.095238095238095, 5.619047619047619 ],
     [ 14.5, 2.5 ] ],
   iteration: 2,
   error: 3.0171467652692345,
   didReachSteadyState: true }
{ centroids:
   [ [ 7.6, 7.5 ],
     [ 2.8181818181818183, 3.909090909090909 ],
     [ 13.444444444444445, 2.4444444444444446 ] ],
   iteration: 2,
   error: 1.878739816915397,
   didReachSteadyState: true }
```

The fourth run of the solver found a different answer from the other runs: it discovered (11.3, 2.3), (5.1, 5.6), (14.5, 2.5) as a solution. Because the other solution is much more common than this one, we can assume the algorithm has been trapped in a local optimum. Let's chart these values against the rest of the data and see what it looks like:

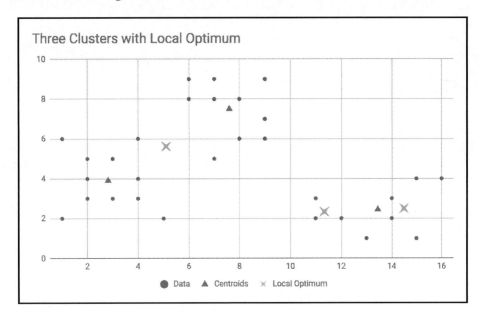

In the preceding chart, our data points are represented by circles, the centroids we'd expect are represented by triangles, and the odd result we got is represented by **X** marks. Looking at the chart, you can understand how the algorithm may have come to this conclusion. One centroid, the **X** mark at (5.1, 5.6), has captured two different clusters and is sitting between them. The other two centroids have divided the third cluster into two. This is a perfect example of a local optimum: it's a solution that makes sense, it logically clusters the data points, but it is not the best available solution (the global optimum) for the data. Most likely, the two centroids on the right were both randomly initialized inside that cluster and got trapped there.

This is always a potential outcome for the k-means algorithm, and indeed all ML algorithms. Based on initial conditions and the quirks of the dataset, the algorithm may occasionally (or even frequently) discover local optima. Fortunately, if you compare the errors of the two solutions from the preceding output, the global solution has an error of 1.9 and the locally optimum solution reports an error of 3.0. In this case, our error calculation has done its job well, and correctly represented the tightness of the clustering.

To combat this issue with the k-means algorithm, you should generally run it more than one time, and look for either consensus (for example, four of five runs all agree), or the minimum error, and use that as your result.

Example 2 – 3D data

Because we've written the k-means algorithm to handle any arbitrary number of dimensions, we can also test it with 3D data (or 10D, or 100D or any number of dimensions that you require). While this algorithm will work for more than three dimensions, we have no way of visually plotting the higher dimensions and therefore can't visually check the results—so we'll test with 3D data and move on.

Open up `data.js` and add the following to the middle of the file—anywhere preceding the `export default` line is OK:

```
const example_3d3k = [
    [1, 1, 1],
    [1, 2, 1],
    [2, 1, 2],
    [2, 2, 3],
    [2, 4, 3],
    [5, 4, 5],
    [5, 3, 4],
    [6, 2, 6],
    [5, 3, 6],
```

```
        [6,  4,  7],
        [9,  1,  4],
        [10, 2,  5],
        [9,  2,  5],
        [9,  2,  4],
        [10, 3,  3]
    ];
```

And then modify the export line to look like this (add the `example_3d3k` variable to the export):

```
export default {
    example_randomCentroids,
    example_2d3k,
    example_3d3k
};
```

The preceding data, when plotted in 3D, looks like this:

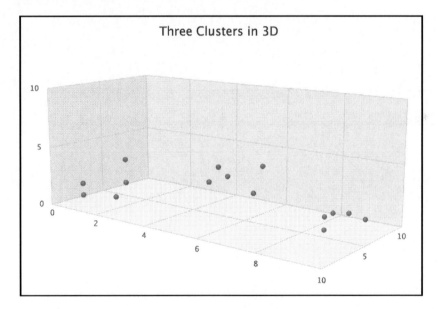

As you can see, there are three clear clusters, and we'd expect k-means to handle this easily. Now, switch to `index.js` and add the following. We are simply creating a new solver for this example, loading the 3D data, and printing the results:

```
console.log("Solving example: 3d data with 3 clusters:");
console.log("=================================================\n");
console.log("Solution for 3d data with 3 clusters:");
```

```
console.log("---------------------------------------");
const ex_2_solver = new KMeans(3, example_data.example_3d3k);
const ex_2_centroids = ex_2_solver.solve();
console.log(ex_2_centroids);
console.log("");
```

Run the program with `yarn start` and you should see something like the following. I've omitted the output from the earlier 2D example:

```
Solving example: 3d data with 3 clusters:
===================================================================

Solution for 3d data with 3 clusters:
-------------------------------------------------------------------
 { centroids: [ [ 1.6, 2, 2 ], [ 5.4, 3.2, 5.6 ], [ 9.4, 2, 4.2 ] ],
   iteration: 5,
   error: 1.3266499161421599,
   didReachSteadyState: true }
```

Thankfully, our solver has given us 3D data points, so we know that, at the very least, the algorithm can differentiate between 2D and 3D problems. We see that it still only took a handful of iterations, and that the error is a reasonable number (meaning it's defined, not negative, and not too large).

If we plot these centroids against our original data we will see the following:

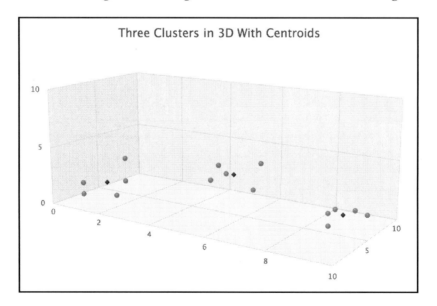

The circles represent the data points, as before, and now we can see our black diamond centroids have found their homes in the middle of their clusters. Our algorithm has proven that it can work for three-dimensional data, and it will work just as well for any number of dimensions you can give it.

k-means where k is unknown

So far, we've been able to define, in advance, how many clusters the algorithm should find. In each example, we've started the project knowing that our data has three clusters, so we've manually programmed a value of 3 for *k*. This is still a very useful algorithm, but you may not always know how many clusters are represented in your data. To solve this problem we need to extend the k-means algorithm.

A major reason I included the optional error calculation in our k-means implementation was to help solve this problem. Using an error metric—in any ML algorithm—doesn't only allow us to search for a solution, it also allows us to search for the best *parameters* that yield the best solution.

In a way, we need to build a meta-ML algorithm, or an algorithm that modifies our algorithm and its parameters. Our approach will be straightforward but effective: we'll build a new class called `KMeansAutoSolver`, and instead of specifying a value of *k*, we'll specify a range of *k* values to test. The new solver will run our k-means code for each value of *k* in the range and determine which value of *k* yields the lowest error. Additionally, we'll also run multiple trials of each *k* value so that we avoid getting caught in local optima.

Add a file to the `src/` folder called `kmeans-autosolver.js`. Add the following code to the file:

```
import KMeans from './kmeans.js';

class KMeansAutoSolver {

    constructor(kMin = 1, kMax = 5, maxTrials = 5, data) {
        this.kMin = kMin;
        this.kMax = kMax;
        this.maxTrials = maxTrials;
        this.data = data;
        this.reset();
    }

    reset() {
        this.best = null;
```

```
        this.log = [];
    }

    solve(maxIterations = 1000) {

        for (let k = this.kMin; k < this.kMax; k++) {

            for (let currentTrial = 0; currentTrial < this.maxTrials;
currentTrial++) {

                const solver = new KMeans(k, this.data);
                // Add k and currentTrial number to the solution before
logging
                const solution = Object.assign({},
solver.solve(maxIterations), {k, currentTrial});
                this.log.push(solution);

                if (this.best === null || solution.error < this.best.error)
{

                    this.best = solution;
                }

            }

        }

        return this.best;

    }
}

    export default KMeansAutoSolver;
```

The `KMeansAutoSolver` class contains a constructor which accepts `kMin`, `kMax`, `maxTrials`, and `data`. The `data` parameter is the same data you would give to the `KMeans` class. Instead of providing the class with a value for *k*, you provide a range of *k* values to test, as specified by `kMin` and `kMax`. Additionally, we'll also program this solver to run the k-means algorithm a number of times for each value of *k*, in order to avoid finding local optima, as we demonstrated earlier.

The main part of the class is the `solve` method, which, like the `KMeans` class, also accepts a `maxIterations` argument. The `solve` method also returns the same thing the `KMeans` class returns, except that we've also added the value of *k* to the output and also the `currentTrial` number. Adding the value of *k* to the output is a bit redundant, as you could just count the number of centroids returned, but it's nice to see in the output.

The body of the `solve` method is straightforward. For each value of *k* in the range between `kMin` and `kMax`, we run the `KMeans` solver `maxTrials` times. If the solution beats the current best solution in terms of error, we record this solution as the best. At the end of the method, we return the solution with the best (lowest) error.

Let's try it out. Open up `data.js` and add the following:

```
const example_2dnk = [
  [1, 2], [1, 1], [2, 3], [2, 4], [3, 3],
  [4, 4], [2, 12], [2, 14], [3, 14], [4, 13],
  [4, 15], [3, 17], [8, 4], [7, 6], [7, 5],
  [8, 7], [9, 7], [9, 8], [8, 14], [9, 15],
  [9, 16], [10, 15], [10, 14], [11, 14], [10, 18]
];
```

And update the export line as follows:

```
export default {
    example_randomCentroids,
    example_2d3k,
    example_3d3k,
    example_2dnk
};
```

Graphing this data, we see four neat clusters:

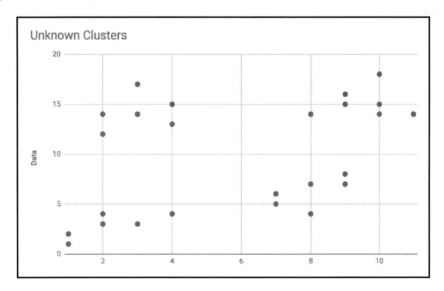

However, for the purposes of this example, we do not know how many clusters to expect, only that it's likely between one and five.

Next, open up `index.js` and import the `KMeansAutoSolver` at the top of the file:

```
import KMeansAutoSolver from './kmeans-autosolver';
```

Then, at the bottom of the file, add the following:

```
console.log("Solving example: 2d data with unknown clusters:");
console.log("=========================================\n");
console.log("Solution for 2d data with unknown clusters:");
console.log("-----------------------------------");
const ex_3_solver = new KMeansAutoSolver(1, 5, 5,
example_data.example_2dnk);
const ex_3_solution = ex_3_solver.solve();
console.log(ex_3_solution);
```

Run `yarn start` and you should see output similar to the following (previous output omitted):

```
Solving example: 2d data with unknown clusters:
============================================================

Solution for 2d data with unknown clusters:
------------------------------------------------------------
 { centroids:
    [ [ 2.166666666666665, 2.8333333333333335 ],
      [ 9.571428571428571, 15.142857142857142 ],
      [ 8, 6.166666666666667 ],
      [ 3, 14.166666666666666 ] ],
   iteration: 2,
   error: 1.6236349578000828,
   didReachSteadyState: true,
   k: 4,
   currentTrial: 0 }
```

Right away, you can see that the solver found an answer with `k: 4`, which is what we expected, and that the algorithm reached steady state in only three iterations with a low error value—all good signs.

Plotting these centroids against our data, we see that the algorithm has determined both the correct value for k and the centroid positions:

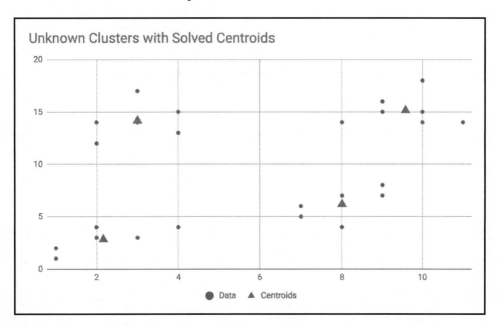

Note that our k-means auto-solver is also susceptible to local optima, and will not always guess the correct value for k. The reason? Increasing the value of k means that we can distribute more centroids amongst the data and reduce the error value. If we have 25 data points and set the range of k to anywhere from 1 to 30, the solver may end up finding a solution where k = 25, and each centroid sits on top of each individual data point for a total error of 0! This can be considered *overfitting*, where the algorithm finds a correct answer but hasn't sufficiently generalized the problem to give us the results we want. Even when using the auto-solver, you must be careful of the range of k values you give it, and keep the range as small as possible.

For example, if we increase `kMax` from 5 to 10 in the preceding example, we find that it gives a result for *k* = 7 as the best. As always, the local optimum makes sense, but it is not quite what we were looking for:

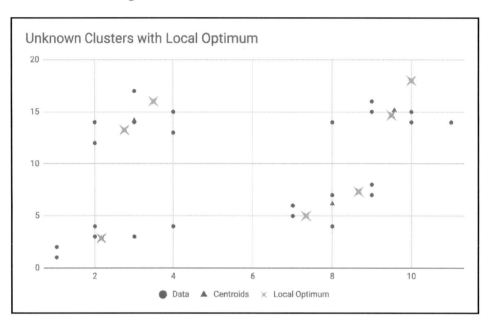

Because the auto-solver uses the error value calculation as its only guidance, you may be able to tune the error calculation to also consider the value of *k* and penalize solutions with too many clusters. The previous error calculation was a purely geometric calculation, representing the average distance each point is from its centroid. We may want to upgrade our error calculation so that it also prefers solutions with fewer centroids. Let's see what that would look like.

Return to the `kmeans.js` file and modify the `calculateError` method. Find the following line:

```
const thisDistance = distance(point, centroid);
```

And modify it to add the value of k to the distance:

```
const thisDistance = distance(point, centroid) + this.k;
```

When running the KMeans class by itself, this modification will do no harm because the value of k will be constant for that solver. The only time this modification may be undesirable is if you're actually interpreting and using the error value as a representation of *distance specifically*, as opposed to just looking for lower error values. Meaning, if you *need* the error to be a representation of distance, then you should not make this change. In all other cases, however, it can be advantageous, as this modification will prefer solutions with fewer clusters.

Now, return to index.js and modify the ex_3_solver to search the range of k values from 1 through 30. Run the program again with yarn start and you will see that the auto-solver once again correctly returns results for *k = 4*! While the previous, locally optimal solution with *k = 7* has a low error rate, adding the value of k to the error penalized the *k = 7* solution enough that the solver now prefers the *k = 4* solution. Because of this modification to the error calculation, we can be a little less careful when choosing our kMin and kMax, which is very helpful when we have no idea what *k* will be.

While our error calculation is no longer a geometrical representation of the cluster tightness, you can see that being thoughtful about the error calculation can give you a lot of leeway when trying to optimize for certain system properties. In our case, we wanted to find not just the tightest geometrical clusters, but the tightest geometrical clusters *with the fewest amount of clusters possible*, so updating the error calculation to consider *k* was a very helpful step.

Summary

In this chapter, we discussed the problem of clustering, or grouping data points into logically similar groups. Specifically, we introduced the k-means algorithm, which is the most popular numerical clustering algorithm in ML. We then implemented the k-means algorithm in the form of a KMeans JavaScript class and tested it with both two and three-dimensional data. We also discussed how to approach the clustering problem when the number of clusters you desire is unknown beforehand, and built a new JavaScript class called KMeansAutoSolver to solve this problem. Along the way, we also discussed the impact of error calculations, and made a modification to our error calculation that helps generalize our solution to avoid overfitting.

In the next chapter we'll take a look at classification algorithms. Classification algorithms are supervised learning algorithms that can be seen as a more sophisticated extension of clustering algorithms. Rather than simply grouping data points by their similarity or proximity, classification algorithms can be trained to learn specific labels that should be applied to data.

5
Classification Algorithms

Classification problems involve detecting patterns in data and using those patterns to assign a data point to a group of similar data points. If that's too abstract, here are some examples of classification problems: analyzing an email to determine whether it's spam; detecting the language of a piece of text; reading an article and categorizing it as finance, sports, politics, opinion pieces, or crime; and determining whether a review of your product posted on Twitter is positive or negative (this last example is commonly called **sentiment analysis**).

Classification algorithms are tools that solve classification problems. By definition, they are supervised learning algorithms, as they'll always need a labeled training set to build a model from. There are lots of classification algorithms, each designed with a specific principle in mind or for a particular type of input data.

In this chapter, we'll discuss four classifiers: **k-Nearest Neighbors** (**KNN**), Naive Bayes, **Support Vector Machines** (**SVMs**), and random forest. Here's a brief introduction to each of the algorithms:

- The KNN algorithm is one of the simplest classifiers, and works well when your dataset has numerical features and clustered patterns. It is similar in nature to the k-means clustering algorithm, in that it relies on plotting data points and measuring distances from point to point.

- The Naive Bayes classifier is an effective and versatile classifier based on Bayesian probability. While it can be used for numerical data, it's most commonly used in text classification problems, such as spam detection and sentiment analysis. Naive Bayes classifiers, when implemented properly, can be both fast and highly accurate for narrow domains. The Naive Bayes classifier is one of my go-to algorithms for classification.

- SVMs are, in spirit, a very advanced form of the KNN algorithm. The SVM graphs your data and attempts to find dividing lines between the categories you've labeled. Using some non-trivial mathematics, the SVM can linearize non-linear patterns, so this tool can be effective for both linear and non linear data.

- Random forests are a relatively recent development in classification algorithms, but they are effective and versatile and therefore a go-to classifier for many researchers, myself included. Random forests build an ensemble of decision trees (another type of classifier we'll discuss later), each with a random subset of the data's features. Decision trees can handle both numerical and categorical data, they can perform both regression and classification tasks, and they also assist in feature selection, so they are becoming many researchers' first tool to grab when facing new problems.

k-Nearest Neighbor

The KNN is a simple, fast, and straightforward classification algorithm. It is very useful for categorized numerical datasets where the data is naturally clustered. It will feel similar in some ways to the k-means clustering algorithm, with the major distinction being that k-means is an unsupervised algorithm while KNN is a supervised learning algorithm.

If you were to perform a KNN analysis manually, here's how it would go: first, plot all your training data on a graph, and label each point with its category or label. When you wish to classify a new, unknown point, put it on the graph and find the *k* closest points to it (the *nearest neighbors*). The number *k* should be an odd number in order to avoid ties; three is a good starting point, but some applications will need more and some can get away with one. Report whatever the majority of the *k* nearest neighbors are classified as, and that will be the result of the algorithm.

Finding the *k* nearest neighbors to a test point is straightforward, but can use some optimizations if your training data is very large. Typically, when evaluating a new point, you would calculate the Euclidean distance (the typical, high school geometry distance measure we introduced in `Chapter 4`, *Grouping with Clustering Algorithms*) between your test point and every other training point, and sort them by distance. This algorithm is quite fast because the training data is generally not more than 10,000 points or so.

If you have many training examples (in the order of millions) or you really need the algorithm to be lightning-fast, there are two optimizations you can make. The first is to skip the square root operation in the distance measure, and use the squared distance instead. While modern CPUs are very fast, the square root operation is still much slower than multiplication and addition, so you can save a few milliseconds by avoiding the square root. The second optimization is to only consider points within some bounding rectangle of distance to your test point; for instance, only consider points within +/- 5 units in each dimension from the test point's location. If your training data is dense, this optimization will not affect results but will speed up the algorithm because it will avoid calculating distances for many points.

The following is the KNN algorithm as a high-level description:

1. Record all training data and their labels
2. Given a new point to evaluate, generate a list of its distances to all training points
3. Sort the list of distances in order of closest to farthest
4. Throw out all but the *k* nearest distances
5. Determine which label represents the majority of your *k* nearest neighbors; this is the result of the algorithm

A more efficient version avoids maintaining a large list of distances that need to be sorted by limiting the list of distances to *k* items. Let's now write our own implementation of the KNN algorithm.

Building the KNN algorithm

Since the KNN algorithm is quite simple, we'll build our own implementation:

1. Create a new folder and name it Ch5-knn.
2. To the folder, add the following package.json file. Note that this file is a little different from previous examples because we have added a dependency for the jimp library, which is an image processing library that we'll use in the second example:

```
{
  "name": "Ch5-knn",
  "version": "1.0.0",
  "description": "ML in JS Example for Chapter 5 - k-nearest-
neighbor",
  "main": "src/index.js",
  "author": "Burak Kanber",
```

```
  "license": "MIT",
  "scripts": {
    "build-web": "browserify src/index.js -o dist/index.js -t [
babelify --presets [ env ] ]",
    "build-cli": "browserify src/index.js --node -o dist/index.js -
t [ babelify --presets [ env ] ]",
    "start": "yarn build-cli && node dist/index.js"
  },
  "dependencies": {
    "babel-core": "^6.26.0",
    "babel-plugin-transform-object-rest-spread": "^6.26.0",
    "babel-preset-env": "^1.6.1",
    "babelify": "^8.0.0",
    "browserify": "^15.1.0",
    "jimp": "^0.2.28"
  }
}
```

3. Run the `yarn install` command to download and install all the dependencies, and then create subfolders called `src`, `dist`, and `files`.
4. Inside the `src` folder, create an `index.js` file and an `knn.js` file.

You will also need a `data.js` file. For these examples, I'm using a larger dataset than can be printed in this book, so you should take a minute to download the `Ch5-knn/src/data.js` file from this book's GitHub account.

Let's start with the `knn.js` file. Like the k-means example in the previous chapter, we will need a distance-measuring function. Let's use the one from Chapter 4, *Grouping with Clustering Algorithms*; add the following to the beginning of `knn.js`:

```
/**
 * Calculate the distance between two points.
 * Points must be given as arrays or objects with equivalent keys.
 * @param {Array.<number>} a
 * @param {Array.<number>} b
 * @return {number}
 */
const distance = (a, b) => Math.sqrt(
    a.map((aPoint, i) => b[i] - aPoint)
        .reduce((sumOfSquares, diff) => sumOfSquares + (diff*diff), 0)
);
```

If you really need a performance optimization for your KNN implementation, this is where you might omit the `Math.sqrt` operation and return just the squared distance. I reiterate, however, that because this is such a fast algorithm by nature, you should only need to do this if you're working on an extreme problem with a lot of data or with very strict speed requirements.

Next, let's add the stub of our KNN class. Add the following to `knn.js`, beneath the distance function:

```
class KNN {

    constructor(k = 1, data, labels) {
        this.k = k;
        this.data = data;
        this.labels = labels;
    }

}

export default KNN;
```

The constructor accepts three arguments: the `k`, or the number of neighbors to consider when classifying your new point; the training data split up into the data points alone; and a corresponding array of their labels.

Next, we need to add an internal method that considers a test point and calculates a sorted list of distances from the test point to the training points. We'll call this a **distance map**. Add the following to the body of the KNN class:

```
generateDistanceMap(point) {

    const map = [];
    let maxDistanceInMap;

    for (let index = 0, len = this.data.length; index < len; index++) {

        const otherPoint = this.data[index];
        const otherPointLabel = this.labels[index];
        const thisDistance = distance(point, otherPoint);

        /**
         * Keep at most k items in the map.
         * Much more efficient for large sets, because this
         * avoids storing and then sorting a million-item map.
         * This adds many more sort operations, but hopefully k is small.
         */
```

```
        if (!maxDistanceInMap || thisDistance < maxDistanceInMap) {

            // Only add an item if it's closer than the farthest of the
candidates
            map.push({
                index,
                distance: thisDistance,
                label: otherPointLabel
            });

            // Sort the map so the closest is first
            map.sort((a, b) => a.distance < b.distance ? -1 : 1);

            // If the map became too long, drop the farthest item
            if (map.length > this.k) {
                map.pop();
            }

            // Update this value for the next comparison
            maxDistanceInMap = map[map.length - 1].distance;

        }
    }


    return map;
}
```

This method could be easier to read, but the simpler version is not efficient for very large training sets. What we're doing here is maintaining a list of points that might be the KNNs and storing them in `map`. By maintaining a variable called `maxDistanceInMap`, we can loop over every training point and make a simple comparison to see whether the point should be added to our candidates list. If the point we're iterating over is closer than the farthest of our candidates, we can add the point to the list, re-sort the list, remove the farthest point to keep the list small, and then update `mapDistanceInMap`.

If that sounds like a lot of work, a simpler version might loop over all points, add each one with its distance measurement to the map, sort the map, and then return the first *k* items. The downside of that implementation is that for a dataset of a million points, you'd need to build a distance map of a million points and then sort that giant list in memory. In our version, you only ever hold *k* items as candidates, so you never need to store a separate million-point map. Our version does require a call to `Array.sort` whenever an item is added to the map. This is inefficient in its own way, as the sort function is called for each addition to the map. Fortunately, the sort operation is only for *k* items, where *k* might be something like 3 or 5. The computational complexity of the sorting algorithm is most likely `O(n log n)` (for a quicksort or mergesort implementation), so it only takes about 30 data points for the more sophisticated version to be more efficient than the simple version when *k* = 3, and for *k* = 5, that happens at around 3,000 data points. However, both versions are so fast that for a dataset smaller than 3,000 points, you won't notice the difference.

Finally, we tie the algorithm together with a `predict` method. The `predict` method must accept a test point, and at the very least return the determined label for the `point`. We will also add some additional output to the method, and report the labels of the *k* nearest neighbors as well as the number of votes each label contributed.

Add the following to the body of the KNN class:

```
predict(point) {

    const map = this.generateDistanceMap(point);
    const votes = map.slice(0, this.k);
    const voteCounts = votes
        // Reduces into an object like {label: voteCount}
        .reduce((obj, vote) => Object.assign({}, obj, {[vote.label]:
(obj[vote.label] || 0) + 1}), {})
    ;
    const sortedVotes = Object.keys(voteCounts)
        .map(label => ({label, count: voteCounts[label]}))
        .sort((a, b) => a.count > b.count ? -1 : 1)
    ;

    return {
        label: sortedVotes[0].label,
        voteCounts,
        votes
    };

}
```

This method requires a little bit of datatype juggling in JavaScript, but is simple in concept. First, we generate our distance map using the method we just implemented. Then, we remove all data except for the *k* nearest points and store that in a `votes` variable. If you're using 3 as *k*, then `votes` will be an array of length three.

Now that we have our *k* nearest neighbors, we need to figure out which label represents the majority of the neighbors. We'll do this by reducing our votes array into an object called `voteCounts`. To get a picture of what we want `voteCounts` to look like, imagine that we're looking for the three nearest neighbors and the possible categories are `Male` or `Female`. The `voteCounts` variable might look like this: `{"Female": 2, "Male": 1}`.

Our job is still not done, however—after reducing our votes into a vote-count object, we still need to sort that and determine the majority label. We do this by mapping the vote counts object back into an array and then sorting the array based on vote counts.

There are other ways to approach this problem of tallying votes; any method you can think of will work, as long as you can return the majority vote at the end of the day. I like thinking about data in terms of structure and the transformations necessary to get from one structure to the next, but as long as you can report the top vote, the algorithm will work.

That's all we need to do in the `knn.js` file. The algorithm is complete, requiring fewer than 70 lines of code.

Let's set up our `index.js` file and get ready to run some examples. Remember that you need to download the `data.js` file first—see Packt's GitHub account or my personal GitHub account at `https://github.com/bkanber/MLinJSBook`.

Add the following to the top of `index.js`:

```
import KNN from './knn.js';
import {weight_height} from './data.js';
```

Let's try our algorithm out on a few simple examples.

Example 1 – Height, weight, and gender

KNN, like k-means, can work on high-dimensional data—but, like k-means, we can only graph example data in a two-dimensional plane so we'll keep our examples simple. The first question we'll tackle is: can we predict a person's biological sex given only their height and weight?

I've downloaded some data for this example from a national longitudinal survey on people's perception of their weight. Included in the data are the respondents' height, weight, and gender. This is what the data looks like, when graphed:

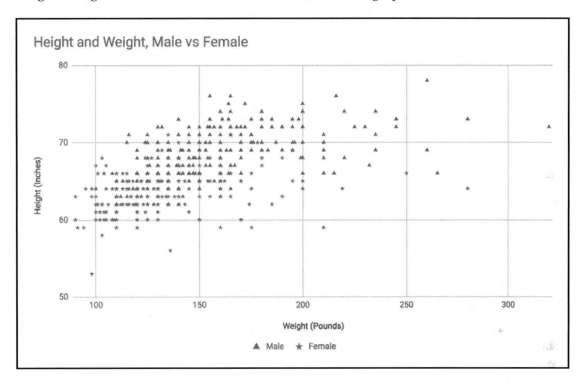

Just by looking at the preceding charted data, you can get a sense as to why KNN is so effective at evaluating clustered data. It's true that there's no neat boundary between male and female, but if you were to evaluate a new data point of a 200 pound, 72 inches-tall person, it's clear that all the training data around that point is male and it's likely your new point is male, too. Conversely, a new respondent at 125 pounds and a height of 62 inches is well into the female area of the graph, though there are a couple of males with those characteristics as well. The middle of the graph, around 145 pounds and 65 inches tall, is the most ambiguous, with an even split of male and female training points. I would expect the algorithm to be uncertain about new points in that area. Because there is no clear dividing line in this dataset, we would need more features or more dimensions to get a better resolution of the boundaries.

In any case, let's try out a few examples. We'll pick five points that we expect to be definitely male, definitely female, probably male, probably female, and indeterminable. Add the following code to `index.js`, beneath the two import lines:

```
console.log("Testing height and weight with k=5");
console.log("==========================");

 const solver1 = new KNN(5, weight_height.data, weight_height.labels);

 console.log("Testing a 'definitely male' point:");
 console.log(solver1.predict([200, 75]));
 console.log("\nTesting a 'probably male' point:");
 console.log(solver1.predict([170, 70]));
 console.log("\nTesting a 'totally uncertain' point:");
 console.log(solver1.predict([140, 64]));
 console.log("\nTesting a 'probably female' point:");
 console.log(solver1.predict([130, 63]));
 console.log("\nTesting a 'definitely female' point:");
 console.log(solver1.predict([120, 60]));
```

Run `yarn start` from the command line and you should see the following output. Since the KNN is not stochastic, meaning it does not use any random conditions in its evaluation, you should see exactly the same output as I do—with the possible exception of the ordering of votes and their indexes, if two votes have the same distance.

If you get an error when you run `yarn start`, make sure your `data.js` file has been correctly downloaded and installed.

Here's the output from the preceding code:

```
Testing height and weight with k=5
======================================================================

 Testing a 'definitely male' point:
 { label: 'Male',
 voteCounts: { Male: 5 },
 votes:
 [ { index: 372, distance: 0, label: 'Male' },
 { index: 256, distance: 1, label: 'Male' },
 { index: 291, distance: 1, label: 'Male' },
 { index: 236, distance: 2.8284271247461903, label: 'Male' },
 { index: 310, distance: 3, label: 'Male' } ] }

 Testing a 'probably male' point:
 { label: 'Male',
 voteCounts: { Male: 5 },
```

```
votes:
[ { index: 463, distance: 0, label: 'Male' },
{ index: 311, distance: 0, label: 'Male' },
{ index: 247, distance: 1, label: 'Male' },
{ index: 437, distance: 1, label: 'Male' },
{ index: 435, distance: 1, label: 'Male' } ] }

Testing a 'totally uncertain' point:
{ label: 'Male',
voteCounts: { Male: 3, Female: 2 },
votes:
[ { index: 329, distance: 0, label: 'Male' },
{ index: 465, distance: 0, label: 'Male' },
{ index: 386, distance: 0, label: 'Male' },
{ index: 126, distance: 0, label: 'Female' },
{ index: 174, distance: 1, label: 'Female' } ] }

Testing a 'probably female' point:
{ label: 'Female',
voteCounts: { Female: 4, Male: 1 },
votes:
[ { index: 186, distance: 0, label: 'Female' },
{ index: 90, distance: 0, label: 'Female' },
{ index: 330, distance: 0, label: 'Male' },
{ index: 51, distance: 1, label: 'Female' },
{ index: 96, distance: 1, label: 'Female' } ] }

Testing a 'definitely female' point:
{ label: 'Female',
voteCounts: { Female: 5 },
votes:
[ { index: 200, distance: 0, label: 'Female' },
{ index: 150, distance: 0, label: 'Female' },
{ index: 198, distance: 1, label: 'Female' },
{ index: 147, distance: 1, label: 'Female' },
{ index: 157, distance: 1, label: 'Female' } ] }
```

The algorithm has determined genders just as we would have done, visually, by looking at the chart. Feel free to play with this example more and experiment with different values of k to see how results might differ for any given test point.

Let's now look at a second example of KNN in action. This time, we'll choose a problem where k = 1 really shines.

Example 2 – Decolorizing a photo

The KNN algorithm is very susceptible to local noise and isn't very useful when there is a lot of overlap between classes expected. It is typically not very useful for more advanced tasks, such as psychographic, demographic, or behavioral analysis. But it's a very useful tool to keep handy in your toolbox, because it can assist with lower-level tasks very easily.

In this example, we'll use our KNN class to de colorize a photo. Specifically, we're going to take colorful input photos and restrict them to a color scheme of only 16 colors. We'll use KNN here to select the appropriate replacement color for a pixel, given that pixel's original color.

Our workflow will look like this:

1. Use the `jimp` library to read an input image

2. Loop over each pixel in the image and:

    1. Find the most similar color in our 16-color scheme

    2. Replace that pixel with the new color

3. Write a new output file, based on the 16-color scheme

Before we start, *verify* that the following exists in your `data.js` file. If you downloaded the `data.js` file from the GitHub for this book, then this should already be in there. However, if you sourced your gender survey data from a different place, you will need the following in the `data.js` file:

```
export const colors_16 = {
 data: [
 [0, 0, 0], // black
 [128, 128, 128], // gray
 [128, 0, 0], //maroon
 [255, 0, 0], // red
 [0, 128, 0], // green
 [0, 255, 0], // lime
 [128, 128, 0], // olive
 [255, 255, 0], // yellow
 [0, 0, 128], // navy
 [0, 0, 255], // blue
 [128, 0, 128], // purple
 [255, 0, 255], // fuchsia
 [0, 128, 128], // teal
```

```
[0, 255, 255], // aqua
[192, 192, 192], // silver
[255, 255, 255], // white
],

labels: [
'Black',
'Gray',
'Maroon',
'Red',
'Green',
'Lime',
'Olive',
'Yellow',
'Navy',
'Blue',
'Purple',
'Fuchsia',
'Teal',
'Aqua',
'Silver',
'White',
]
};
```

The preceding color definitions represent a common color scheme of 16 colors. You can also experiment with color schemes on your own; you can use this approach to colorize to shades of blue, or to warm colors, or to sepia tones, and so on. You can also allow for far more than 16 colors by increasing the training data size.

Let's start by writing a couple of helper functions. Create a new file, in the src folder, called decolorize.js. Make sure you added jimp to your package.json—if you're unsure, run yarn add jimp from the command line. Add the following imports to the top of the file:

```
import KNN from './knn.js';
import {colors_16} from './data.js';
import jimp from 'jimp'
```

Then, create and export a function that accepts an image filename and writes a new file with the decolorized image. I've left some gentle comments in the code snippet that describe the workflow; most of the code is just juggling data formats. In general, our approach is to open and read the input file, iterate over all pixels, use a KNN to find a substitute color for that pixel, write the new color to the pixel, and then finally write a new output file using the modified colors:

```
const decolorize = filename => {

  return jimp.read(filename)
    .then(image => {

      // Create a KNN instance with our color scheme as training data
      // We use k=1 to find the single closest color
      // k > 1 wouldn't work, because we only have 1 label per training
point
      const mapper = new KNN(1, colors_16.data, colors_16.labels);
      const {width, height} = image.bitmap;

      // For every pixel in the image...
      for (let x = 0; x < width; x++) {
      for (let y = 0; y < height; y++) {

      // Do some work to get the RGB value as an array: [R,G,B]
      const originalColorHex = image.getPixelColor(x, y);
      const originalColorRgb = jimp.intToRGBA(originalColorHex);
      const pixelPoint = [originalColorRgb.r, originalColorRgb.g,
originalColorRgb.b];

      // Ask the KNN instance what the closest color from the scheme is
      const closestColor = mapper.predict(pixelPoint);

      // Then get that color in hex format, and set the pixel to the new
color
      const newColor =
colors_16.data[colors_16.labels.indexOf(closestColor.label)];
      const newColorHex = jimp.rgbaToInt(newColor[0], newColor[1],
newColor[2], 255);
      image.setPixelColor(newColorHex, x, y);

    }
  }

  const ext = image.getExtension();
  image.write(filename.replace('.'+ext, '') + '_16.' + ext);

  })
```

```
      .catch(err => {
        console.log("Error reading image:");
        console.log(err);
      })
  };

  export default decolorize
```

We now have a function that will accept a filename and create a new de-colorized photo. If you haven't already, create a folder called `files` in the `Ch5-knn` directory. Find a few of your favorite pictures and add them to the `files` folder. Or, you can use the image examples from the book's GitHub, which are `landscape.jpeg`, `lily.jpeg`, and `waterlilies.jpeg`.

Finally, open up `index.js` and add the following to the bottom of the file:

```
['landscape.jpeg', 'lily.jpeg', 'waterlilies.jpeg'].forEach(filename => {
  console.log("Decolorizing " + filename + '...');
  decolorize('./files/' + filename)
    .then(() => console.log(filename + " decolorized"));
});
```

If you are using your own example files, make sure to update the filenames shown in bold in the preceding code.

Run the code with `yarn start` and you should see output like the following (you may have the results from the other KNN experiment in your output, as well):

```
Decolorizing images
========================================================
Decolorizing landscape.jpeg...
Decolorizing lily.jpeg...
Decolorizing waterlilies.jpeg...
lily.jpeg decolorized
waterlilies.jpeg decolorized
landscape.jpeg decolorized
```

If there are any errors with filenames or permissions, resolve them. Look in the `files` folder for your new photos. I don't know which format you're reading this book in and how these images will look to you, but the following is my `landscape.jpeg` file, original and processed.

The original:

And the de-colorized version:

I think it did a very good job on the foreground and the scenery, however, the limited color palette definitely affects the sky, water, and mountains in the background. Try adding another 8 or 16 colors to the training data to see what happens.

I like this project as a KNN example because it shows you that **machine learning** (ML) algorithms don't always have to be used for sophisticated analyses. Many of them can be used as part of your everyday toolbox, trained with smaller models to help you with simpler data-processing tasks.

I should also make a note here about measuring the distance between colors. The approach we have taken, using the Euclidean distance formula to measure distances between RGB values, is not perceptually accurate. The RGB space is slightly warped when it comes to human visual perception, so our Euclidean distance measurements are not totally accurate. For our purposes, they are close enough because we are downgrading to a very low resolution. If you need perceptually-accurate image processing, you will either need to transform all RGB values into a more accurate color space, such as *Lab*, or update your distance function to measure perceptual distance rather than just the geometric distance between points.

Let's move on from KNN and look at a more sophisticated way to classify objects, based on centuries-old probability theory that is still powerful today: Bayesian classification.

Naive Bayes classifier

A Naive Bayes classifier is a type of probabilistic classifier, or an algorithm that assigns a probability distribution to the potential outcomes. As opposed to a binary classification, such as `Male` or `Female`, the probabilistic classifier tells you there is an 87% chance this data point is `Male` and a 13% chance it is `Female`.

Not all probabilistic classifiers are Bayesian, nor are they all necessarily naive. The term *Naive*, in this context, is not a veiled insult to the classifier—it's a mathematical term that has a meaning in probability theory, which we'll discuss further later. The term *Bayes* or *Bayesian* means that the principles used in the classifier were first published by Reverend Thomas Bayes, an 18th century mathematician, popular for his *Bayes theorem* in probability theory.

Let's first have a probability refresher. First, you should know that probability can work with both *continuous distributions* and *discrete distributions*. Continuous distributions are those where your variable is a number and can have any value. Discrete distributions have only a fixed number of possible states, even if that number is large. Continuous values are things such as *activity of 54.21 minutes per week; $23.34 per share; 18 total logins*. Discrete values are *true/false; Hollywood, gossip, politics, sports, local events*, or *world news*, or even the frequency of individual words in an article. Most of the theorems in probability can be used both for continuous and discrete distributions, though the implementation details between the two will differ.

In discrete probability, which we will use for our example, you work with the probability of various *events* occurring. An event is a set of possible outcomes from an experiment. The classical illustrative example of this involves a pack of playing cards; imagine you draw a card at random from a shuffled deck. What's the probability that the card you pulled is a heart? When we ask this question, we're asking about the probability of a certain event, specifically *that the card is a heart*. We can give our event a label, such as H for heart, and then we can shorten the phrase *probability that the card is a heart* to simply, P(H). The answer is 13/52, or 1/4, or 0.25, so you could also say that P(H) = 0.25. There are many other possible events in our scenario. What's the chance the card is the five of diamonds? What's the chance the card is black? What's the chance the card is a face card? What's the chance the value is less than five? All of those are types of events, and each one has its own probability.

Not all events are independent. For instance, let's say the experiment is *did you drink a soda yesterday?*, and we are surveying Americans. We can define the event S as *drank a soda yesterday*. By surveying everyone in America (or at least a representative sample), we find that nearly 50% of respondents said yes! (It is actually 48%, according to Yale University.) So we can say that the probability of S is 50%, or P(S) = 0.5. We can also define an event as S',, which is the probability of the event *did not drink a soda yesterday*, or the inverse.

We want to develop more insight into citizens' eating habits, so we add another question to the survey: did you eat at a fast food restaurant yesterday? We'll name this event M, for McDonald's, and we find that P(M) = 0.25, or a quarter of the nation.

We can now ask more sophisticated questions, such as: does eating fast food affect whether people drink soda? We can ask about the probability that someone drank a soda given that they ate fast food yesterday. This is called the **conditional probability** of S events given M, or P(S|M).

If we asked the questions about drinking a soda and eating fast food in the same survey, then we can calculate P(S|M) by finding the probability of a respondent doing both events (this is written P(S ∩ M), pronounced *probability of S intersect M*), and dividing by P(M). The full formula is P(S|M) = P(S ∩ M) / P(M).

Let's say that 20% of respondents both drank a soda and ate fast food. We can now calculate that P(S|M) = 0.2 / 0.25 = 0.8. The probability of having drunk a soda yesterday is 80%, given that you ate fast food yesterday.

Note that this is *not* the probability that you drank a soda *while* eating fast food. To answer that question, you'd have to go to a fast food restaurant and survey the people there. Our version is less committal in terms of causation.

Now you want to ask the reverse question: what's the probability of someone having eaten fast food given that they drank a soda yesterday? This is asking about P(M|S). We could just reverse the preceding formula, but let's say that we lost the original survey data and can no longer determine P(S ∩ M).

We can use the Bayes theorem to correctly reverse our probability:

$$P(M|S) = P(S|M) * P(M) / P(S)$$

Fortunately, we remember those three values and find that:

$$P(M|S) = 0.8 * 0.25 / 0.5 = 0.4$$

The probability that someone ate fast food yesterday, knowing that they drank a soda, is 40%. That's up from the baseline of 25% for anyone eating fast food.

How does this apply to naive Bayes classifiers? We use the preceding conditional probability theorems to relate features to their respective classes. In a spam filter, we ask the question: what's the probability that this document is spam given that it has the word *credit* in it? And what's the probability this document is spam given that it has the word *transfer* in it? We ask that question for every word in the document, and then we combine those probabilities to get the overall probability that the document is spam. The naive Bayes classifier is naive because it assumes that the events are all independent. Truthfully, this is a bad assumption. Emails with the word *credit* are more likely to also have the word *transfer* in them, but in practice it turns out that these classifiers are still very accurate despite the incorrect assumption.

Tokenization

We also must briefly discuss the concept of *tokenization*. We will discuss tokenization in depth in Chapter 10, *Natural Language Processing in Practice* when we discuss natural language programming, but we do need a short introduction to it now. Tokenization is the act of breaking up a document into individual *tokens*. You can think of a token as a word, but not all words are necessarily tokens and not all tokens are necessarily words.

The simplest tokenizer would be to split a document up by spaces. The result would be an array of words, including their capitalization and their punctuation. A slightly more advanced tokenizer might convert everything to lowercase and remove any non-alphanumeric characters. Now the tokens are all lowercase words, numbers, and words with numbers in them. Your tokenizer can remove common words, such as *and* and *the*—this is called **stopword filtering**. You can also *stem* as part of your tokenizer, which is to remove extraneous endings from a word. For instance *parties*, *partied*, and *party* might all become *parti*. This is a great dimensionality reduction technique, and helps your classifier focus on the meaning of words rather than the particular tense or usage. You can take it even farther by *lemmatizing*, which is similar to stemming but actually grammatically transforms words to their root form, so that *running*, *runs*, and *ran* would all become *run*.

Tokenization can take more advanced forms. A token does not need to be a single word; it can be pairs or trios of words. These are called **bigrams** and **trigrams**, respectively. Tokens can also be generated from metadata. Email spam filters, in particular, do very well when some information from the message's headers are included as tokens: whether the email passed or failed its SPF check, whether it has a valid DKIM key, the sender's domain, and so on. Tokenizers can also modify tokens from certain fields; for instance, it was found that prefixing tokens from email subject lines (as opposed to body content) improved spam filtering performance. Rather than tokenizing *buy pharmaceuticals now* as *buy*, *pharmaceuticals*, *now*, you can tokenize those as *SUBJ_buy*, *SUBJ_pharmaceuticals*, *SUBJ_now*. The effect of this prefixing is to allow the classifier to consider subject and body words separately, which may increase performance.

Do not underestimate the importance of the tokenizer. Often, you can get significant accuracy improvements by being thoughtful about your tokenizer algorithm. In this example, we'll use a simple, intuitive one that is still quite effective.

Building the algorithm

Let's now build the naive Bayes classifier. These are the steps that are to be followed to build the algorithm :

1. Create a new folder for the project called Ch5-Bayes. As usual, create src and data and dist folders, and add the following package.json file:

```json
{
  "name": "Ch5-Bayes",
  "version": "1.0.0",
  "description": "ML in JS Example for Chapter 5 - Bayes",
  "main": "src/index.js",
  "author": "Burak Kanber",
  "license": "MIT",
  "scripts": {
  "build-web": "browserify src/index.js -o dist/index.js -t [
babelify --presets [ env ] ]",
  "build-cli": "browserify src/index.js --node -o dist/index.js -t [
babelify --presets [ env ] ]",
  "start": "yarn build-cli && node dist/index.js"
  },
  "dependencies": {
  "babel-core": "^6.26.0",
  "babel-plugin-transform-object-rest-spread": "^6.26.0",
  "babel-preset-env": "^1.6.1",
  "babelify": "^8.0.0",
  "browserify": "^15.1.0"
  }
}
```

2. Once you've added the package.json file, run yarn install from the command line to install all the project dependencies.

3. Navigate to the book's GitHub account, and download the four files in the data folder. They should be called train_negative.txt, train_positive.txt, test_negative.txt, and test_positive.txt. These files contain reviews of movies from https://www.imdb.com/, and are pre-sorted into positive reviews and negative reviews, using IMDB's star-rating system. We will use this data to train and later validate an algorithm to detect movie review sentiment.

4. Create a `bayes.js` file in the `src` folder. Add the following tokenizer function to the top of the file:

```
export const simpleTokenizer = string => string
  .toLowerCase()
  .replace(/[^\w\d]/g, ' ')
  .split(' ')
  .filter(word => word.length > 3)
  .filter((word, index, arr) => arr.indexOf(word, index+1) === -1);
```

This function accepts a string as an input, and returns an array of tokens as the output. The string is first converted to lowercase, because our analysis is case-sensitive. Then any characters that are not word or number characters are removed and replaced with spaces. We split the string up by spaces to get an array of tokens. Next, we filter out any tokens that are three characters or shorter (so the words *the* and *was* would be removed, while words like *this* and *that* are preserved). The last line of the tokenizer filters out non-unique tokens; we will consider only the existence of words in documents, not the number of times those words are used.

> Note that the `filter` function in the tokenizer does not preserve word order. To preserve word order, you would need to add `.reverse()` before and after the final filter line. However, our algorithm doesn't consider word order, so preserving it is not necessary.

5. Create the `BayesClassifier` class and export it from `bayes.js`. Add the following to the file:

```
class BayesClassifier {

  constructor(tokenizer = null) {
    this.database = {
    labels: {},
    tokens: {}
  };

    this.tokenizer = (tokenizer !== null) ? tokenizer :
  simpleTokenizer;
  }
}

export default BayesClassifier;
```

The constructor for the classifier accepts only a `tokenizer` function, however, it defaults to the simple preceding tokenizer we created. Making the tokenizer configurable like this will allow you to experiment with better tokenizers that fit your particular dataset.

Training a Naive Bayes classifier is a straightforward process. First, simply count the number of documents in each category that you have seen. If your training set has 600 positive movie reviews and 400 negative movie reviews, then you should have 600 and 400 as your document counts, respectively. Next, tokenize the document to be trained. You must always make sure to use the same tokenizer during training as you do during evaluation. For each token in the training document, record how many times you've seen that token amongst all documents in the category. For example, if your training data has 600 positive movie reviews and the word *beautiful* appears in 100 of them, you would need to maintain a count of 100 for the token *beautiful* in the *positive* category. If the token *beautiful* only appears three times in your negative review training data, then you must maintain that count separately.

Let's translate this into code. It's a very simple operation, but we are also dividing up the work between many small count and incrementing functions; we will use these counting functions in our evaluation stage as well:

```
/**
 * Trains a given document for a label.
 * @param label
 * @param text
 */
train(label, text) {
  this.incrementLabelDocumentCount(label);
  this.tokenizer(text).forEach(token => this.incrementTokenCount(token,
label));
}

/**
 * Increments the count of documents in a given category/label
 * @param label
 */
incrementLabelDocumentCount(label) {
  this.database.labels[label] = this.getLabelDocumentCount(label) + 1;
}

/**
 * Returns the number of documents seen for a given category/label.
 * If null is passed as the label, return the total number of training
documents seen.
 * @param label
 */
getLabelDocumentCount(label = null) {
  if (label) {
    return this.database.labels[label] || 0;
  } else {
    return Object.values(this.database.labels)
```

```
        .reduce((sum, count) => sum + count, 0);
    }
}

/**
 * Increment the count of a token observed with a given label.
 * @param token
 * @param label
 */
incrementTokenCount(token, label) {
  if (typeof this.database.tokens[token] === 'undefined') {
    this.database.tokens[token] = {};
  }

  this.database.tokens[token][label] = this.getTokenCount(token, label) +
1;
}

/**
 * Get the number of times a token was seen with a given category/label.
 * If no label is given, returns the total number of times the token was
seen
 * across all training examples.
 * @param token
 * @param label
 * @returns {*}
 */
getTokenCount(token, label = null) {
  if (label) {
    return (this.database.tokens[token] || {})[label] || 0;
  } else {
    return Object.values(this.database.tokens[token] || {})
      .reduce((sum, count) => sum + count, 0);
  }
}
```

As you can see, the `train()` method is quite simple: increment the document count for the given label (for example, `spam` or `not spam`, `positive sentiment` or `negative sentiment`); then, for each token in the document, increment the token count for the given label (for example, *beautiful* was seen 100 times in positive-sentiment documents, and was seen three times in negative-sentiment documents). These counts are maintained in an instance variable called `this.database` in the `BayesClassifier` class.

In order to make a prediction on a new document, we'll need to consider each of the labels we encountered during training separately, calculate a probability for that label, and return the most probable label. Let's work backwards in terms of implementing the prediction; we'll start by adding the `predict` method and then work backwards, filling in all the other methods we'll need.

First, add the following `predict` method to the `BayesClassifier` class:

```
/**
 * Given a document, predict its category or label.
 * @param text
 * @returns {{label: string, probability: number, probabilities: array}}
 */
predict(text) {
  const probabilities = this.calculateAllLabelProbabilities(text);
  const best = probabilities[0];

  return {
    label: best.label,
    probability: best.probability,
    probabilities
  };

}
```

This method accepts an input string or document, and returns a `result` object with the most likely label or category, the probability of that label or category, and an array of all the probabilities for all labels encountered during training.

Next, add the method that `predict` relies upon to calculate the probability of each label on the input document:

```
/**
 * Given a document, determine its probability for all labels/categories
encountered in the training set.
 * The first element in the return array (element 0) is the label/category
with the best match.
 * @param text
 * @returns {Array.<Object>}
 */
calculateAllLabelProbabilities(text) {
  const tokens = this.tokenizer(text);
  return this.getAllLabels()
    .map(label => ({
      label,
      probability: this.calculateLabelProbability(label, tokens)
```

```
      }))
      .sort((a, b) => a.probability > b.probability ? -1 : 1);
  }
```

This method tokenizes the input text, and then generates an array of all labels and their probabilities, sorted in order of most probable to least probable. You will now need to add these two methods to the class—first, the simple getAllLabels() method:

```
/**
 * Get all labels encountered during training.
 * @returns {Array}
 */
getAllLabels() {
  return Object.keys(this.database.labels);
}
```

And then add the more complex calculateLabelProbability, which is responsible for calculating the probability of an individual label fitting a document:

```
/**
 * Given a token stream (ie a tokenized document), calculate the
probability that
 * this document has a given label.
 * @param label
 * @param tokens
 * @returns {number}
 */
calculateLabelProbability(label, tokens) {

  // We assume that the a-priori probability of all labels are equal.
  // You could alternatively calculate the probability based on label
frequencies.
  const probLabel = 1 / this.getAllLabels().length;

  // How significant each token must be in order to be considered;
  // Their score must be greater than epsilon from the default token score
  // This basically filters out uninteresting tokens from consideration.
  // Responsible for 78% => 87.8% accuracy bump (e=.17) overall.
  const epsilon = 0.15;

  // For each token, we have to calculate a "token score", which is the
probability of this document
  // belonging to a category given the token appears in it.
  const tokenScores = tokens
    .map(token => this.calculateTokenScore(token, label))
    .filter(score => Math.abs(probLabel - score) > epsilon);
```

```
    // To avoid floating point underflow when working with really small
    numbers,
    // we add combine the token probabilities in log space instead.
    // This is only used because of floating point math and should not affect
    the algorithm overall.
    const logSum = tokenScores.reduce((sum, score) => sum + (Math.log(1-
    score) - Math.log(score)), 0);
    const probability = 1 / (1 + Math.exp(logSum));

    return probability;
}
```

The inline comments in the `calculateLabelProbability` method illuminate the specifics of how the method works, but the basic goal of this step is to calculate a probability for each token in the document, and then to combine the individual token probabilities into one overall probability for the label.

For instance, if a movie review states *beautiful [but] awful garbage*, this method is responsible for looking at all of the tokens (*but* is omitted by the tokenizer) and determining how well they fit a given label (for example, *positive* or *negative*).

Let's imagine we're running this method for the *positive* category label. The word *beautiful* would get a strong score, maybe 90%, but the tokens *awful* and *garbage* would both get weak scores, for instance 5%. This method would then report that the probability of the *positive* label is low for this document. On the other hand, when this method is run for the *negative* category label, the *beautiful* token gets a low score but both *awful* and *garbage* get high scores, so the method will return a high probability of the document being negative.

This method involves a couple of tricks. The first one is an accuracy enhancement. If a token is ambiguous (a word such as *that* or *movie*, something that applies equally to all categories), it is removed from consideration. We do this by filtering out token scores that are close to 50%; specifically, we ignore all tokens that have a score between 35-65%. This is a very effective technique and increases accuracy by about 10%. The reason it works so well is that it filters out noise in those marginal tokens. If the word *movie* has a positive score of 55% but is generally seen in both positive and negative documents, it'll skew all documents toward the positive category. Our approach is to instead only consider the most impactful tokens.

The second trick is our log sum approach. Normally, the way to combine individual words or token probabilities into an overall probability looks like this—assuming you already have an array variable called `tokenScores`:

```
const multiplyArray = arr => arr.reduce((product, current) => current *
product, 1);
```

```
const tokenScores = []; // array of scores, defined elsewhere
const inverseTokenScores = tokenScores.map(score => 1 - score);
const combinedProbability = multiplyArray(tokenScores) /
(multiplyArray(tokenScores) + multiplyArray(inverseTokenScores));
```

Put another way, assume you have probabilities for individual tokens called p1, p2, p3, ... pN; the way to get the combined probability of all those tokens would be:

```
p = (p1 * p2 * p3 * ... pN) / ( (p1 * p2 * p3 * ... pN) + (1-p1 * 1-p2 * 1-
p3 * ... 1-pN) )
```

This approach has some issues when dealing with small, floating-point numbers. If you start multiplying small, floating-point numbers by each other, you risk creating numbers so small that floating-point math can't deal with it, and you get *floating-point underflow*, or NaN in JavaScript. The solution is to convert this calculation to log space, and manage the whole calculation by adding natural log values of each of the probabilities and removing the log at the end.

The final piece of the puzzle is to generate the probabilities of each individual token given a label. This is where the Bayes theorem truly comes into play. What we're looking for is a probability like P(L|W), or the probability that the document has a **label** given a **word**. We need this probability for each token in the document, and for each label that we're considering. However, we don't have the P(L|W) value on hand, so we can use Bayes' theorem to get an equivalent expression:

$$P(L|W) = P(W|L)P(L) / P(W|L)P(L) + P(W|L')P(L')$$

This may look complicated, but it's not bad. We are transforming the P(L|W) goal into much easier probabilities, such as P(W|L) (the probability the word appears given a label, or its frequency in that label) and P(L) (the probability of any given label). The denominator also uses the inverse probabilities, P(W|L') (the probability the word appears in any other label) and P(L') (the probability of any other label).

We make this transformation because we can get the word frequencies just by counting tokens and labels when we see them during training; we do not need to record which tokens appear in which documents, and we can keep our database simple and fast.

The preceding expression is what we've been calling the *token score*, or the probability that a document has a label, given that the document has a word in it. Making things a little more concrete, we can ask the question P("positive review" | "beautiful"), or the probability that a document is a positive movie review, given that the word beautiful is in it.

If there is a 50/50 chance of reviews being positive or negative, and we see the word *beautiful* in 10% of positive reviews and only 1% of negative reviews, then our P(L|W) probability is around 91%. (The calculation for this was (0.1 * 0.5) / ((0.1 * 0.5) + (0.01 * 0.5)), using the preceding formula.) You can interpret this 91% figure as the *positivity* of the word *beautiful*. By analyzing all words in a document in this manner, we can combine their positivity scores to get an overall probability that a document is positive. The same holds for any type of classification, whether it's positive/negative movie reviews, spam/ham emails, or English/French/Spanish language detection.

There is one other thing we need to consider when calculating token scores. What do we do if we've never seen a token before? Or if we've only seen it once or twice? The best approach for us is to adjust the token score that we calculate by a weighted average; we want to weight the average so that rare words are pulled toward a 50/50 score.

Let's implement all of the preceding logic. This method is long, but as you can see, much of the work is simply grabbing the correct counts for the various variables we need to calculate. We also define a *strength* for our rare word weighting; we define the strength as three so that we must see the token in question three times for it to have an equivalent weight as the default 50/50 weighting:

```
/**
 * Given a token and a label, calculate the probability that
 * the document has the label given that the token is in the document.
 * We do this by calculating the much easier to find Bayesian equivalent:
 * the probability that the token appears, given the label (the word
frequency in that category).
 * This method also adjusts for rare tokens.
 * @param token
 * @param label
 * @returns {number}
 */
calculateTokenScore(token, label) {
  const rareTokenWeight = 3;

  const totalDocumentCount = this.getLabelDocumentCount();
  const labelDocumentCount = this.getLabelDocumentCount(label);
  const notLabelDocumentCount = totalDocumentCount - labelDocumentCount;

  // Assuming equal probabilities gave us 1% accuracy bump over using the
frequencies of each label
  const probLabel = 1 / this.getAllLabels().length;
  const probNotLabel = 1 - probLabel;

  const tokenLabelCount = this.getTokenCount(token, label);
  const tokenTotalCount = this.getTokenCount(token);
```

```
    const tokenNotLabelCount = tokenTotalCount - tokenLabelCount;

    const probTokenGivenLabel = tokenLabelCount / labelDocumentCount;
    const probTokenGivenNotLabel = tokenNotLabelCount /
  notLabelDocumentCount;
    const probTokenLabelSupport = probTokenGivenLabel * probLabel;
    const probTokenNotLabelSupport = probTokenGivenNotLabel * probNotLabel;

    const rawWordScore =
      (probTokenLabelSupport)
      /
      (probTokenLabelSupport + probTokenNotLabelSupport);

    // Adjust for rare tokens -- essentially weighted average
    // We're going to shorthand some variables to make reading easier.
    // s is the "strength" or the "weight"
    // n is the number of times we've seen the token total
    const s = rareTokenWeight;
    const n = tokenTotalCount;
    const adjustedTokenScore =
      ( (s * probLabel) + (n * (rawWordScore || probLabel)) )
      /
      ( s + n );

    return adjustedTokenScore;
  }
```

To review the way this algorithm works, here is a brief summary:

To train:

1. Accept an input document and known label or category
2. Tokenize the input document into an array of tokens
3. Record the total number of documents you've seen for this specific label
4. For each token, record the number of times you've seen this token *with this specific label*

To predict:

1. Accept an input document and tokenize it
2. For each possible label (all the labels you encountered during training), and for each token in the document, calculate the *token score* for that token (mathematically, the probability of a document having that label, given that specific token)

3. You may need to filter token scores for significance
4. You may need to adjust token scores for rare words
5. For each possible label, combine the token scores into a single, overall label probability (for example, the probability that the document is in this category or label)
6. Report the label with the highest overall probability

With all of our code added, we're ready to train and test our Naive Bayes classifier. We'll train it on IMDB movie reviews, and try to guess the sentiment of never-before-seen reviews.

Example 3 – Movie review sentiment

We're going to use our Naive Bayes classifier to tackle the *sentiment analysis* problem, or the problem of inspecting a piece of text and determining whether it has an overall positive or negative sentiment. This is a common analysis done in advertising, marketing, and public relations; most brand managers want to know whether people on Twitter have good things or bad things to say about their brand or product.

The training data for this example will come from https://www.imdb.com/. We'll train our classifier on positive and negative movie reviews, and then use our classifier to check untrained (but pre-labeled) reviews to see how many it gets right.

If you haven't done so yet, download the data files from the data directory from this project's GitHub page. You will need all four text files: train_positive.txt, train_negative.txt, test_positive.txt, and test_negative.txt. We will use the two training files for training, and the two test files for validation.

Next, create an index.js file in the src folder. Add the following code to the top of the file:

```
import readline from 'readline';
import fs from 'fs';
import BayesClassifier, {simpleTokenizer} from "./bayes";

const classifier = new BayesClassifier(simpleTokenizer);
```

We import the `readline` and `fs` libraries to help us process the training files. Next, create a `utility` function to help us train the classifier:

```
const trainer = (filename, label, classifier) => {

  return new Promise((resolve) => {
    console.log("Training " + label + " examples...");
    readline.createInterface({
      input: fs.createReadStream(filename)
    })
      .on('line', line => classifier.train(label, line))
      .on('close', () => {
        console.log("Finished training " + label + " examples.");
        resolve();
      });
  });
}
```

This `helper` function accepts a filename, a label, and an instance of a `BayesClassifier` class. It reads an input file line by line, and trains the classifier on each line for the given label. All the logic is wrapped up in a promise so that we can externally detect when the trainer has completed.

Next, add a helper utility to test the classifier. In order to test the classifier, it must be trained first. The testing function will open up a test file with a known label, and test each line in the file using the classifier's `predict` method. The utility will count how many examples the classifier got right and how many it got wrong, and report back:

```
const tester = (filename, label, classifier) => {

  return new Promise((resolve) => {
    let total = 0;
    let correct = 0;
    console.log("Testing " + label + " examples...");
    readline.createInterface({ input: fs.createReadStream(filename) })
      .on('line', line => {
        const prediction = classifier.predict(line);
        total++;
        if (prediction.label === label) {
          correct++;
        }
      })
      .on('close', () => {
        console.log("Finished testing " + label + " examples.");
        const results = {total, correct};
        console.log(results);
```

```
        resolve(results);
    });
  });
}
```

We also wrap this in a promise, and make sure to deliver the results as part of the resolution of the promise, so we can inspect the results from without.

Finally, add some bootstrap code. This code will train the classifier on the two training files, wait for training to complete, and then test the classifier on the two test files, reporting the overall results when finished:

```
Promise.all([
  trainer('./data/train_positive.txt', 'positive', classifier),
  trainer('./data/train_negative.txt', 'negative', classifier)
])
  .then(() => {
    console.log("Finished training. Now testing.");

    Promise.all([
      tester('./data/test_negative.txt', 'negative', classifier),
      tester('./data/test_positive.txt', 'positive', classifier)
    ])
      .then(results => results.reduce(
        (obj, item) => ({total: obj.total + item.total, correct:
obj.correct + item.correct}), {total: 0, correct: 0}
      ))
      .then(results => {
        const pct = (100 * results.correct / results.total).toFixed(2) +
'%';
        console.log(results);
        console.log("Test results: " + pct);
      });
  })
```

Once this code is added, you can run the program by issuing yarn start from the command line. You should see output like the following:

```
Training positive examples...
Training negative examples...
Finished training positive examples.
Finished training negative examples.
Finished training. Now testing.
Testing negative examples...
Testing positive examples...
Finished testing positive examples.
{ total: 4999, correct: 4402 }
```

```
Finished testing negative examples.
{ total: 5022, correct: 4738 }
{ total: 10021, correct: 9140 }
Test results: 91.21%
```

This simple, probabilistic classifier has an accuracy of over 91%! A 9% error rate may not seem impressive, but in the ML world this is actually a very good result, especially considering the ease of implementation and speed of operation of the classifier. These results are why the Naive Bayes classifier is so popular when classifying text. With more thoughtful tokenization, especially in narrow fields, such as spam detection, you can get the accuracy of a Naive Bayes classifier over 95%.

Let's see what an individual example looks like. You can add the following code to the index.js file if you would like to test out some documents on your own:

```
Promise.all([
  trainer('./data/train_positive.txt', 'positive', classifier),
  trainer('./data/train_negative.txt', 'negative', classifier)
])
  .then(() => {

    const tests = [
       "i really hated this awful movie, it was so bad I didn't even know
what to do with myself",
       "this was the best movie i've ever seen. it was so exciting, i was on
the edge of my seat every minute",
       "i am indifferent about this"
    ];

    tests.forEach(test => {
      console.log("Testing: " + test);
      const result = classifier.predict(test);
      console.log(result);
    });
  });
```

Running the preceding code results in the following code:

```
Training positive examples...
Training negative examples...
Finished training positive examples.
Finished training negative examples.

Testing: i really hated this awful movie, it was so bad I didn't even know
what to do with myself
{ label: 'negative',
  probability: 0.9727173302897202,
  probabilities:
  [ { label: 'negative', probability: 0.9727173302897202 },
    { label: 'positive', probability: 0.027282669710279664 } ] }

Testing: this was the best movie i've ever seen. it was so exciting, i was
on the edge of my seat every minute
{ label: 'positive',
  probability: 0.8636681390743286,
  probabilities:
  [ { label: 'positive', probability: 0.8636681390743286 },
    { label: 'negative', probability: 0.13633186092567148 } ] }

Testing: i am indifferent about this
{ label: 'negative',
  probability: 0.5,
  probabilities:
  [ { label: 'negative', probability: 0.5 },
    { label: 'positive', probability: 0.5 } ] }
```

The classifier works as expected. Our strongly negative statement has a 97% probability of being negative. Our positive statement has an 86% probability of being positive. And our indifferent statement, even though it returns the negative label, also reports an even 50/50 probability split between positive and negative sentiments.

We did all this, and achieved great accuracy, by simply counting the number of times we saw words in documents and using centuries-old probability theory to interpret the data. We didn't need a neural network, an advanced framework, or a deep natural language programming knowledge to get these results; for these reasons, the Naive Bayes classifier should be one of the core algorithms you pay attention to when researching ML.

In the following sections, we'll take a look at two more classification algorithms that should not be ignored: the SVM and the random forest.

Support Vector Machine

An SVM is a numerical classifier that in some ways is similar to the KNN algorithm, although the SVM is far more mathematically advanced. Rather than comparing a test point to the points closest to it, an SVM attempts to draw boundary lines between the classes of data points, creating regions where all points inside that region will be considered a member of that class.

Consider this image (from Wikipedia's article on SVMs). The two categories of data points are separated by a straight line. The line that separates the classes is chosen as the line of *maximum margin*, meaning this dividing line has the most room on either side of it, as compared to any other separating line you can draw:

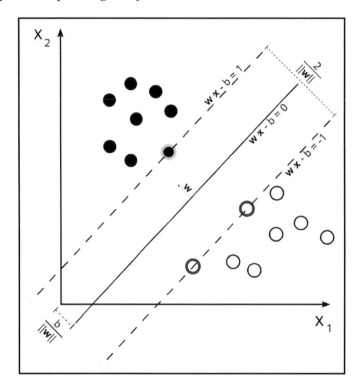

The SVM, exactly as implemented here, is useful in some limited situations, but is not a powerful tool, because it requires that the classes be *linearly separable*; that is, it requires that you can draw a straight line through the two classes. This SVM is also a *binary classifier*, meaning it only works with two categories or classes.

Consider the following data (this image and the one after are both courtesy of Shiyu Ji, licensed under Creative Commons CC BY-SA 4.0). While there are only two classes, they are not linearly separable; only a circle or ellipse can separate the two classes:

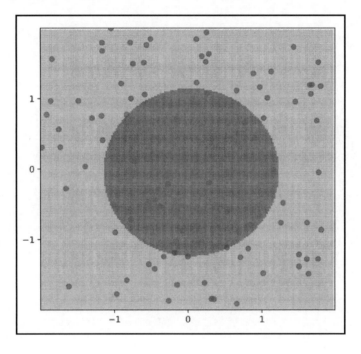

While the SVM has been around since the 1960s, it wasn't until 1992 that researchers figured out how to approach this problem. By using a technique called the **kernel trick**, you can transform the non-linearly-separable data into linearly-separable data in a higher number of dimensions. In this case, transforming the data through a kernel will add a third dimension, and it's that new third dimension that becomes linearly separable:

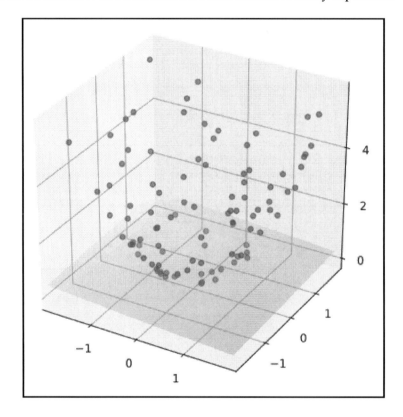

After applying the kernel trick, the data has been mapped onto three dimensions. The class of red data points have been pulled downward in the third dimension, while the purple points have been pulled upward. It's now possible to draw a plane (the three-dimensional equivalent of a straight line in two dimensions) that separates the two categories.

Through appropriate selection of kernels and parameters, the support vector machine can work its way through all sorts of shapes of data. While the support vector machine will always draw a line, plane, or hyperplane (a higher-dimensional version of a plane) through the data—these are always *straight*—the algorithm first transforms the data into something that can be separated by straight lines.

There are many types of kernels that can be used with an SVM. Each kernel transforms the data in a different manner, and the appropriate selection of kernel will depend on the shape of your data. In our case, we will use the *radial basis function kernel*, which is a good general-purpose kernel to use for clustered data. The SVM itself has settings and parameters that you must tweak, such as the error cost parameter, but keep in mind that the kernel you select may also have its own configurable parameters. The radial basis function, for instance, uses a parameter called **gamma**, which controls the curvature of the kernel.

Because SVMs require a lot of math, we won't attempt to build our own. Instead, we'll use an off-the-shelf library with a popular, classical dataset. The dataset we'll use is called the `iris flower` dataset. This particular dataset was created around 1936 by Edgar Anderson (a botanist) and Ronald Fisher (a statistician and biologist). Anderson chose three species of iris flowers, specifically the *Iris setosa*, the *Iris versicolor*, and the *Iris virginica*. For each species, Anderson chose 50 samples and measured the petal length, petal width, sepal length, and sepal width, and recorded the measurements along with the species name (a *sepal* is the green leaf that protects the flower bud before it blooms).

The `Iris` dataset is a common toy or test dataset for many ML algorithms for a few reasons. It's a small dataset: there are only 150 samples, four dimensions or features, and three categories. The data is multidimensional, but with only four features, it is still easy to visualize and understand intuitively. The pattern in the data is also interesting and poses a non-trivial challenge for classifiers: one species (*Iris setosa*) is clearly separated from the other two, but *Iris versicolor* and *Iris virginica* are more intermingled.

Because the data is four-dimensional, it cannot be visualized directly, but we can plot each combination of two features separately into a grid. This image is courtesy of Wikipedian Nicoguaro, and is licensed CC BY 4.0:

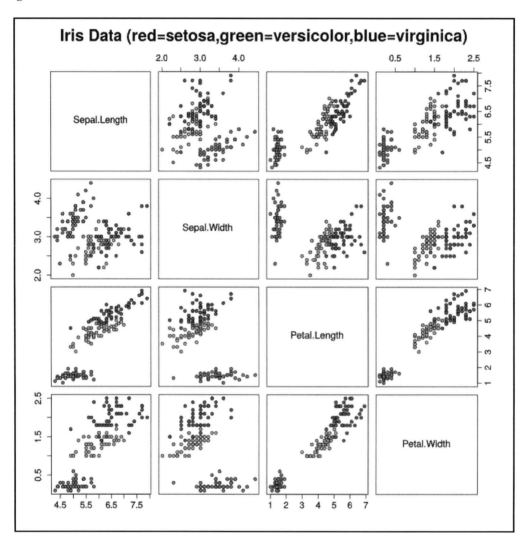

You can see why this dataset would be interesting to researchers. In several dimensions, such as sepal length versus sepal width, the *Iris versicolor* and *Iris virginica* overlap a great deal; in others, they look nearly linearly separable, for instance, in the petal length versus petal width plots.

Create a new folder called Ch5-SVM and add the following package.json file:

```
{
  "name": "Ch5-SVM",
  "version": "1.0.0",
  "description": "ML in JS Example for Chapter 5 - Support Vector Machine",
  "main": "src/index.js",
  "author": "Burak Kanber",
  "license": "MIT",
  "scripts": {
  "build-web": "browserify src/index.js -o dist/index.js -t [ babelify --
presets [ env ] ]",
  "build-cli": "browserify src/index.js --node -o dist/index.js -t [
babelify --presets [ env ] ]",
  "start": "yarn build-cli && node dist/index.js"
  },
  "dependencies": {
  "babel-core": "^6.26.0",
  "babel-plugin-transform-object-rest-spread": "^6.26.0",
  "babel-preset-env": "^1.6.1",
  "babelify": "^8.0.0",
  "browserify": "^15.1.0",
  "libsvm-js": "^0.1.3",
  "ml-cross-validation": "^1.2.0",
  "ml-dataset-iris": "^1.0.0",
  "ml-random-forest": "^1.0.2"
  }
}
```

Once the file is in place, run yarn install to install all the dependencies. Rather than using a data.js file, we will use the Iris dataset that comes with the MLJS library.

Next, create an src folder and an index.js file. At the top of index.js, import the following:

```
import SVM from 'libsvm-js/asm';
import IrisDataset from 'ml-dataset-iris';
```

Next, we need to extract the data from the `IrisDataset` library. This implementation of the SVM algorithm requires our labels to be integers (it doesn't support strings as labels), so we must simply map the species names from the dataset to integers:

```
const data = IrisDataset.getNumbers();
const labels = IrisDataset.getClasses().map(
  (elem) => IrisDataset.getDistinctClasses().indexOf(elem)
);
```

Let's also write a simple function that measures accuracy, or more specifically *loss* (or error). This function must accept an array of expected values as well as an array of actual values, and return the proportion of incorrect guesses:

```
const loss = (expected, actual) => {
  let incorrect = 0,
  len = expected.length;
  for (let i in expected) {
    if (expected[i] !== actual[i]) {
      incorrect++;
    }
  }
  return incorrect / len;
};
```

We're now ready to implement the SVM class. We will test our classifier in two ways: first, we'll train the classifier on the full dataset and then test it on the full dataset; this will test the algorithm's ability to fit data. Then we will use a cross-validation method to train the classifier on only subsets of the data and test it on unseen data; this will test the algorithm's ability to generalize its learning.

Add the following code to `index.js`:

```
console.log("Support Vector Machine");
console.log("======================");

const svm = new SVM({
  kernel: SVM.KERNEL_TYPES.RBF,
  type: SVM.SVM_TYPES.C_SVC,
  gamma: 0.25,
  cost: 1,
  quiet: true
});

svm.train(data, labels);

const svmPredictions = svm.predict(data);
```

```
const svmCvPredictions = svm.crossValidation(data, labels, 5);

console.log("Loss for predictions: " + Math.round(loss(labels,
svmPredictions) * 100) + "%");
console.log("Loss for crossvalidated predictions: " +
Math.round(loss(labels, svmCvPredictions) * 100) + "%");
```

We initialize the SVM with some reasonable parameters. We choose the radial basis function as our kernel, we choose a specific algorithm called **CSVC** for our SVM (this is the most common SVM algorithm), and we choose values of 1 for cost and 0.25 for gamma. Cost and gamma will both have similar effects on how the classifier draws boundaries around your classes: the larger the values, the tighter the curves and boundaries around the clusters will be.

The `svm.crossValidation` method accepts three arguments: the data, the labels, and the number of segments to divide the data into, reserving one segment for validation on each pass.

Run `yarn start` from the command line and you should see the following:

```
Support Vector Machine
================================================
Loss for predictions: 1%
Loss for crossvalidated predictions: 3%
```

This is a very strong result. The SVM was able to correctly recall 99% of training examples, meaning only a couple of data points were guessed incorrectly after being fully trained. When crossvalidating, we see a loss of only 3%; only perhaps five examples out of 150 were guessed incorrectly. The crossvalidation step is important because it more accurately represents what real-world performance would be; you should tune your algorithm's parameters so that the crossvalidated accuracy is maximized.

It is easy to get 100% accuracy for the fully-trained algorithm: we can simply overfit the data and memorize the category of each datapoint. Change the values of both gamma and cost to 50 and re-run the algorithm. You should see something like this:

```
Support Vector Machine
================================================
Loss for predictions: 0%
Loss for crossvalidated predictions: 25%
```

By cranking up the cost and the gamma, we're drawing really tight boundaries around our existing data points. With a high enough value of cost and gamma, we might even be drawing individual circles around each and every data point! The result is a perfect score when testing the fully-trained classifier (for example, every training point has been memorized), but an awful score when cross-validating the dataset. Our cross-validation uses 80% of the data for training and reserves 20% for validation; in this case, we've overfit the training data so much that the classifier simply cannot categorize unseen data points. The classifier has memorized the data, but has not learned from it.

As a rule of thumb, a good starting point for the cost value is around 1. A higher cost will penalize training errors more harshly, meaning that your classification boundaries will try to more tightly wrap the training data. The cost parameter attempts to balance the simplicity of the boundaries with the recall of the training data: a lower cost will favor simpler, smoother boundaries, while a higher cost will favor higher training accuracy even if it means drawing more complex boundaries. This might lead to large sections of the sample space being misclassified with real-world data, especially if your dataset is highly dispersed. A higher cost value works better for very tightly clustered and neatly separated data; the more you trust your data, the higher you can make the cost. Values between 0.01 and 100 are most common for the cost parameter, though there are certainly cases where you may need a larger or smaller cost.

Similarly, the gamma value also controls the shape and curvature of the SVM's boundaries, however, this value influences the data preprocessing when applying the kernel trick to transform the data. The result is similar to that of the cost parameter, but arises from a completely different mechanism. The gamma parameter essentially controls the influence of a single training example. Lower values for gamma will result in smoother, broader boundaries around training points, while higher values will result in closer, tighter boundaries. One common rule of thumb for gamma is to set it to roughly 1/M, where M is the number of features in your data. In our case, we have four features or dimensions in our data, so we've set gamma to 1/4 or 0.25.

When training an SVM for the first time, you should always use cross-validation to tune your parameters. As with any ML algorithm, you'll have to tune the parameters to fit your data set and make sure that you're sufficiently generalizing the problem and not overfitting your data. Tune and test parameters methodically: for instance, choose five possible values for cost and five possible values for gamma, test all 25 combinations with cross-validation, and choose the parameters with the highest accuracy.

Next, we'll take a look at a modern workhorse of ML: the random forest.

Random forest

The random forest algorithm is modern, versatile, robust, accurate, and is deserving of consideration for nearly any new classification task that you might encounter. It won't always be the best algorithm for a given problem domain, and it has issues with high dimensional and very large datasets. Give it more than 20-30 features or more than, say, 100,000 training points and it will certainly struggle in terms of resources and training time.

However, the random forest is virtuous in many ways. It can easily handle features of different types, meaning that some features can be numerical and others can be categorical; you can blend features such as `number_of_logins: 24` with features such as `account_type: guest`. A random forest is very robust to noise and therefore performs well with real-world data. Random forests are designed to avoid overfitting, and therefore are quite easy to train and implement, requiring less tweaking and tuning than other algorithms. Random forests also automatically evaluate the importance of each feature of your data, and therefore can help you reduce dimensionality or select better features *for free*, so to speak. And while random forests can be expensive for high dimensional data, in my experience, most real-world ML problems involve only about a dozen features and a few thousand training points, which random forests can handle. These virtues make the random forest a great go-to algorithm for general-purpose classification tasks.

I am therefore heartbroken to report that, at the time of writing, I have found no high-quality random forest classifiers in the JavaScript ecosystem. Regardless, I'm going to continue writing this section—and even show you one existing library that I believe may have some bugs or problems—in the hopes that by the time you read this everything will be fixed and high-quality random forests will be readily available in JavaScript.

Random forests are a type of *ensemble* classifier built on top of decision trees. An ensemble classifier comprises several or many individual classifiers that all vote on the prediction. In `Chapter 2`, *Data Exploration*, we ran the k-means algorithm several times with different random initial conditions in order to avoid getting caught in local optima; that was a rudimentary example of ensemble classification.

A random forest is an ensemble of *decision trees*. You're probably already familiar with decision trees: in everyday life, decision trees are more commonly called **flowcharts**. In an ML context, decision trees are automatically trained and built by an algorithm, rather than drawn by hand.

First, let's discuss a single decision tree. Decision trees predate random forests, but have historically been of only moderate usefulness to ML. The concept behind a decision tree is the same as a hand-drawn flowchart. When a decision tree evaluates a data point, it'll check each feature in turn: *is petal length less than 1.5 centimeters? If so, check the sepal length; if not, check the petal width.* Eventually, the decision tree will come to a final leaf or node where no more decisions are possible, and the tree will predict the category of the data point.

Decision trees are automatically trained by using a couple of concepts from information theory, such as information gain, entropy, and a metric called **Gini impurity**. In essence, these techniques are used to determine what the most important branching decisions are. A decision tree wants to be as small and simple as possible, so these techniques are used to determine how best to split the dataset between decisions and when. Should the first branch in the tree check petal width or sepal length? If it checks sepal length, should it split at 2.0 centimeters or 1.5 centimeters? Which comparisons will result in the best splits for the whole dataset? This training is done recursively, and each feature and each training point is evaluated to determine its effect on the whole.

The result is a lightning-fast classifier that is also easy to understand and debug. Unlike a neural network, where the influence of each neuron is highly abstract, and unlike a Bayesian classifier, which requires skill in probability to understand, a decision tree can be rendered as a flowchart and interpreted directly by a researcher.

Unfortunately, a decision tree by itself is not very accurate, they are not robust to changes in training data or noise, they can get trapped in local optima, and there are certain categories of problems that a decision tree cannot handle well (like the classic XOR problem, which will result in a very complex tree).

In the mid-1990s, researchers figured out two new ensemble approaches to decision trees. First, the technique of *sample bagging* (or *bootstrap aggregating*) was developed. In this approach, you create a number of decision trees, each based on a totally random subset of the training data (with replacement), and you use the majority vote of all the trees when coming up with a prediction. Bagging works because the variance due to noise is high for a single tree, but for many uncorrelated trees the noise tends to cancel out. Think of concertgoers singing along to their favorite band in an arena—the crowd always sounds in tune because the people singing sharp get canceled out by the people singing flat.

The random forest builds on the idea of bagging by not only randomizing the samples that are given to each tree, but also the *features* that are given to each tree. As opposed to *sample bagging,* you could call this *feature bagging*. If you build a random forest of 50 trees for our Iris dataset (which has four features and 150 data points), you might expect each tree to have only 100 unique data points and only two of the four features. Like sample bagging, feature bagging serves to decouple each of the decision trees and reduce the overall variance of the ensemble. Feature bagging also serves to identify the most important features, and if you need to save resources you can always remove the least important features from the dataset. When you attempt to predict a data point, each of the 50 trees will submit its vote; some trees will be wildly incorrect, but the ensemble as a whole will make a very good prediction that is robust to noise.

Let's build a random forest and test our Iris data against it. You should already have the random forest and cross-validation libraries installed in your package.json file from the SVM section; if not, you should yarn add both ml-cross-validation and ml-random-forest.

At the top of the existing index.js file for the Ch5-SVM example, import the appropriate classes:

```
import {RandomForestClassifier} from 'ml-random-forest';
import crossValidation from 'ml-cross-validation';
```

You should already have labels and data set up from the SVM section. Now, add the following to the bottom of the file, beneath the SVM example:

```
console.log("=====================");
console.log("Random Forest");
console.log("=====================");

const rfOptions = {
  maxFeatures: 3,
  replacement: true,
  nEstimators: 100,
  useSampleBagging: true
};

const rf = new RandomForestClassifier(rfOptions);
rf.train(data, labels);
const rfPredictions = rf.predict(data);

const confusionMatrix = crossValidation.kFold(RandomForestClassifier, data,
labels, rfOptions, 10);
const accuracy = confusionMatrix.getAccuracy();
```

```
console.log("Predictions:");
console.log(rfPredictions.join(","));
console.log("\nLoss for predictions: " + Math.round(loss(labels,
rfPredictions) * 100) + "%");
console.log("Loss for crossvalidated predictions: " + Math.round( (1 -
accuracy) * 100) + "%\n");
console.log(confusionMatrix);
```

Similar to the SVM example, we're evaluating the random forest in two ways. We first train the forest on the full training data and evaluate its recall, then we use cross-validation to get an idea of its real-world performance. In this example, we're using MLJS's cross-validation and confusion matrix tools to evaluate the classifier's performance.

Run the code with `yarn start` and you should see something like the following:

```
Random Forest
==================================================================
Predictions:
0,0,0,0,0,0,0,0,0,0,0,0,0,0,2,0,0,0,0,0,0,0,0,0,0,0,0,0,0,0,0,0,0,1,0,
0,1,0,0,0,0,0,0,0,0,0,0,0,0,0,2,2,2,1,2,0,2,0,2,0,0,2,2,2,1,2,1,2,2,1,
2,2,2,2,2,2,2,2,2,0,1,1,2,2,0,2,2,2,1,1,1,2,2,0,1,0,0,2,0,0,2,2,2,2,2,
2,0,2,2,2,2,2,2,0,2,2,2,2,2,2,2,1,2,2,2,2,2,2,2,2,2,2,2,2,2,2,2,2,2,2,
2,2,2,2,2,2,2,2,2,2

Loss for predictions: 31%
Loss for crossvalidated predictions: 33%

ConfusionMatrix {
    labels: [ 0, 1, 2 ],
    matrix: [ [ 43, 6, 1 ], [ 8, 11, 31 ], [ 1, 2, 47 ] ] }
```

Unfortunately, the accuracy of this algorithm is very poor. In fact, this performance is atypical of random forests, especially for the `Iris` dataset, which should be very easy for an algorithm to interpret.

I wanted to be certain that these poor results were an implementation problem rather than a conceptual one, so I ran the same exact Iris data through a familiar random forest library that I use daily, using the same options and parameters, and I got very different results: **my random forest has a cross-validated loss of 2% only**. Unfortunately, I must blame this poor accuracy not on the random forest itself, but this specific implementation of the algorithm. While I did spend some time looking into the matter, I was not able to quickly identify the issue with this implementation. There is a possibility I am misusing this tool, however, it is more likely that there's a minus sign where there should be a plus (or something similarly silly and disastrous) somewhere in the library. My personal prediction for the performance of a random forest on the Iris dataset was around 95% accuracy, my familiar random forest library resulted in 98% accuracy, yet this library resulted in only 70% accuracy.

Even worse is the fact that I was unable to find a single random forest library in JavaScript that works for the Iris dataset. There are a couple of random forest libraries out there, but none that are modern, maintained, and correct. Andrej Karpathy has an abandoned random forest library that seems to work, but it can only handle binary classifications (only 1 and -1 as labels), and a few other random forest libraries are limited in similar ways. The MLJS random forest library that we used previously is the closest thing to a working, maintained library that I've found, so I hope the issue—whatever it is—will be discovered and resolved by the time you read this.

I do not want you to be discouraged from using random forests. If you are working in languages other than JavaScript, there are many random forest libraries available to you. You should become familiar with them as they'll quickly become your go-to first choice for the majority of classification problems. In terms of JavaScript, while random forests are harder to build from scratch than Bayesian classifiers, they are still quite achievable. If you are able to correctly implement a decision tree, or port one from a different language, building a random forest becomes very easy—the trees do most of the work in the forest.

While JavaScript's ML toolset is advancing all the time, this random forest example perfectly highlights that there's still work to be done. You must proceed cautiously. I started writing this example with the expectation of 95% accuracy or greater, based on my prior experience with random forests. But what if I had no expectations or experience going into it? Would I have just accepted the 70% accuracy from this tool? Would I have convinced myself that a random forest is the wrong tool for the job? Would it have discouraged me from using random forests in the future? Maybe! The ML in the JavaScript ecosystem will have more land mines like this one; look out for them.

Before we finish this chapter, I would like to revisit the confusion matrix we just saw, as this may be a new concept for you. We discussed precision, recall, and accuracy in an earlier chapter. The confusion matrix is the raw data from which these values can be derived for any classification. Here's the confusion matrix from the random forest, again:

```
ConfusionMatrix {
    labels: [ 0, 1, 2 ],
    matrix: [ [ 43, 6, 1 ], [ 8, 11, 31 ], [ 1, 2, 47 ] ] }
```

If we organize this into a table, it might look like this:

	Guessed *I. setosa*	Guessed *I. versicolor*	Guessed *I. virginica*
Actual *I. setosa*	43	6	1
Actual *I. versicolor*	8	11	31
Actual *I. virginica*	1	2	47

The confusion matrix is the matrix (or table) of guesses versus actual categories. In a perfect world, you want the confusion matrix to be all zeros except for the diagonal. The confusion matrix tells us that the random forest did a pretty good job of guessing *Iris setosa* and *Iris virginica*, but it got most *Iris versicolor* wrong and incorrectly labeled them as *Iris virginica*. This is not too surprising, considering the shape of the data; recall that the latter two species overlap quite a bit (however, a random forest still should have been able to resolve this).

The code we wrote for the random forest also printed out the individual predictions for each data point, which looked like this:

```
0,0,0,0,0,0,0,0,0,0,0,0,0,0,2,0,0,0,0,0,0,0,0,0,0,0,0,0,0,0,0,0,0,0,1,0,0,1,0
,0,0,0,0,0,0,0,0,0,0,0,0,2,2,2,1,2,0,2,0,2,0,0,2,2,2,1,2,1,2,2,1,2,2,2,2,2,
2,2,2,2,0,1,1,2,2,0,2,2,2,1,1,1,2,2,0,1,0,0,2,0,0,2,2,2,2,2,2,0,2,2,2,2,2,2
,0,2,2,2,2,2,2,2,1,2,2,2,2,2,2,2,2,2,2,2,2,2,2,2,2,2,2,2,2,2,2,2,2,2,2
```

The numbers are not exactly the same as in the confusion matrix, because these predictions came from the fully-trained tree while the confusion matrix came from the cross-validation process; but you can see that they are still similar. The first 50 predictions should all be 0s (for *Iris setosa*), and they mostly are. The next 50 predictions should be all 1s, but they are primarily 2s; the confusion matrix tells us the same thing (that most I. versicolor were incorrectly labeled I. virginica). The last 50 predictions should be all 2s, and are for the most part correct. The confusion matrix is a more compact and intuitive way of looking at the difference between expected and actual guesses, and this is exactly the type of information you'll need when fine-tuning an algorithm.

In short, the random forest is an excellent classifier algorithm that currently has no convincing JavaScript implementation. I encourage you to be part of JavaScript's evolution and build your own random forest, or at least keep this algorithm in mind for the future.

Summary

Classification algorithms are a type of supervised learning algorithm whose purpose is to analyze data and assign unseen data points to a pre-existing category, label, or classification. Classification algorithms are a very popular subset of ML, and there are many classification algorithms to choose from.

Specifically, we discussed the simple and intuitive k-nearest-neighbor algorithm, which compares a data point to its neighbors on a graph. We discussed the excellent and very popular Naive Bayes classifier, which is a classic probability-based classifier that dominates the text classification and sentiment analysis problem spaces (though it can be used for many other types of problems). We also discussed the support vector machine, an advanced geometric classifier that works well for non-linearly-separable data. Finally, we discussed the random forest classifier, a robust and powerful ensemble technique that relies on decision trees but unfortunately has only a questionable implementation in JavaScript.

We also discussed cross-validation and the confusion matrix, two powerful techniques for evaluating the accuracy of your models.

In the next chapter, we'll look at association rules, which give us some more predictive power. If someone buys bread and butter from a store, are they more likely to also buy milk, or to buy deli meat? Association rules can help us model and interpret those relationships.

Association Rule Algorithms

6

Association rule learning, or association rule mining, is a relatively modern unsupervised learning technique originally used to discover associations between purchased items in grocery stores. The goal of association rule mining is to discover interesting relationships between sets of items, for instance, discovering that shoppers preparing for a hurricane often buy Pop-Tarts along with their bottled water, batteries, and flashlights.

In Chapter 5, *Classification Algorithms*, we introduced the concept of conditional probability. In this chapter, we're going to take the concept a bit further and apply conditional probability to association rule learning. Recall that conditional probability asks (and answers) the question: given that we know something, what's the probability of something else happening? Or, what's the probability that someone will buy Pop-Tarts given that they also bought bottled water and batteries? The probability is high, as we will shortly see.

In association rule learning, our goal is to look at a database of transactions or events and relate the most common subsets to each other through probabilities. This may be easier to understand with an example. Imagine you run an e-commerce store, and your task is to create a personalized widget on the homepage suggesting products to the shopper. You have the full database of their order history available to you, and you must use the shopper's browsing history to suggest items that have a high probability of being purchased by them.

Naturally, there are several ways to solve this problem. There's no reason you can't train a neural network on the entire order history of your store to suggest new products—except for time and complexity. Training the neural network on millions of transactions is both time-consuming and very difficult to inspect and understand intuitively. Association rule learning, on the other hand, gives us a simple and quick tool that's grounded in basic probability concepts.

Let's say your e-commerce store is a drop-shipping business that sells boutique, curated home decorations, and furniture. Your goal is to determine the sets of items that are most frequently bought together, for instance: 90% of people who bought the recliner chair and end table also bought the ottoman, and 80% of people who bought the giant wall clock also bought the drywall-mounting anchor set.

If you have a fast and efficient way to search through millions of previous orders to find these relationships, you can compare the current shopper's browsing history to other shoppers' purchase histories and display the items that the shopper is most likely to purchase.

Association rule learning is not limited to e-commerce. Another obvious application is physical stores, such as your local supermarket. If 90% of shoppers who buy milk and eggs also buy bread, it might be good to keep the bread close by so your shoppers can find it more easily. Alternatively, you might want to put bread on the *opposite* side of the store, because you know the shopper is going to have to walk through a bunch of aisles and probably pick up some more items along the way. How you use this data is up to you, and depends on what you want to optimize for: shopper convenience or total shopping basket value.

At first blush, it seems like this would be an easy algorithm to write—we're just counting probabilities, after all. However, with a large database and a large number of possible items to select from, it becomes very time-consuming to check every combination of items for their frequencies, and therefore we need something a little more involved than the brute-force, exhaustive-search approach.

In this chapter, we will discuss:

- Association rule learning from a mathematical perspective
- A description of the Apriori algorithm
- Various applications of association rule learning
- Worked examples of various association rule algorithms

Let's get started by looking at association rule learning from a mathematical perspective.

The mathematical perspective

Association rule learning assumes that you have a *transactional database* to learn from. This doesn't refer to any specific technology, but rather the concept of a database that stores transactions—the database can be an array in memory, an Excel file, or a table in your production MySQL or PostgreSQL instance. Since association rule learning was developed for products in supermarkets, the original transactional database was a list of items bought by each individual shopper on a given shopping trip—essentially an archive of receipts from the checkout aisle. However, a transactional database can be any list of items or events that occur during a single session, whether that session is a shopping trip, a website visit, or a trip to a doctor. For the time being, we'll consider the supermarket example. We'll discuss other uses of the association rule in a later section.

A transactional database is a database where the rows are sessions and the columns are *items*. Consider the following:

Receipt	Eggs	Milk	Bread	Cheese	Shampoo
1	Yes	Yes	No	Yes	No
2	No	No	Yes	Yes	No
3	No	No	No	No	Yes
4	Yes	Yes	Yes	Yes	No
5	Yes	Yes	No	Yes	No

Such a table can be considered a transactional database. Note that we are not recording the quantities of each item purchased, just whether or not the item was purchased. This is the case for most association rule learning: both the quantities and the ordering of items are typically ignored.

Based on the information in the table, we can put together probabilities for the occurrences of various events. For instance, the probability that a shopper buys Shampoo, or $P(E_{Shampoo})$, is 20%. The probability that a shopper buys both Cheese and Bread is 40%, since two of the five shoppers bought both Cheese and Bread.

Mathematically speaking, *milk* and *bread* is called an **itemset** and is typically written as {milk, bread}. Itemsets are similar to the concept of the probability *events* we introduced in Chapter 5, *Classification Algorithms*, except that itemsets are specifically used for situations such as this, and events are a more general concept in probability.

In association rule learning, the probability that an itemset appears as part of a transaction is called the **support** for that itemset. Just a moment ago, we mentioned that the probability of someone buying both milk and bread was 40%; this is another way of saying that the support for the {milk, bread} itemset is 40%. Noted mathematically, we can write supp({milk, bread}) = 40%.

Calculating the support of an itemset does not get us all the way to association rule learning, however. We first need to define what an association rule is. An association rule has the form X -> Y, where *X* and *Y* are both itemsets. Written out fully, an example association rule could be {eggs, milk} -> {cheese}, which relates the buying of eggs and milk to the buying of cheese. Association rules almost always only have a single item on the right-hand side, though the left-hand side can have any number of items. The association rule, by itself, tells us nothing about the association; we also need to look at various metrics, such as the association's *confidence* and *lift*, to understand how strong the association is.

The most important metric to consider for an association rule is its *confidence*, which is essentially how often the rule is found to be true. The *confidence* also happens to be the conditional probability of $P(E_Y|E_X)$, or the probability that someone buys the items in itemset Y given that they bought the items in X.

Using our knowledge of conditional probability from Chapter 5, *Classification Algorithms*, and the new concepts of *support* and *confidence* in association rule learning, let's write a few equivalences that will help us solidify these mathematical concepts.

First, let's say that the itemset X is eggs and milk, or X = {eggs, milk}, and that Y = {cheese}.

The support of X, or supp(X), is the same as the probability of finding the items in X in a transaction, or $P(E_X)$. In this case, eggs and milk appears in three out of five transactions, so its support is 60%. Similarly, the support of Y (just cheese) is 80%.

The confidence of an association rule, X -> Y, is defined as conf(X -> Y) = supp(X ∪ Y) / supp(X). Another way to say this is that the confidence of a rule is the support of all items in the rule divided by the support of the left-hand side. The ∪ symbol is used in probability theory to mean *union*—basically a Boolean OR operation. The *union* of the X and Y itemsets is therefore any item that appears in either X or Y. In our case, the union is eggs, milk, and cheese.

If `supp(X) = P(EX)`, then `supp(X ∪ Y) = P(EX ∩ XY)`. Recall that ∩ is the symbol for *intersection*, or essentially a Boolean AND. This is one scenario in which the semantics of itemsets differ from the semantics of probability events—the *union* of two itemsets is related to the *intersection* of two events containing those itemsets. Despite the slightly confusing notations, what we're getting at is this: this *confidence* formula is starting to look exactly like the formula for conditional probability, once we start translating the association rule notation into a standard probability notation.

Since, in conditional probability, the $P(E_Y \mid E_X) = P(E_X \cap E_Y) / P(E_X)$ relation defines the conditional probability, and we know that `supp(X ∪ Y) = P(E_X ∩ E_Y)`, and we also know that $P(E_X) = supp(X)$, we find that the confidence of an association rule is just its conditional probability.

Returning to our example rule of `{eggs, milk} ⇒ {cheese}`, we find that the confidence of this rule is 1.0. The union of X and Y (or `{eggs, milk, cheese}`) appears in three of the five transactions, and has a support of 0.6. We divide that by the support of the left-hand side, or just `supp({eggs, milk})`, which we also find in three of the five transactions. Dividing 0.6 by 0.6 gives us 1.0, which is the highest possible confidence value. Every time a shopper bought eggs and milk, they also bought cheese. Or, stated in terms of conditional probability, the probability that someone bought cheese given that they bought eggs and milk is 100%. Compare that to the probability of someone buying cheese, which is only 80%. We clearly have a positive relationship between eggs, milk, and cheese.

This coincidental relationship can be further explored with a concept called **lift**. Lift is defined as the support of the combined items, divided by the support for the left- and right-hand sides individually (that is, assuming they are independent). The formula is `lift(X -> Y) = supp(X ∪ Y) / ( supp(X) * supp(Y) )`. This formula essentially measures how dependent or independent `X` and `Y` are on each other. If the support of `X` and `Y` together is the same as the support of `X` and `Y` separately, the lift of the rule will be 1, and `X` and `Y` can be considered completely independent from one another. As the co-dependence of the two itemsets increases, the value of *lift* will increase as well. In our case, the support for `{eggs, milk, cheese}` is once again 0.6, the support for `{eggs, milk}` is 0.6, and the support for `{cheese}` is 0.8. Combining these values with the lift equation gives us `lift(X -> Y) = 0.6 / (0.6 * 0.8) = 1.25`. This rule is said to have a lift of 25%, which indicates that there is some dependent relationship between `{eggs, milk}` and `{cheese}`.

There are several other metrics that researchers can use when developing association rules, though we will not encounter any of these in our examples. There are metrics such as *conviction, leverage,* and *collective strength,* but for the most part, the familiar concepts of support, confidence, and lift will be all you need.

If you take one thing away from this section, let it be this: many modern problems in computer science and machine learning can be solved with centuries-old probability theory. Association rule learning was developed in the 1990s, but the core concepts can be traced back hundreds of years. As we saw in `Chapter 5`, *Classification Algorithms*, we can use probability theory to develop powerful **machine learning** (**ML**) algorithms, and association rule learning is another argument for honing your knowledge of probability theory.

Let's now take a look at the challenges of analyzing a transactional database, and how an association rule algorithm might work.

The algorithmic perspective

We now come to the much more difficult task of identifying frequent itemsets in a database. Once we know which itemsets and associations we want to generate rules for, calculating the support and confidence of the rules is quite easy. The difficulty, however, lies in automatically discovering the frequent and interesting itemsets in a database of millions of transactions among thousands of possible items.

Imagine that your e-commerce store only carries 100 unique items. Obviously, your customers can purchase any number of items during a session. Let's say a shopper buys only two items—there are 4,950 different combinations of two items from your catalog to consider. But you also must consider shoppers who buy three items, of which there are 161,700 combinations to search for. If your product catalog contains 1,000 items, there are a whopping 166 million combinations of three items that you'd have to consider when searching for frequent itemsets.

Clearly, a more evolved algorithm is necessary to search the transactional database for frequent itemsets. Note that the frequent itemset search is only half of the solution; once you find frequent itemsets, you still must generate association rules from them. However, as the search for frequent itemsets is much more difficult than generating association rules, the itemset search becomes the key focus for most algorithms.

In this section, we'll describe one of the original frequent itemset search algorithms: the Apriori algorithm. We're doing this for educational purposes only; it's unlikely you'd ever need to implement your own version of the Apriori algorithm, as there are newer and faster frequent itemset search algorithms available. However, I think it's important to study and understand these classic algorithms, especially algorithms that tackle a very large search space. Most algorithms that search a very large space use some kind of axiomatically or heuristically justified trick to drastically reduce the search space, and Apriori is no different.

The Apriori algorithm begins by scanning the database of transactions and recording the support (or frequency) of each individual item. The result of this is a list or hash table of items such as eggs = 0.6, milk = 0.6, shampoo = 0.2.

The next step is to find combinations of two items and determine their support (or frequency) in the database. The result of this step would be something like {eggs, milk} = 0.6, {eggs, bread} = 0.2, {eggs, cheese} = 0.6, {eggs, shampoo} = 0.0, and so on. The problem with the brute-force, exhaustive-search approach starts at this step. If you have 100 items in your catalog, you need to calculate the support for 4,950 pairs. If you have 1,000 items in your catalog, you must calculate the support for nearly 500,000 pairs. I don't know how many products Amazon (https://www.amazon.com/) sells (the latest report from January 2017 states 368 million), but assuming they now have 400 million products, there are 8×10^{16} pairs of items to consider (that's eighty million billion pairs of items). And that's just *pairs* of items. We'd also need to look at every triplet of items, every quadruplet of items, and so on.

The clever trick that Apriori uses to reduce the search space is to filter the list of unique products by a minimum support level, or minimum frequency of interest. If we set the minimum support to 0.25, for instance, we find that {shampoo} doesn't make the cut, and shampoo can never be part of our frequent itemset analysis because it's simply not purchased frequently enough.

If shampoo, by itself, is not purchased frequently enough to be considered frequent, it also follows that any pair of items containing shampoo will *also* not be frequent enough for consideration. If shampoo appears in 20% of purchases, then the {eggs, shampoo} pair must appear *less* frequently than (or equal to) 20% of purchases. We cannot only eliminate shampoo from our search, we can also eliminate *any* set that contains shampoo from consideration. If shampoo by itself is infrequent enough that we can ignore it, then {eggs, shampoo}, {bread, shampoo}, and {eggs, bread, shampoo} will all also be so infrequent that we can ignore them. This cuts down on our search space *drastically*.

We can take this approach a step further as we inspect larger combinations of items. In our example, {eggs} has a support of 60% and {bread} has a support of 40%. If we've set our minimum support to 25%, both of these items individually make the cut and should be considered in our frequent dataset analysis. However, the combination of {eggs, bread} has a support of only 20% and can be discarded. In the same way we were able to eliminate any combination containing {shampoo} from our second-degree search, we can now eliminate any combination containing {eggs, bread} from our third-degree search. Because eggs and bread together is rare, any combination of three or more items that contains both eggs and bread must also be rare. We can therefore eliminate combinations such as {eggs, bread, cheese}, {eggs, bread, milk}, and {eggs, bread, shampoo} from consideration, as they all contain the rare combination of eggs and bread.

While this approach drastically reduces the time required to find frequent itemsets, you should use this approach with caution as it's possible to accidentally skip over interesting, but somewhat rare, combinations. Most Apriori implementations will allow you to set both a minimum support and a minimum confidence for the resultant association rules. If you set the minimum support to a high value, your search will be faster but you may get more obvious or less interesting results; if you set the support lower, you're in danger of waiting for a very long time for the search to complete. Typically, association rules are generated after the frequent itemsets are found, so any minimum confidence level you set will not have an impact on the search time—only the minimum support variable will have a significant effect on search time.

It should also be noted that there are more advanced and faster algorithms for frequent itemset searches. In particular, we will experiment with the FP-Growth algorithm later in this chapter. However, the Apriori algorithm is a great starting point for understanding how frequent itemset searches work in practice.

Before we implement libraries, let's take a look at a few situations in which association rules might be helpful.

Association rule applications

The original use of association rule algorithms was for market basket analysis, such as the grocery store example we've been using throughout this chapter. This is a clear-cut application for association rule mining. Market basket analysis can be used both in physical stores and in e-commerce stores, and different models can be maintained for different days of the week, seasons, or even for specific rare events, such as an upcoming concert or a hurricane.

In fact, in 2004, The New York Times (and others) reported that Walmart used association rule mining to figure out how to stock stores in advance of hurricanes. Walmart discovered that the association with the highest lift right before a hurricane wasn't bottled water or flashlights, but in fact strawberry Pop-Tarts. Another association with a high confidence was beer. I'm not too surprised about the beer, but the strawberry Pop-Tarts is the type of insight that you can really only get from ML!

Imagine you were a data scientist at Walmart back in 2004. It would be easy to look up the individual sales volumes of various products during different time periods. It's possible that the strawberry Pop-Tarts, being a small-ticket item, only showed a very minor percentage change in the relative sales volume during hurricane periods. That's the kind of data point you might naturally ignore as being insignificant. Pop-Tarts get a slight bump, so what? But if you were to mine the data for frequent itemsets and association rules, you might have found that the `{bottled water, batteries} -> {Strawberry Pop-Tarts}` rule appeared with an unusually strong confidence, and a lift of around 8.0 (a very high value for lift) in the days before a hurricane. Outside of hurricane season, this association may have been nonexistent or too weak to make the cut. But when a hurricane is about to hit, strawberry Pop-Tarts become a necessary hurricane supply, almost certainly due to their long shelf life and their ability to make both children and adults happy. Seeing this association, you'd tell stores to stock up on strawberry Pop-Tarts and put them right at the front of the store—next to the bottled water and batteries—and make a killing on Pop-Tart sales.

While this type of scenario is what association rules were designed for, you can apply frequent itemset mining and association rules to any transactional database. If you consider a website session to be a transaction, and if you can capture actions taken (such as *logged in*, *wishlisted item*, *downloaded case study*) as your items, you can apply the same algorithms and association rule mining to website visitor behaviors. You can develop association rules, such as `{downloaded case study, viewed pricing page} -> {entered credit card}`, to model your visitor behavior and optimize the layout and functionality of your site to encourage the behavior you want.

Keep in mind that association rules are not just valuable when they're positive. They're valuable when they're negative, too. Oftentimes you need cold, hard facts to change your mind about a stubborn belief that you previously held. Performing association rule mining on a dataset and *not* seeing an association you expected to see can be just as powerful as discovering an unexpected association. Seeing that the confidence for a rule you intuitively thought to be a strong association is actually very low, or below your cut-off, can help you let go of outdated thinking that might be holding you or your product back.

There are stories of association rule mining being used in many and varied fields. Yes, association rules can be used to maximize Pop-Tarts profits before a hurricane, but association rules can also be used to characterize the hurricanes themselves in terms of their features and power output. Even though association rule learning was developed for market basket analysis, its foundation in conditional probability makes it applicable to nearly any statistical system that can be represented by items and transactions.

Consider, for instance, medical diagnoses. If each diagnosis by a doctor is considered a transaction, and every medical condition or environmental factor an item, we can apply association rule mining to find surprising associations between pre-existing conditions, environmental factors, and new diagnoses. You might find that the `{poor air quality, poor diet} -> {asthma}` rule has a high confidence or lift, and that can inform the way researchers and doctors treat asthma, perhaps by taking a closer look at diet.

Association rules can be used in many other fields, such as genetics, bioinformatics, and IT security. Because these approaches can be used so broadly, it's often difficult to recognize when association rules should be applied. A good rule of thumb to use is this: if your dataset contains transactions, or if you can see yourself calculating conditional probabilities for many combinations of events, you may want to consider association rule mining.

Let's take a look at a couple of JavaScript libraries for association rule mining.

Example – retail data

In this example, we'll use the Apriori algorithm to analyze a retail dataset. Start by creating a new folder for this project called Ch6-Apriori, and add the following `package.json` file:

```
{
  "name": "Ch6-Apriori",
  "version": "1.0.0",
  "description": "ML in JS Example for Chapter 6 - Association Rules",
  "main": "src/index.js",
  "author": "Burak Kanber",
  "license": "MIT",
  "scripts": {
    "build-web": "browserify src/index.js -o dist/index.js -t [ babelify --
presets [ env ] ]",
    "build-cli": "browserify src/index.js --node -o dist/index.js -t [
babelify --presets [ env ] ]",
    "start": "yarn build-cli && node dist/index.js"
  },
```

```
    "dependencies": {
      "apriori": "^1.0.7",
      "babel-core": "^6.26.0",
      "babel-plugin-transform-object-rest-spread": "^6.26.0",
      "babel-preset-env": "^1.6.1",
      "babelify": "^8.0.0",
      "browserify": "^15.1.0",
      "node-fpgrowth": "^1.0.0"
    }
}
```

After adding the `package.json` file, run `yarn install` from the command line to install the dependencies.

Next, create a `src` directory and download the required data file from this book's GitHub repository, `retail-data.json`, into the folder.

Now add an `index.js` file to the `src` folder and add the following code:

```
import receipts from './retail-data.json';
import Apriori  from 'apriori';
import {FPGrowth} from 'node-fpgrowth';

const results = (new Apriori.Algorithm(0.02, 0.9, false))
    .analyze(receipts.slice(0, 1000));

console.log(results.associationRules
    .sort((a, b) => a.confidence > b.confidence ? -1 : 1));
```

The preceding code imports the data and the Apriori library. It then initializes a new Apriori solver with a minimum support of `0.02` (2%) and a minimum rule confidence of 90%. We're also only analyzing the first 1,000 receipts in the dataset; the Apriori algorithm is a bit slow by nature, so you'll likely want to limit the dataset as you experiment initially.

Run the program with `yarn start` and you should see output similar to the following. The output will be longer than what I show here; take a minute to explore your own console output:

```
[ a {
    lhs:
      [ 'KNITTED UNION FLAG HOT WATER BOTTLE',
        'RED WOOLLY HOTTIE WHITE HEART.',
        'SET 7 BABUSHKA NESTING BOXES' ],
    rhs: [ 'WHITE HANGING HEART T-LIGHT HOLDER' ],
    confidence: 1 },
  a {
```

```
lhs:
 [ 'RETRO COFFEE MUGS ASSORTED',
   'SAVE THE PLANET MUG',
   'VINTAGE BILLBOARD DRINK ME MUG',
   'WHITE HANGING HEART T-LIGHT HOLDER' ],
 rhs: [ 'KNITTED UNION FLAG HOT WATER BOTTLE' ],
 confidence: 1 },
a {
lhs:
 [ 'RETRO COFFEE MUGS ASSORTED',
   'SAVE THE PLANET MUG',
   'VINTAGE BILLBOARD DRINK ME MUG' ],
 rhs: [ 'WHITE HANGING HEART T-LIGHT HOLDER' ],
 confidence: 1 },
```

These association rules all have a confidence of 1.0, which means that the right-hand side (labeled `rhs`) appeared in a transaction 100% of the times that the left-hand side appeared.

Scroll down through the results a little more and you might find this rule:

```
a {
lhs: [ 'HAND WARMER BABUSHKA DESIGN', 'HAND WARMER RED RETROSPOT' ],
rhs: [ 'HAND WARMER BIRD DESIGN' ],
confidence: 0.9130434782608696 },
```

This rule essentially tells us that when a shopper buys the babushka and red retrospot design hand warmers, they have a 91% likelihood of also buying the bird design hand warmer. Have you ever wondered why, when shopping on Amazon, you often see suggestions similar to items you've just bought or added to your cart? This is why—apparently shoppers buy groups of similar items often enough that the association rule passes the various thresholds it needs to pass, despite the fact that the *average* shopper has no need for three differently designed hand warmers. But catering to the average shopper is not always the goal; you want to cater to the shopper who's going to spend more money, and you can find that shopper with statistics.

Experiment a little with the Apriori settings. What happens if you decrease the minimum confidence? What happens if you increase the minimum support?

Keeping the minimum support the same while decreasing the minimum confidence should give you more association rule results with no real impact on execution time. Most of the execution time is spent discovering frequent itemsets, where confidence is not yet a defined parameter; confidence only comes into play when composing rules, and does not affect individual itemsets.

Raising the minimum support will speed up the algorithm, however, you will find that you get less interesting results. As you raise the minimum support, you'll find that the left-hand side of the rules become simpler. Where you used to see rules with three and four items on the left-hand side, you'll now start seeing simpler left-hand itemsets, with only one or maybe two items. Itemsets with more than one item naturally tend toward having lower support values, so as you raise the minimum support, you will end up with simpler associations.

Lowering the minimum support, on the other hand, will drastically increase execution time but also yield more interesting results. Note that it's possible to have rules with generally low support but very high confidence; these are rules that hold to be true often, but are rare in occurrence. As you lower the minimum support, you will find that the new rules that appear are evenly spread across a range of confidence values.

Also try increasing the limit given to `receipts.slice`. Not only will the program become slower, but you'll also have *fewer* rules in the output if you keep the minimum support parameter constant. The reason for this is that the support value depends on the size of the dataset. An itemset that appeared in 2% of 1,000 transactions *might* only appear in 1% of 2,000 transactions, depending on the distribution of items. If you have a very large selection of items, or if your distribution of items is exponentially decaying (that is, the *long-tail distribution*), you will find that you need to scale the minimum support value as you scale the number of items considered.

To demonstrate this, I started with a minimum support of 0.02, a minimum confidence of 0.9, and a limit of 1,000 items from the receipts variable. With these parameters, the Apriori algorithm found 67 association rules. When I update the limit from 1,000 to 2,000, the algorithm finds zero rules. The frequent itemsets in the first 1,000 transactions are different enough from the itemsets in the second 1,000 transactions that most itemsets' support values were reduced when I increased the limit.

In order to find more results, I must decrease the minimum support. I first tried setting a minimum support of 0.01, however, I had to cancel that attempt after two hours of waiting for the program to complete. I tried again at 0.015. This time, the program finished in 70 seconds and gave me 12 results. There must be some point between 0.010 and 0.015 where the number of itemsets dramatically increases—and indeed, the program found 584 rules with a minimum support of 0.0125.

The support of an itemset is simply its frequency among all transactions. We can reframe everything related to support in terms of frequency. If we're considering 2,000 transactions, a support of 0.0125 corresponds to 25 occurrences. Put another way, the list of 584 rules I just generated only includes items that were purchased at least 25 times in my 2,000-transaction dataset. In order to generate rules for products that were only purchased, say, 5 or more times, I'd need to set a minimum support of 0.0025—a value I'm pretty sure would set my laptop on fire.

Here, the need for an algorithm more refined than Apriori becomes apparent. Unfortunately, the JavaScript ecosystem is still lacking in this department. Another popular frequent itemset mining algorithm, ECLAT, seems not to have any JavaScript implementations.

There is another frequent itemset mining algorithm available to us: the FP-Growth algorithm. This algorithm should be able to handle our task quite readily, however, the library available to us only does the frequent itemset search and does not generate association rules. It is much easier to generate association rules once the frequent itemsets have been discovered, however, I will leave this exercise up to the reader. For now, let's take a look at the FP-Growth library.

In the `index.js` file, you may comment out the existing lines related to the Apriori solver and add the following code:

```
const fpgrowth = new FPGrowth(0.01);
fpgrowth.exec(receipts)
    .then(result => {
        console.log(result.itemsets);
        console.log("Completed in " + result.executionTime + "ms.");
});
```

The FP-Growth implementation does not generate association rules, therefore the only parameter it takes is the minimum support value. In this example, we are not truncating the `receipts` transaction database, since the algorithm should be able to handle the larger dataset. The full transaction database has approximately 26,000 records, so a minimum support of `0.01` corresponds to products that were purchased `260` times or more.

Run `yarn start` from the command line and you should see output similar to this:

```
[ { items: [ 'DECORATIVE WICKER HEART LARGE' ], support: 260 },
  { items: [ 'MINIATURE ANTIQUE ROSE HOOK IVORY' ], support: 260 },
  { items: [ 'PINK HEART SHAPE EGG FRYING PAN' ], support: 260 },
  ... 965 more items ]
  Completed in 14659ms.
```

Notice that the value for support is given as an absolute value, that is, the number of times the items were found in the database. While these are only frequent itemsets and not association rules, they are still useful. If you see a frequent itemset similar to the following, you might want to show the user the rose teapot if they're browsing the sugar bowl page:

```
{ items: [ 'REGENCY SUGAR BOWL GREEN', 'REGENCY TEAPOT ROSES ' ],
    support: 247 }
```

While I think there is still some work to be done in terms of association rule learning in the JavaScript ecosystem, the Apriori and FP-Growth algorithms are both available and useful. The Apriori implementation in particular should be useful in most real-world use cases, which often contain fewer transactions and smaller item catalogs. While the FP-Growth implementation doesn't bother to generate association rules, there are still many things you can do by finding sets that an item frequently occurs in.

Summary

In this chapter, we discussed association rule learning, or the approach of finding frequent sets of items in a transactional database and relating them to one another via probabilities. We learned that association rule learning was invented for market basket analysis but has applications in many fields, since the underlying probability theory and the concept of transactional databases are both broadly applicable.

We then discussed the mathematics of association rule learning in depth, and explored the canonical algorithmic approach to frequent itemset mining: the Apriori algorithm. We looked at other possible applications of association rule learning before trying out our own example on a retail dataset.

Forecasting with Regression Algorithms

7

In this chapter, we're going to take a brief look at forecasting using regression algorithms. We'll additionally discuss time-series analysis and how we can use techniques from digital-signal processing to aid in our analysis. By the end of the chapter, you will have seen a number of patterns commonly found in time-series and continuous-valued data and will have an understanding of which types of regressions fit on which types of data. Additionally, you will have learned a few digital signal processing techniques, such as filtering, seasonality analysis, and Fourier transformations.

Forecasting is a very broad concept that covers many types of tasks. This chapter will provide you with an initial toolbox of concepts and algorithms that apply broadly to time-series data. We will focus on the fundamentals, and discuss the following topics:

- Regression versus classification
- Regression basics
- Linear, exponential, and polynomial regression
- Time-series analysis basics
- Low-pass and high-pass filtering
- Seasonality and subtractive analysis
- Fourier analysis

These concepts build an essential toolbox that you can use when working with real-world forecasting and analysis problems. There are many other tools that apply to specific situations, but I consider these topics to be the absolute essentials.

Let's begin by looking at the similarities—and differences—between regression and classification in **machine learning (ML)**.

Regression versus classification

Much of this book has been involved with classification tasks, where the objective of the analysis is to fit a data point to one of a number of predefined classes or labels. When classifying data, you are able to judge your algorithm's accuracy by comparing predictions to true values; a guessed label is either correct or incorrect. In classification tasks, you can often determine the likelihood or probability that a guessed label fits the data, and you typically choose the label with the maximum likelihood.

Let's compare and contrast classification tasks to regression tasks. Both are similar in that the ultimate goal is to make a prediction, informed by prior knowledge or data. Both are similar in that we want to create some kind of function or logic that maps input values to output values, and make that mapping function both as accurate and as generalized as possible. However, the major difference between regression and classification is that in regression, your goal is to determine the *quantity* of a value rather than its label.

Imagine you have historical data about the processing load over time on a server that you manage. This data is *time-series*, because the data evolves over time. The data is also *continuous* (as opposed to *discrete*), because the output values can be any real number: 1, or 2.3, or 2.34353, and so on. The goal in time-series analysis or regression analysis is not to label the data, but rather to predict what your server load will be next Thursday evening at 20:15 p.m., for instance. To accomplish this goal, you must analyze the time-series data and attempt to extract patterns from it, and then use those patterns to make a future prediction. Your prediction will also be a real and continuous number, such as *I predict the server load next Thursday night will be 2.75.*

In classification tasks, you can judge the accuracy of your algorithm by comparing predictions to true values and counting how many predictions were correct or incorrect. Because regression tasks involve themselves with continuous values, one cannot simply determine whether a prediction was correct or incorrect. If you predict that server load will be 2.75 and it ends up truly being 2.65, can you say that the prediction was correct? Or incorrect? What about if it ends up being 2.74? When classifying *spam* or *not spam*, you either get the prediction right or you get it wrong. When you compare continuous values, however, you can only determine how close you got the prediction and therefore must use some other metric to define the accuracy of your algorithm.

In general, you will use a different set of algorithms to analyze continuous or time-series data than you would use for classification tasks. However, there are some ML algorithms that can handle both regression and classification tasks with minor modifications. Most notably, decision trees, random forests, and neural networks can all be used both for classification and regression tasks.

In this chapter, we will look at the following concepts:

- Least-squares regressions techniques, such as linear regression, polynomial regression, power law regression, and others
- Trend analysis or smoothing
- Seasonality analysis or pattern subtraction

Regression basics

When performing regression analysis, there are two primary and overarching goals. First, we want to determine and identify any underlying, systemic patterns in the data. If we can identify the systemic patterns, we may be able to identify the phenomena underlying the patterns and develop a deeper understanding of the system as a whole. If, through your analysis, you find that there is a pattern that repeats itself every 16 hours, you will be in a much better position to figure out what phenomenon is causing the pattern and take action. As with all ML tasks, that 16-hour pattern may be buried deep within the data and may not be identifiable at a glance.

The second major goal is to use the knowledge of the underlying patterns to make future predictions. The predictions that you make will only be as good as the analysis that powers the predictions. If there are four different systemic patterns in your data, and you've only identified and modeled three of them, your predictions may be inaccurate since you haven't fully modeled the real-world phenomena involved.

Achieving both of these goals relies on your ability to identify and formally (that is, mathematically) describe the patterns and phenomena. In some cases, you may not be able to fully identify the root cause of a pattern; even then, if the pattern is reliable and your analysis is good, you will still be able to predict the future behavior of the system even if you don't fully understand the cause. This is the case with all ML problems; ML ultimately analyzes behaviors and results—the things we can measure—but having a deep understanding of the causes can only help.

In all ML problems, we must also contend with noise. In classification problems, noise can take many forms, such as missing or incorrect values, or undefinable human behavior. Noise can take many forms in regression problems as well: sensors may be susceptible to environmental noise, there can be random fluctuations in the underlying processes, or noise can be caused by many small, hard-to-predict, systemic factors.

Noise always makes patterns more difficult to identify, whether you're performing regression or classification analysis. In regression analysis, your goal is to be able to separate the systemic behaviors (the actual patterns) from the random sources of noise in the data. In some cases, it's important to also model the noise as a behavior, because the noise itself can have a significant effect on your predictions; in other cases, the noise can be ignored.

To illustrate the difference between systemic patterns and noise, consider the following dataset. There are no units on the graph, as this is just a conceptual example of some dependent parameter, *Y*, that varies with some independent parameter, *X*:

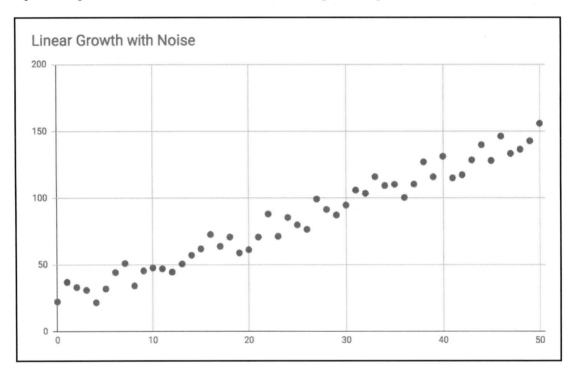

In this example, we can clearly see the difference between the systemic pattern and the noise. The systemic pattern is the steady, linear growth—the Y-values generally increase as the X-values increase, despite some fluctuations from point to point due to noise. By modeling the systemic pattern in this data, we would be able to make a reasonable prediction for what the Y-value will be when the X-value is 75, or 100, or -20. Whether or not the noise is significant will depend on the specific application; you can either ignore the noise, or you can model it and include it in your analysis.

In `Chapter 1`, *Exploring the Potential of JavaScript*, we learned about one technique for dealing with noise: smoothing with a moving average. Instead of graphing individual points, we can take groups of three points together and plot their averages. If the noise is truly random and distributed evenly (that is, the average of all the effects of noise comes out close to zero), a moving average will tend to cancel out some of the noise. If you are averaging three points, and the effect due to noise on each of those points adds +1, -2, and +1.2 to each point, respectively, the moving average will reduce the total effect of the noise to +0.2. When we graph the moving average, we will typically find a smoother pattern:

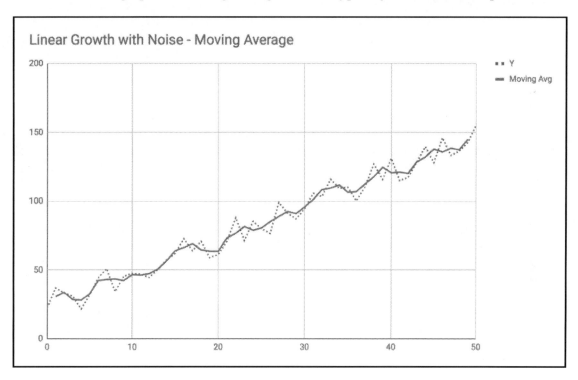

The moving average has reduced the effect of the noise, and helps us focus on the systemic pattern a bit more—but we are not much closer to being able to predict future values, such as when X is 75. The moving average only helps us reduce the effect of noise on the data points within the dataset. When you look at the Y-value when $X = 4$, for instance, the measured value is around 21 while the smoothed value is 28. In this case, the smoothed value of 28 better represents the *systemic pattern* at $X = 4$, even though the actual measured value at this point was 21. Most likely, the big difference between the measurement and the systemic pattern was caused by a significant source of random noise when this measurement was taken.

Be cautious when dealing with noise. It's important to recognize that, in the preceding example, the actual measured Y-value was indeed 21 at $X = 4$. The smoothed, moving average version is an idealization. It is our attempt to cut through the noise in order to see the signal, but we cannot forget that the actual measurement was significantly affected by noise. Whether this fact is important to your analysis depends significantly on the problem you are trying to solve.

How, then, do we approach the problem of predicting a future value of this data? The moving average may help us when *interpolating* data, but not when *extrapolating* to a future X-value. You can, of course, make a guess as to what the value will be when $X = 75$, since this example is simple and easy to visualize. However, since this is a book about ML, we can assume that real-world problems will not be so easy to analyze by eye, and we will need to introduce new tools.

The solution to this problem is the *regression*. As with all predictive ML problems, we want to create some kind of abstract function that can map input values to output values, and use that function to make predictions. In classification tasks, that mapping function may be a Bayesian predictor or a heuristic based on random forests. In regression tasks, the mapping function will often be a mathematical function that describes a line, or a polynomial, or some other kind of shape that fits the data well.

If you've ever graphed data in Excel or Google Sheets, there's a good chance you have already used linear regressions. The *trendline* feature of these programs performs a linear regression in order to determine a mapping function that best fits the data. The following graph is a trendline determined by a *linear regression*, which is a type of algorithm that is used to find the mathematical line that best fits the data:

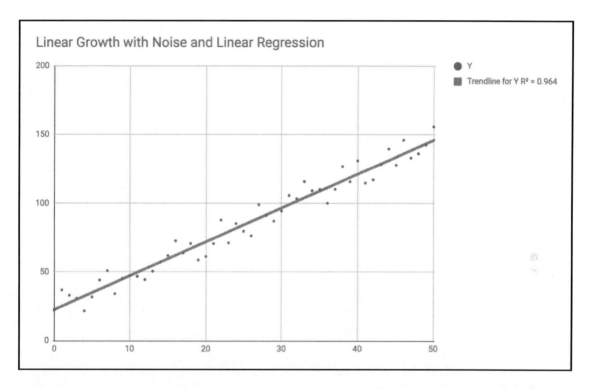

Additionally, Excel gives us another piece of information, called the **R² value**, which is a representation of how well the trendline fits the data. An R^2 value closer to 1.0 indicates that the trendline explains much of the variance between points; a low R^2 value indicates that the model does not explain the variance.

The major difference between the trendline and the moving average we saw earlier is that the trendline is an actual mathematical model. When you find a trendline with a linear regression, you will have a mathematical formula that describes the entire line. The moving average only exists where the data points exist; we can only have a moving average between X = 0 and X = 50. The trendline, on the other hand, is described by the mathematical formula for a straight line, and it extends out to infinity both to the left and to the right. If you know the formula for the trendline, you can plug in *any* value of X to that formula and get a prediction for the value of Y. If, for example, you find that the formula for a line is Y = 2.5 x X + 22, you can plug in X = 75 and you will get a prediction of Y = 2.5 x 75 + 22, or Y = 209.5. There is no way to get such a prediction from a moving average.

Linear regression is just one type of regression algorithm, specifically used to find a straight line that fits the data. In this chapter, we will explore several other types of regression algorithms, each with a different shape. In all cases, you can use a metric that describes how well the regression fits the data. Typically, this metric will be **root mean squared error (RMSE)**, which is the square root of the average of the squared error for each point compared to the trendline. Most regression algorithms are *least-squares* regressions, which aim to find the trendline that minimizes the RMSE.

Let's take a look at several examples of regression shapes and how to fit them to data in JavaScript.

Example 1 – linear regression

Before we dive into the first example, let's take a minute to set up our project folder and dependencies. Create a new folder called Ch7-Regression, and inside that folder add the following package.json file:

```
{
  "name": "Ch7-Regression",
  "version": "1.0.0",
  "description": "ML in JS Example for Chapter 7 - Regression",
  "main": "src/index.js",
  "author": "Burak Kanber",
  "license": "MIT",
  "scripts": {
    "build-web": "browserify src/index.js -o dist/index.js -t [ babelify --presets [ env ] ]",
    "build-cli": "browserify src/index.js --node -o dist/index.js -t [ babelify --presets [ env ] ]",
    "start": "yarn build-cli && node dist/index.js"
  },
  "dependencies": {
    "babel-core": "^6.26.0",
    "babel-plugin-transform-object-rest-spread": "^6.26.0",
    "babel-preset-env": "^1.6.1",
    "babelify": "^8.0.0",
    "browserify": "^15.1.0",
    "dspjs": "^1.0.0",
    "regression": "^2.0.1"
  }
}
```

Then run the `yarn install` command from the command line to install all dependencies. Next, create a folder called `src`, and add an empty file called `index.js`. Finally, download the `data.js` file from the book's GitHub repository into the `src` folder.

In this example, we're going to work on the noisy linear data from the previous section. As a reminder, the data itself looks like this:

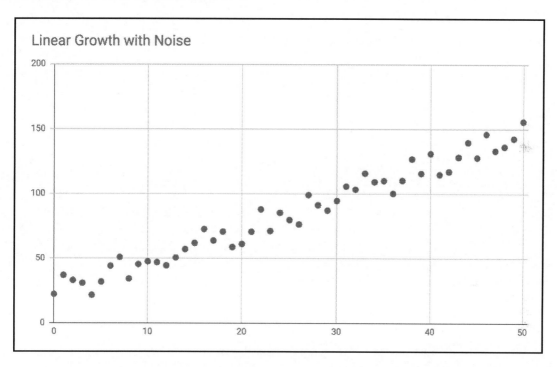

Our goal is to find the formula for a line that fits the data and make a prediction for a future value when $X = 75$. We'll use Tom Alexander's `regression` library, which can perform a number of types of regressions and also provides the capability to make predictions based on the resultant regression.

In the `index.js` file, add the following import statements to the top of the file:

```
import * as data from './data';
import regression from 'regression';
```

As with all ML problems, you should start by visualizing your data and trying to understand the overall shape of the data before you choose the algorithm. In this case, we can see that the data follows a linear trend so we will choose the linear regression algorithm.

In linear regression, the goal is to determine the parameters for the formula for a line that best fits the data. The formula for a straight line has the following form: $y = mx + b$, sometimes written as $y = ax + b$, where x is the input variable or independent variable, y is the target or dependent variable, m (or a) is the *slope* or *gradient* of the line, and b is the *y-intercept* of the line (the Y-value of the line when $X = 0$). Therefore, the minimum requirements for the output of a linear regression are the values for a and b, the only two parameters that determine the shape of the line.

Add the following import lines to `index.js`:

```
console.log("Performing linear regression:");
console.log("==============================");
const linearModel = regression.linear(data.linear);
console.log("Slope and intercept:");
console.log(linearModel.equation);
console.log("Line formula:");
console.log(linearModel.string);
console.log("R^2 fitness: " + linearModel.r2);
console.log("Predict X = 75: " + linearModel.predict(75)[1]);
```

Performing a linear regression on the data will return a model; the model essentially encapsulates the values of a and b, or the slope and the intercept of the line. This particular library not only returns the line's parameters in the `linearModel.equation` property, but also gives us a string representation of the line formula, calculates the R^2 fit of the regression, and gives us a method, called `predict`, which we can use to plug a new X-value into the model.

Run the code by issuing the `yarn start` command from the command line. You should see the following output:

```
Performing linear regression:
==============================
Slope and intercept:
[ 2.47, 22.6 ]
Line formula:
y = 2.47x + 22.6
R^2 fitness: 0.96
Predict X = 75: 207.85
```

The regression has determined that the formula for the line that best fits our data is $y = 2.47x + 22.6$. The original formula I used to create this test data was $y = 2.5x + 22$. The slight difference between the determined equation and the actual equation is due to the effect of the random noise I added to the dataset. As you can see, the linear regression has done a good job of looking past the noise and discovering the underlying pattern. If we chart these results, we will see the following:

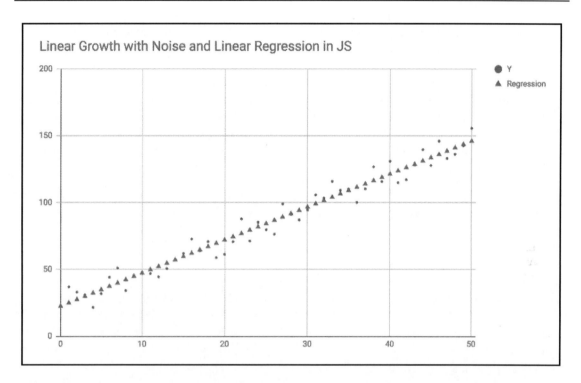

The results of the regression, as seen in the preceding graph, are exactly the same as the results given by the trendline feature of Excel or Google Sheets, with the difference being that we generated the trendline in JavaScript.

When asked to predict a future value where $X = 75$, the regression returns $Y = 207.85$. Using my original formula, the true value would have been 209.5. The amount of noise I added to the data amounts to a random and uniform noise level of +/- 12.5 for any given point, so the predicted value turns out to be very close to the actual value when you account for the uncertainty due to noise.

It should be noted, however, that errors in regression compound as you make predictions further away from the domain of the original data. When predicting for $X = 75$, the error between the prediction and the actual value is only 1.65. If we were to predict for $X = 1000$, on the other hand, the true formula would return 2,522, but the regression would predict 2,492.6. The error between the actual value and the prediction at $X = 1000$ is now 29.4, nearly 30, far beyond the uncertainty due to noise. Regressions are very useful predictors, but you must always keep in mind that these errors can compound and therefore the predictions will become less accurate as you get further away from the domain of the dataset.

The reason for this type of prediction error lies in the regression for the slope of the equation. The slope of the line in the original equation is 2.5. This means that for every unit change in the X value, we should expect a change of 2.5 units in the Y value. The regression, on the other hand, determines a slope of 2.47. Therefore, for every unit change in the X value, the regression is inheriting a slight error of -0.03. Predicted values will be slightly lower than actual values by that amount, multiplied by the X distance for your prediction. For every 10 units of X, the regression inherits a total error of -0.3. For every 100 units of X, the regression inherits an error of -3.0, and so on. When we extrapolate out to X=1000, we've inherited an error of -30, because that slight per-unit error of -0.03 gets multiplied by the distance we travel along the x axis.

When we look at values within our data domain—values between $X = 0$ and $X = 50$—we only get very small prediction errors due to this slight difference in slope. Within our data domain, the regression has corrected for the error in slope by slightly increasing the y-intercept value (the original is +22, the regression returned +22.6). Due to the noise in our data, the regression formula of $y = 2.47x + 22.6$ is a better fit than the actual formula of $y = 2.5x + 22$. The regression finds a slightly less-steep slope and makes up for it by raising the entire line by 0.6 units (the difference in y-intercepts), because this fits both the data and the noise better. This model fits the data very well between $X = 0$ and $X = 50$, but when we try to predict the value when $X = 1000$, the slight +0.6 modification in the y-intercept is no longer enough to make up for the decreased slope over such a vast distance.

Linear trends like the one found in this example are very common. There are many types of data that exhibit linear relationships and can be modeled simply yet accurately as long as you don't attempt to over-extrapolate the data. In the next example, we'll take a look at exponential regressions.

Example 2 – exponential regression

Another common trend in continuous data patterns is *exponential growth,* which is also commonly seen as *exponential decay.* In exponential growth, a future value is proportionally related to the current value. The general formula for this type of growth can be written as:

$$y = y_0 \, (1 + r) \, x$$

Where y_0 is the quantity's initial value (when $x = 0$), and r is the growth rate of the quantity.

For instance, if you are investing money in the stock market and expect a 5% rate of return per year ($r = 0.05$) with an initial investment of $10,000, after five years you can expect $12,763. The exponential growth formula applies here because the amount of money you have next year is proportionally related to the amount of money you have this year, and the amount of money you have two years from now is related to the money you have next year, and so on. This only applies if you reinvest your returns, causing the amount of money you're actively investing to increase with each passing year.

Another form for the exponential growth equation is given as:

$$y = ae^{bx}$$

Where $b = ln(1 + r)$, a is the initial value y_0, and e is Euler's constant of approximately 2.718. This slight transformation in form is easier to manipulate mathematically and is typically the preferred form used by mathematicians for analysis. In our stock market investment example, we can rewrite the formula for five year growth as $y = 10000*e^{ln(1.05)*5}$, and we will get the same result of $12,763.

Exponential growth is sometimes called **hockey-stick growth** due to the shape of the curve resembling the outline of a hockey stick:

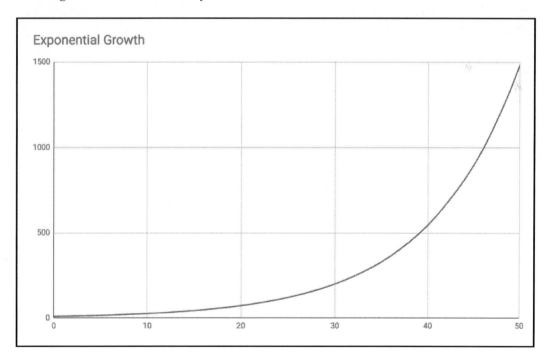

Some examples of exponential growth include:

- Population growth; that is, world population or bacterial culture growth
- Viral growth, such as analysis of disease infections or the viral spread of YouTube videos
- Positive feedback loops in mechanics or signal processing
- Economic growth, including compound interest
- Processing power of computers under Moore's law

It is important to note that, in almost all circumstances, exponential growth is unsustainable. For example, if you are predicting the growth of a bacterial colony in a Petri dish, you may observe exponential growth for a short time, however once the Petri dish runs out of food and space, other factors will take over and the growth will no longer be exponential. Similarly, if your website incentivizes new users to invite their friends, you may see exponential growth in your membership for a while, but eventually you will saturate the market and growth will slow. Therefore, you must be cautious in analyzing exponential growth models and understand that the conditions that fuel exponential growth may ultimately change. Similar to linear regression, an exponential regression will only apply to modest extrapolations of your data. Your website's membership may grow exponentially for a year, but not for ten years; you cannot have 20 billion members if there are only seven billion people on Earth.

If the growth rate, r, or the parameter k (called the **growth constant**), is negative, you will have exponential decay rather than exponential growth. Exponential decay is still exponential growth in the sense that future values are proportional to the current value, however in exponential decay, future values are proportionately *smaller* than the current value.

One real-world use of exponential decay is in carbon-dating analysis. Because the radioactive carbon-14 isotope decays into non-radioactive carbon-12 with a half-life of 5,730 years—meaning that, in aggregate, half the carbon-14 decays into carbon-12 every 5,730 years—scientists can use the exponential decay formula to figure out how old an object must be in order to have the appropriate ratio of carbon-14 to carbon-12.

Exponential decay is also seen in physics and mechanics, particularly in the spring-mass-damper problem. It can also be used by coroners and medical examiners to determine the time of death of a subject, based on the fact that a warm body will cool down and approach the ambient temperature of the room in an exponentially decaying fashion.

In exponential regression, our goal is to determine the values of the parameters a and b—the initial value and the growth constant. Let's try this in JavaScript. The data we wish to analyze is exponentially decaying, with random sensor noise added:

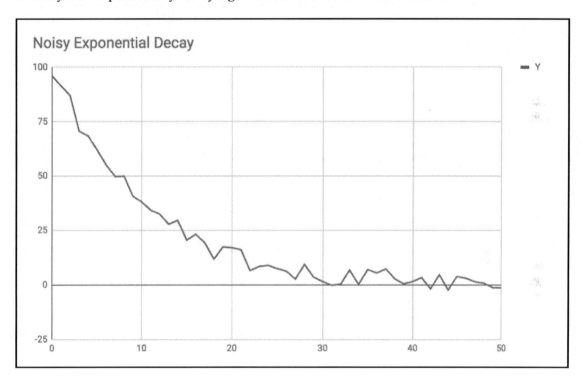

The preceding chart exhibits some quantity that starts near 100 and decays down to approximately 0. This could represent, for instance, the number of visitors over time to a post that was shared on Facebook.

Attempting to fit a trendline with Excel or Google Sheets does not help us in this case. The linear trendline does not fit the exponential curve, and the inappropriateness of the fit is indicated by the poor R^2 value:

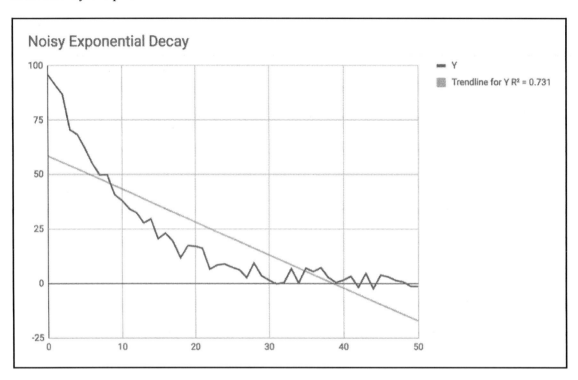

Let's now use JavaScript to find the regression for this data and also make a prediction of the value for one second before the dataset started. Add the following code to index.js; it is the linear regression code:

```
console.log("Performing exponential regression:");
console.log("=================================");
const expModel = regression.exponential(data.exponential);
console.log("Initial value and rate:");
console.log(expModel.equation);
console.log("Exponential formula:");
console.log(expModel.string);
console.log("R^2 fitness: " + expModel.r2);
console.log("Predict X = -1: " + expModel.predict(-1)[1]);
```

Run the program with `yarn start` and you should see the following output, following the output for the linear regression example:

```
Performing exponential regression:
==============================
Initial value and rate:
[ 94.45, -0.09 ]
Exponential formula:
y = 94.45e^(-0.09x)
R^2 fitness: 0.99
Predict X = -1: 103.34
```

We can immediately see the high R^2 value of 0.99, indicating that the regression has found a good fit to the data. If we chart this regression along with the original data, we see the following:

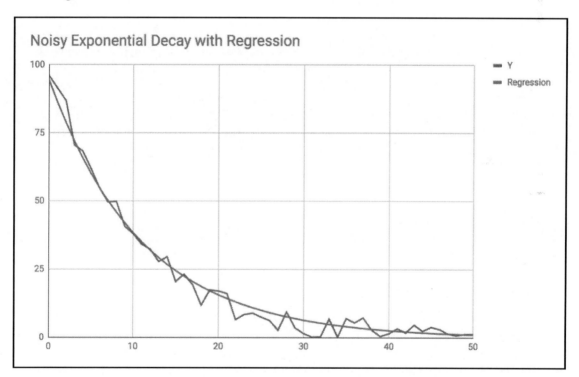

Additionally, we get a prediction for X = -1 of 103, which fits our data well. The original parameters for the equation I used to generate the test data were *a = 100* and *b = -0.1*, while the predicted parameters were *a = 94.5* and *b = -0.09*. The presence of noise has made a significant impact on the starting value, which would have been 100 if there were no noise in the system, but was actually measured at 96. When comparing the regressed value for *a* to the actual value of *a*, you must also consider the fact that the regressed value of *a* was close to the measured, noisy value, even though it is pretty far from the systemic value.

In the next section, we will take a look at the polynomial regression.

Example 3 – polynomial regression

The polynomial regression can be considered a more generalized form of the linear regression. A polynomial relationship has the form:

$$y = a_0 + a_1x^1 + a_2x^2 + a_3x^3 + ... + a_nx^n$$

A polynomial can have any number of terms, which is called the **degree** of the polynomial. For each degree of the polynomial, the independent variable, x, is multiplied by some parameter, a_n, and the X-value is raised to the power n. A straight line is considered a polynomial of degree *1*; if you update the preceding polynomial formula to remove all degrees above one, you are left with:

$$y = a_0 + a_1x$$

Where a_0 is the y-intercept and a_1 is the slope of the line. Despite the slight difference in notation, this is equivalent to $y = mx + b$.

Quadratic equations, which you may recall from high school math, are simply polynomials of degree 2, or $y = a_0 + a_1x + a_2x^2$. Cubic equations are polynomials of degree 3, quadratic equations are polynomials of degree 4, and so on.

The property of polynomials and polynomial regressions that makes them so powerful is the fact that nearly any shape can be described by a polynomial of sufficient degree, within a limited range of values. Polynomial regressions can even fit sinusoidal shapes, as long as you don't try to extrapolate too far. Polynomial regressions exhibit properties similar to other machine learning algorithms in the sense that they can overfit and become very inaccurate for new data points if you attempt to extrapolate too far.

Because polynomials can be of any degree, you must also configure the regression with an additional parameter; this parameter can be guessed or you can search for the degree that maximizes the R^2 fit. This approach is similar to the approach we used for k-means when you don't know the number of clusters in advance.

The data we wish to fit, when graphed, looks like this:

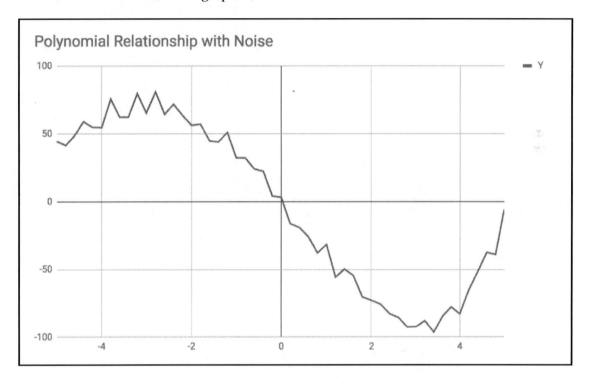

This small window of data looks sinusoidal but is in fact polynomial; remember that polynomial equations can reproduce many types of shapes.

Add the following code to the bottom of index.js:

```
console.log("Performing polynomial regression:");
console.log("================================");
const polyModel = regression.polynomial(data.polynomial, {order: 2});
console.log("Polynomial parameters");
console.log(polyModel.equation);
console.log("Polynomial formula:");
console.log(polyModel.string);
console.log("R^2 fitness: " + polyModel.r2);
console.log("Predict X = 6: " + polyModel.predict(6)[1]);
```

Note that we have configured the regression with `{order: 2}`, that is, we are attempting to fit the data with a quadratic formula. Run the program with `yarn start` to see the following output:

```
Performing polynomial regression:
==============================
Polynomial parameters
[ 0.28, -17.83, -6.6 ]
Polynomial formula:
y = 0.28x^2 + -17.83x + -6.6
R^2 fitness: 0.75
Predict X = 6: -103.5
```

The R^2 fit for this data is quite low, at 0.75, indicating that we have probably used an incorrect value for the `order` parameter. Try increasing the order to `{order: 4}` and re-run the program to get the following:

```
Performing polynomial regression:
==============================
Polynomial parameters
[ 0.13, 1.45, -2.59, -40.45, 0.86 ]
Polynomial formula:
y = 0.13x^4 + 1.45x^3 + -2.59x^2 + -40.45x + 0.86
R^2 fitness: 0.99
Predict X = 6: 146.6
```

The regression is a much better fit now, at the expense of having added extra polynomial terms to the equation. If we graph this regression against the original data, we will see the following output, which indeed fits the data very well:

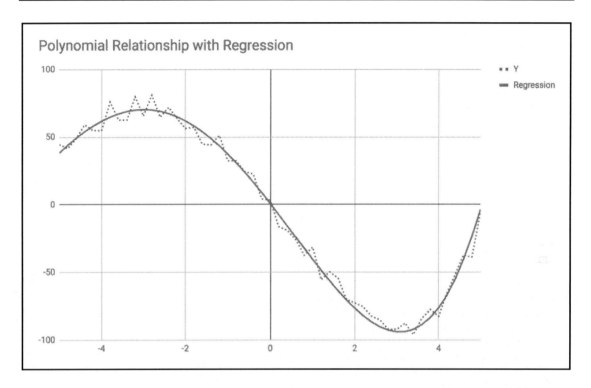

In the next section, we will explore some other types of analyses that can be performed on time-series data, including low-pass and high-pass filters, and seasonality analysis.

Other time-series analysis techniques

Regressions are a great starting point for analyzing continuous data, however, there are many other techniques one can employ when analyzing time-series data specifically. While regressions can be used for any continuous data mapping, time-series analysis is specifically geared toward continuous data that evolves over time.

There are many examples of time-series data, for instance:

- Server load over time
- Stock prices over time
- User activity over time
- Weather patterns over time

The objective when analyzing time-series data is similar to the objective in analyzing continuous data with regressions. We wish to identify and describe the various factors that influence the changing value over time. This section will describe a number of techniques above and beyond regressions that you can use to analyze time-series data.

In this section, we will look at techniques that come from the field of digital signal processing, which has applications in electronics, sensor analysis, and audio signals. While your specific time-series problem may not be related to any of these fields, the tools used in digital signal processing applications can be applied to any problem domain that deals with digital signals. Among the most significant tools and techniques are filtering, seasonality detection, and frequency analysis. We'll discuss these techniques, but I will leave it up to you to implement your own examples and experiments.

Filtering

Filtering, in a digital signal processing context, is a technique used to filter out either high-frequency or low-frequency components of a signal. These are called **low-pass filters** and **high-pass filters**, respectively; a low-pass filter allows low-frequency signals to *pass* while removing high-frequency components from the signal. There are also *band-pass* and *notch* filters, which either allow a range of frequencies to pass or cut a range of frequencies from the signal.

In electronics, filters are designed by using capacitors, resistors, and other simple electronic components in order to allow only frequencies above or below a *cut-off frequency* to pass through the circuit. In digital signal processing, the same effect can be achieved with an *infinite impulse response* filter, which is an algorithm that can reproduce the effects of an electronic circuit on time-series data.

To illustrate this, consider the following data:

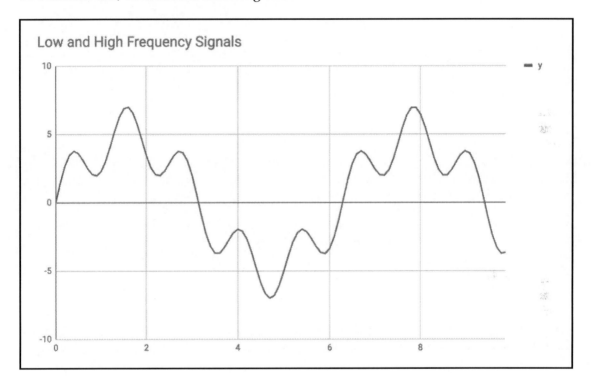

This data was generated by combining two sinusoidal signals, one low-frequency signal and one high-frequency signal. If we chart the two signals individually, we can see how they combine to create the overall signal:

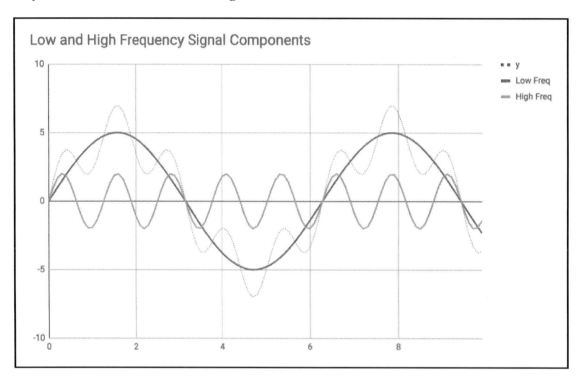

When filtering the overall signal, the goal is to extract either the low-frequency or the high-frequency component of the signal, while filtering the other out. This is called **subtractive processing,** since we are removing (filtering) a component from the signal.

In general, you should use low-pass filtering to isolate large, general, periodic trends in time-series data while ignoring faster periodic trends. High-pass filtering, on the other hand, should be used when you wish to explore the short-term periodic trends while ignoring the long-term trends. One example of this approach is when analyzing visitor traffic; you can use high-pass and low-pass filtering to selectively ignore monthly trends versus daily trends.

Seasonality analysis

Building on the previous section, we can also use digital signal processing to analyze seasonal trends. Seasonal trends are long-term periodic (that is, low-frequency) trends that you wish to subtract from your overall data in order to analyze other, potentially non-periodic trends in data. Consider the following graph:

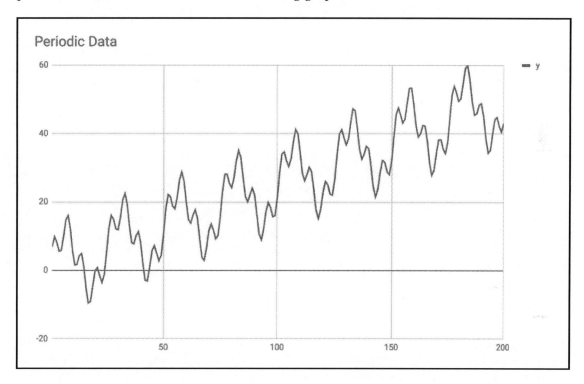

This data exhibits a combination of linear growth on top of periodic fluctuations in activity. Specifically, there are two periodic components (one low-frequency and one high-frequency) and one linear component to this data trend.

In order to analyze this data, the approach would be to first identify the linear trend, either through a large moving-average window or through a linear regression. Once the linear trend has been identified, you can subtract it from the data to isolate the periodic portions only. This approach is illustrated as follows:

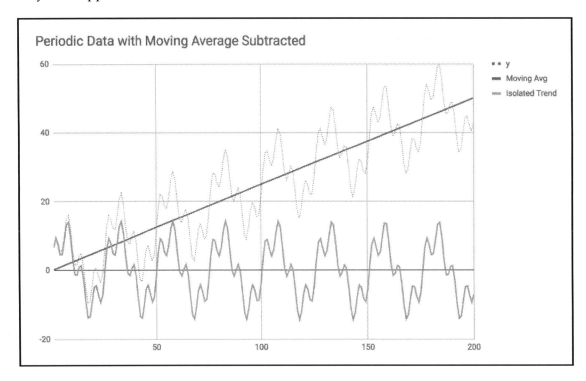

Because signals are additive, you are able to subtract the linear trend from the original data in order to isolate the non-linear components of the signal. If you've identified multiple trends, either through regressions or other means, you can continue to subtract the trends that you've identified from the original signal and you'll be left with only the unidentified signal components. Once you've identified and subtracted all of the systemic patterns, you'll have only the sensor noise remaining.

In this case, once you've identified and subtracted the linear trend from the data, you can either perform filtering on the resultant signal in order to isolate the low- and high-frequency components, or you can perform a *Fourier analysis* on the leftover signal to identify the specific frequencies and amplitudes of the remaining components.

Fourier analysis

Fourier analysis is a mathematical technique used to decompose a time-series signal into its individual frequency components. Recall that polynomial regressions of arbitrary degree can reproduce nearly any signal shape. In a similar manner, the sum of a number of sinusoidal oscillators can reproduce nearly any periodic signal. If you've ever seen an *oscilloscope* or *spectrum analyzer* in action, you've seen the real-time results of a Fourier transform being applied to a signal. In short, a Fourier transformation turns a periodic signal, such as the ones we saw in the last section, into a formula similar to:

$$a_1 sin(f_1+\varphi_1) + a_2 sin(f_2+\varphi_2) + a_3 sin(f_3+\varphi_3) + ... + a_n sin(f_n+\varphi_n)$$

Where f_n represents a frequency, a_n represents its amplitude, and φ_n represents a phase offset. By combining an arbitrary number of these sinusoidal signals together, one can replicate nearly any periodic signal.

There are many reasons to perform a Fourier analysis. The most intuitive examples relate to audio and sound processing. If you take a one-second-long audio sample of the note A4 being played on a piano and perform a Fourier transform on it, you would see that the frequency of 440 Hz has the largest amplitude. You would also see that the harmonics of 440 Hz, like 880 Hz and 1,320 Hz, also have some energy. You can use this data to aid in audio fingerprinting, auto-tuning, visualizing, and many other applications. The Fourier transformation is a sampling algorithm, and so it is susceptible to aliasing and other sampling errors. A Fourier transformation can be used to partially recreate an original signal, but much detail would be lost in translation. This process would be similar to down-sampling an image and then trying to up-sample it again.

There are many other applications for Fourier transforms in nearly every domain. The Fourier transform's popularity is due to the fact that, mathematically, many types of operations are easier to perform in the frequency domain than the time domain. There are many types of problems in mathematics, physics, and engineering that are very difficult to solve in the time domain but easy to solve in the frequency domain.

A Fourier transformation is a mathematical process that specific algorithms perform. The most popular Fourier transform algorithm is called the **Fast Fourier Transform (FFT)**, named s0 because it was much faster than its predecessor, the *Discrete Fourier Transform*. The FFT has one significant limitation in that the number of samples to be analyzed must be a power of 2, that is, it must be 128, 256, 512, 1,024, 2,048, and so on, samples long. If you have 1,400 samples to analyze, you must either truncate it down to 1,024 samples or pad it up to 2,048 samples. Most often, you will be *windowing* a larger sample; in the example of the piano note recording, we have windowed one second of samples from a live or recorded signal. If the audio sample rate is 44,100 Hz, then we would have 44,100 samples (one second's worth) to give to the Fourier transformation.

When padding, truncating, or windowing samples from a larger signal, you should use a *window function*, which is a function that tapers the signal at both ends so that it is not sharply cut off by your window. There are many types of window functions, each with their own mathematical properties and unique effects on your signal processing. Some popular window functions include the rectangular and triangular windows, as well as the Gaussian, Lanczos, Hann, Hamming, and Blackman windows, which each have desirable properties in different types of analyses.

The output of a Fourier transform algorithm, like the FFT algorithm, is a *frequency domain spectrum*. More concretely, the output of the FFT algorithm will be an array or a hash table where the keys are frequency buckets (such as 0-10 Hz, 10-20 Hz, and so on), and the values are amplitude and phase. These may be represented as complex numbers, multidimensional arrays, or some other structure specific to the algorithm implementation.

Some limitations apply to all sampling algorithms; these are limitations of signal processing itself. For instance, aliasing can occur if your signal contains components at frequencies above the *Nyquist frequency*, or half the sampling rate. In audio, where a sampling rate of 44,100 Hz is common, any frequencies above 22,050 Hz will be aliased, or misrepresented as low-frequency signals. Preprocessing signals with a low-pass filter is therefore a common technique. Similarly, the FFT algorithm can only resolve frequencies up to the Nyquist frequency. The FFT algorithm will return only as many frequency buckets as the sample buffer size, so if you give it 1,024 samples you will only get 1,024 frequency buckets. In audio, this means that each frequency bucket will have a bandwidth of 44,100 Hz / 1,024 = 43 Hz. This means that you would not be able to tell the difference between 50 Hz and 55 Hz, but you would easily be able to tell the difference between 50 Hz and 500 Hz. In order to get a higher resolution, you would need to provide more samples, however, this, in turn, will reduce the time resolution of your windows.

You can use the FFT to analyze the periodic portion of the time-series data we saw in the last section. It would be best to perform the FFT after you have subtracted the linear trend from the signal. However, if you have a high enough frequency resolution, the linear trend may only be interpreted as a low-frequency component of the Fourier transformation, so whether or not you need to subtract the linear trend will depend on your specific application.

By adding the FFT to the other tools you have learned about in this chapter, you are prepared to tackle most real-world regression or time-series analysis tasks. Each problem will be unique, and you will have to carefully consider which specific tools you will need for your task.

Summary

In this chapter, you learned a number of techniques used in forecasting, signal processing, regression, and time-series data analysis. Because forecasting and time-series analysis is a broad category, there is no single algorithm you can use that covers every case. Instead, this chapter has given you an initial toolbox of important concepts and algorithms that you can start applying to your forecasting and regression tasks.

Specifically, you learned about the difference between regression and classification. While classification assigns labels to data points, regression attempts to predict the numerical value of a data point. Not all regression is necessarily forecasting, but regression is the single most significant technique used in forecasting.

After learning the basics of regression, we explored a few specific types of regression. Namely, we discussed linear, polynomial, and exponential regression. We saw how regression deals with noise and how we can use it to predict future values.

We then turned to the broader concept of time-series analysis, and discussed core concepts, such as extracting trends from signals. We discussed tools used in digital signal processing that are applicable to time-series analysis, such as low-pass and high-pass filters, seasonality analysis, and Fourier transformations.

In the next chapter, we're going to look at more advanced machine learning models. Specifically, we're going to learn about the neural network—which, by the way, can also perform regressions.

8
Artificial Neural Network Algorithms

Artificial Neural Networks (ANNs) or, simply NNs, are arguably the most popular **machine learning (ML)** tool today, if not necessarily the most widely used. The tech media and commentary of the day love to focus on neural networks, and they are seen by many as the magical algorithm. It is believed that neural networks will pave the way to **Artificial General Intelligence (AGI)**—but the technical reality is much different.

While they are powerful, neural networks are highly specialized ML models that focus on solving individual tasks or problems—they are not magical *brains* that can solve problems out of the box. A model that exhibits 90% accuracy is typically considered good. Neural networks are slow to train and require thoughtful design and implementation. That said, they are indeed highly proficient problem solvers that can unravel even very difficult problems, such as object identification in images.

It is likely that neural networks will play a large part in achieving AGI. However, many other fields of ML and **natural language processing (NLP)** will need to be involved. Because ANNs are only specialized problem solvers, it is popularly believed that the way toward AGI is with a large ensemble of thousands of ANNs, each specialized for an individual task. I personally believe that we will see something resembling AGI surprisingly soon. However, AGI will only be achievable initially through immense resources—not in terms of computation power, but rather in terms of training data.

You will learn the basics of neural networks in this chapter. There are many ways to use neural networks, and many possible topologies for them—we'll discuss a number of these in this chapter and Chapter 9, *Deep Neural Networks*. Each neural network topology has its own purpose, strengths, and weaknesses.

First, we'll discuss neural networks conceptually. We'll examine their components and construction and explore their applications and strengths. We'll have a discussion on the backpropagation algorithm and how ANNs are trained. Then we'll take a brief peek at the mathematics of ANNs, before diving into some practical advice for neural networks in the wild. Finally, we'll demonstrate an example of a simple neural network using the `TensorFlow.js` library.

The following are the topics that we will be covering in this chapter:

- Conceptual overview of neural networks
- Backpropagation training
- Example—XOR in `TensorFlow.js`

Conceptual overview of neural networks

ANNs have been around almost as long as computers have, and indeed were originally constructed out of electrical hardware. One of the first ANNs was developed in the 1970s to adaptively filter echoes out of phone line transmissions. Despite their initial early success, ANNs waned in popularity until the mid-1980s, when the backpropagation training algorithm was popularized.

ANNs are modeled on our understanding of biological brains. An ANN contains many neurons that connect to one another. The manner, structure, and organization of these neuronal connections is called the **topology** (or **shape**) of the network. Each individual neuron is a simple construct: it accepts several numerical input values and outputs a single numerical value, which may in turn be transmitted to several other neurons. The following is a simple, conceptual example of a neuron:

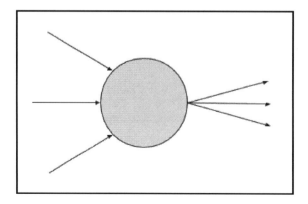

Neurons are typically, but not always, arranged into layers. The specific arrangement and connections between neurons is defined by the network's topology. However, most ANNs will have three or four fully-connected layers, or layers where each neuron in the layer connects to every neuron in the next layer. In these common topologies, the first layer is the input layer and the last layer is the output layer. Input data is fed directly to the input neurons, and the results of the algorithm are read from the output neurons. In between the input and output layers, there are typically one or two hidden layers made up of neurons that the user or programmer doesn't interact with directly. The following diagram shows a neural network with three layers:

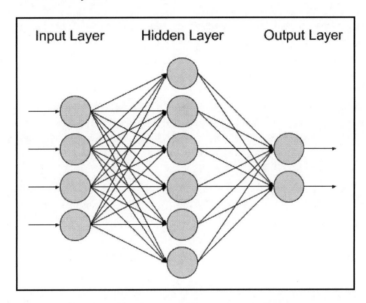

The input layer has four neurons, the single hidden layer has six neurons, and the output layer has two neurons. A shorthand for describing this type of network is to list the number of neurons in each layer, so this could be called a **4-6-2 network** for short. Such a network is capable of accepting four different features and can output two pieces of information, such as X/Y coordinates, true/false values for two properties, or even the numbers 0-3 if the output is taken as binary bits.

When using an ANN to make a prediction, you are using the network in feed-forward mode, which is actually quite straightforward. We will discuss the mechanics of neurons in depth, but for now all you need to know is that a neuron takes a number of inputs and generates a single output based on simple weighted sums and a smoothing function (called the **activation function**).

To make a prediction, you load your input data directly into the input neurons. If your problem is an image recognition problem, then each input neuron might be fed the grayscale intensity of a single pixel (you would need 2,500 input neurons to process a 50 x 50 pixel grayscale image). The input neurons are activated, meaning their inputs are summed up, weighted, biased, and the result fed into an activation function which will return a numerical value (typically between -1 and +1, or between 0 and +1). The input neurons in turn send their activation outputs to the neurons in the hidden layer, which experience the same process, and send their results to the output layer, which again becomes activated. The result of the algorithm is the values of the activation functions at the output layer. If your image recognition problem is a classification problem with 15 possible classes, you would have 15 neurons in the output layer, each representing a class label. The output neurons will either return values of 1 or 0 (or fractions in between), and the output neurons with the highest values are the classes that are most likely represented by the image.

In order to understand how networks like these actually produce results, we need to take a closer look at the neuron. Neurons in ANNs have a few different properties. First, a neuron maintains a set (a vector) of weights. Each input to the neuron is multiplied by its corresponding weight. If you look at the topmost neuron in the hidden layer in the preceding image, you can see that it receives four inputs from the neurons in the input layer. The hidden-layer neurons therefore must each have a vector of four weights, one for each of the neurons in the previous layer that send it signals. The weights essentially determine how important a specific input signal is to the neuron in question. For instance, the topmost hidden-layer neuron might have a weight of 0 for the bottom-most input neuron; in that case, the two neurons are essentially unconnected. On the other hand, the next hidden neuron might have a very high weight for the bottom-most input neuron, meaning that it considers its input very strongly.

Each neuron also has a bias. The bias does not apply to any one single input, but instead is added to the sum of the weighted inputs before the activation function is invoked. The bias can be seen as a modifier to the threshold of the neuron's activation. We'll discuss activation functions shortly, but let's take a look at an updated diagram of the neuron:

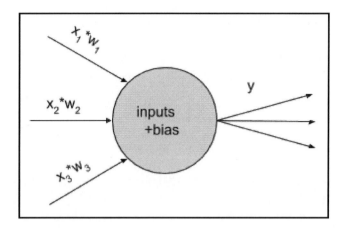

A mathematical form for the description of the neuron goes something like this, where bold figures **w** and **x** represent vectors of inputs and weights (that is, $[x_1, x_2, x_3]$), non-bold b and y represent the bias of the neuron and output of the neuron, respectively, and *fn(...)* represents the activation function. Here goes:

$$y = fn(\textbf{\textit{w}} \cdot \textbf{\textit{x}} + b)$$

The dot in between **w** and **x** is the vector dot product of the two vectors. Another way to write **w·x** would be $w_1{}^*x_1 + w_2{}^*x_2 + w_3{}^*x_3 + \ldots + w_n{}^*x_n$, or simply $\Sigma_j\, w_j{}^*x_j$.

Taken together, it is the weights and the biases of the neurons in the network that actually do the learning and calculation. When you train a neural network, you are gradually updating the weights and biases with the goal of configuring them to solve your problem. Two neural networks with the same topology (for example, two fully-connected 10-15-5 networks) but different weights and biases are different networks that will solve different problems.

How does the activation function factor into all of this? The original model for an artificial neuron was called the perceptron, and its activation function was a step function. Basically, if $\textbf{\textit{w}} \cdot \textbf{\textit{x}} + b$ for a neuron was greater than zero, the neuron would output 1. If, on the other hand, $\textbf{\textit{w}} \cdot \textbf{\textit{x}} + b$ were less than zero, the neuron would output zero.

This early perceptron model was powerful because it was possible to represent logic gates with an artificial neuron. If you've ever taken a course on Boolean logic or circuits, you would have learned that you can use NAND gates to build any other type of logic gate, and it is trivially easy to build a NAND gate with a perceptron.

Imagine a perceptron that takes two inputs, each with a weight of -2. The perceptron's bias is +3. If both inputs are 0, then $w \cdot x + b = +3$ (just the weight, because all inputs are zero). Since the perceptron's activation function is a step function, the output of the neuron in this case will be 1 (+3 is greater than zero, so the step function returns +1).

If the inputs are 1 and 0, in any order, then $w \cdot x + b = +1$, and therefore the output of the perceptron will also be 1. However, if both inputs are instead 1, then $w \cdot x + b = -1$. The two inputs, both weighted -2, will overcome the neuron's bias of +3, and the activation function (which returns 1 or 0), will return 0. This is the logic of the NAND gate: the perceptron will return 0 if both inputs are 1, otherwise it will return 1 for any other combination of inputs.

These early results excited the computer science and electronics community in the 1970s, and ANNs received a lot of hype. However, we had difficulty automatically training neural networks. Perceptron's could be crafted by hand to represent logic gates, and some amount of automated training for neural networks was possible, but large-scale problems remained inaccessible.

The problem was the step function used as the perceptron's activation function. When training an ANN, you want small changes to the weights or biases of the network to similarly result in only small changes to the network's output. But the step function gets in the way of the process; one small change to the weights might result in no change to the output, but the next small change to the weights could result in a huge change to the output! This happens because the step function is not a smooth function—it has an abrupt jump from 0 to 1 once the threshold is crossed, and it is exactly 0 or exactly 1 at all other points. This limitation of the perceptron, and thus the major limitation of ANNs, resulted in over a decade of research stagnation.

Eventually, researchers in 1986 rediscovered a training technique that had been discovered a few years prior. They found that this technique, called **backpropagation**, made training much faster and more reliable. Thus artificial neural networks experienced their second wind.

Backpropagation training

There was one key insight that brought neural network research out of stagnation and into the modern era: the choice of a better activation function for neurons. Step functions caused issues with the automated training of networks because tiny changes in the network parameters (the weights and biases) could alternately have either no effect or an abrupt major effect on the network. Obviously, this is not a desired property of a trainable system.

The general approach to automatically training ANNs is to start with the output layer and work backwards. For each example in your training set, you run the network in feed-forward mode (that is, **prediction mode**) and compare the actual output to the desired output. A good metric to use for comparing desired versus actual results is **mean squared error** (**MSE**); test all training examples, and for each calculate and square the difference in output from the desired values. Sum all the squared errors up and average over the number of training examples, and you have a cost function or loss function. The cost function is a function of the weights and biases of a given network topology. The goal in training ANNs is to reduce the cost function to—ideally—zero. You could potentially use the ANN's accuracy over all training examples as a cost function, but mean-squared error has better mathematical properties for training.

The backpropagation algorithm hinges on the following insight: if you know the weights and biases of all neurons, if you know the inputs and desired outputs, and if you know the activation function the neurons use, you can work backwards from an output neuron to discover which weights or biases are contributing to a large error. That is, if neuron Z has neuron inputs A, B, and C with weights of 100, 10, and 0, respectively, you would know that neuron C has no effect on neuron Z and therefore neuron C is not contributing to neuron Z's error. On the other hand, neuron A has an outsized impact on neuron Z, so if neuron Z has a large error it is likely that neuron A is to blame. The backpropagation algorithm is named such because it propagates the error in output neurons backwards through the network.

Taking this concept a step further, if you also know the activation function and its relationship between the weights, biases, and the errors, you can determine how much a weight would need to change in order to get a corresponding change to a neuron's output. Of course, there are many weights in an ANN and it is a highly complex system, so the approach we use is to make tiny changes to the weights—we can only predict changes to the network's output if we use a simplifying approximation for small changes in weights. This part of the approach is called gradient descent, which is named such because we are trying to descend the gradient (the slope) of the cost function by making small modifications to weights and biases.

To picture this, imagine a nylon hammock hanging between two trees. The hammock represents the cost function, and the x and y axes (viewed from the sky) abstractly represent the biases and weights of the network (in reality, this is a multi-thousand-dimensional picture). There is some combination of weights and biases where the hammock hangs the lowest: that point is our goal. We are a tiny ant sitting somewhere on the surface of the hammock. We don't know where the lowest point of the hammock is, and we're so small that even wrinkles or creases in the fabric can throw us off. But we do know that the hammock is smooth and continuous, and we can feel around our immediate area. As long as we keep heading downhill for each individual step we take, we will eventually find the lowest point in the hammock—or, at least, a low point close to where we started (a local minimum), depending on how complex the shape of the hammock is.

This approach of gradient descent requires us to mathematically understand and be able to describe the gradient of the cost function, which means we must also understand the gradient of the activation function. The gradient of a function is essentially its slope, or derivative. The reason we can't use the perceptron's original step function as an activation function is because the step function is not differentiable at all points; the giant, instantaneous leap between 0 and 1 in the step function is a non-differentiable discontinuity.

Once we figured out that we should be using gradient descent and backpropagation to train our neural networks, the rest came easily. Instead of using a step function for neuron activation functions, we started using sigmoid functions. Sigmoid functions are generally shaped like step functions, except they are smoothed out, continuous, and differentiable at all points. Here's an example of a sigmoid function versus a step function:

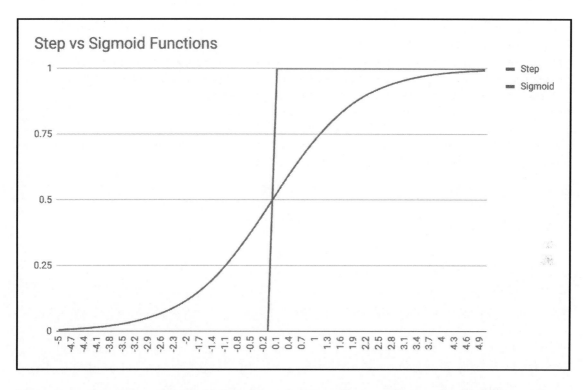

There are many types of sigmoid functions; the preceding one is described by the equation $y = 1 / 1+e^x$ and is called the **logistic function** or **logistic curve**. Other popular sigmoid functions are hyperbolic tangent (that is, tanh), which has a range from -1 to +1 as opposed to the logistic function's range of 0 to +1. Another popular activation function is the **rectified linear unit (ReLU)**, which is often used in image processing and output layers. There is also the *softplus* function, whose derivative is in fact the logistic function itself. The activation function you choose will depend on the specific mathematical properties you desire. It is also not uncommon to use different activation functions in different layers of the network; hidden layers will often use logistic or tanh activation functions, while the output layer might use *softmax* and the input layer might use ReLU. You can invent your own activation function for your neurons, however, you must be able to differentiate the function and determine its gradient in order to integrate it with the backpropagation algorithm.

This singular, minor change to the neuron's activation function made a world of difference to our training of ANNs. Once we started using differentiable activation functions, we were able to calculate the gradient of the cost and activation functions, and use that information to determine precisely how to update weights in the backpropagation algorithm. Neural network training became faster and more powerful, and neural networks were propelled into the modern era, though they still had to wait for hardware and software libraries to catch up. More importantly, neural network training became a study in mathematics—particularly vector calculus—rather than being limited to study by computer scientists.

Example - XOR in TensorFlow.js

In this example, we're going to solve the XOR problem using a `TensorFlow.js` feedforward neural network. First, let's explore the XOR problem, and why it's a good starting point for us.

The XOR, or *exclusive or* operation, is a Boolean operator that returns true if only one, but not both, of its inputs is truth. Compare this to the regular Boolean OR that you're more commonly familiar with, which will return true if both inputs are true—the XOR will return false if both inputs are true. Here is a table comparing XOR to OR; I've highlighted the case where OR and XOR differ:

Input 1	Input 2	OR	XOR
False	False	False	False
False	True	True	True
True	False	True	True
True	True	**True**	**False**

Why is the XOR problem a good test for us? Let's plot the XOR operations on a graph:

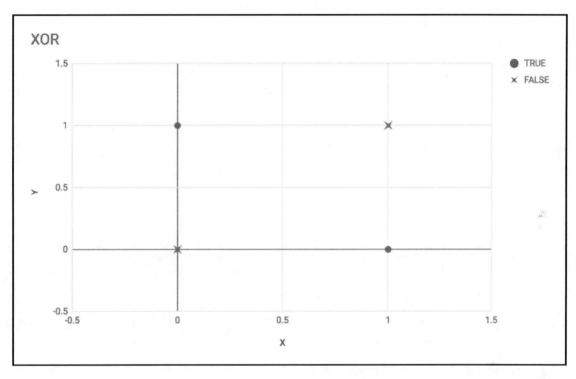

Viewing the preceding graph, we can see that the two classes involved in the **XOR** operation are not linearly separable. In other words, it is impossible to draw a straight line that separates the circles from the X in the preceding graph.

The combined facts that the XOR operation is very simple but also that the classes are not linearly separable make the XOR operation an excellent entry point when testing out a new classification algorithm. You don't need a fancy dataset to test out whether a new library or algorithm will work for you.

Before jumping into the TensorFlow example, let's first discuss how we might build an XOR-solving neural network by hand. We will design our own weights and biases and see whether we can develop a manual neural network that solves XOR.

First, we know that the network requires two inputs and one output. We know that the inputs and output are binary, so we must pick activations functions that have the range [0, 1]; ReLU or sigmoid would be appropriate, while tanh, whose range is [-1, 1] would be less appropriate.

Finally, we know that XOR is not linearly separable and thus cannot be trivially solved; we need a hidden layer in our network. Let's therefore attempt to build a 2-2-1 neural network:

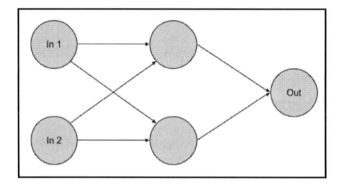

Next, we need to think about the weights and biases of the neurons in the network. We know that the network needs to be designed such that there is a penalty for both inputs being true. Therefore, one hidden-layer neuron should represent a weakly positive signal (that is, it activates when the inputs are activated) and the other hidden-layer neuron should represent a strongly negative signal (that is, if both inputs are true, this neuron should overwhelm the weakly-positive neuron).

Here's an example of one set of weights that would work to achieve XOR:

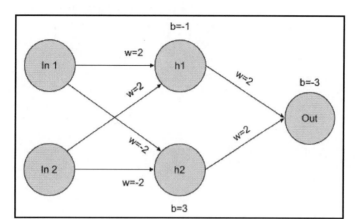

Let's run a few example calculations. I'll start with the differentiating case of both inputs being true. The hidden **h1** neuron will have a total weighted input of 4, because the weight for each input is 2 and both inputs are true. The h1 neuron also has a bias of -1, however, the bias is not enough to deactivate the neuron. The total sum of the biased inputs is therefore 3 for the h1 neuron; since we haven't decided on a specific activation function, we will not try to guess what the actual activation will become—suffice to say that an input of +3 is enough to activate the neuron.

We now turn our attention to the hidden **h2** neuron. It also receives input from both input neurons, however, these weights are negative, and so the unbiased input sum it receives is -4. The bias on h2 is +3, so the total biased input for h2 is -1. If we were to choose the ReLU activation function, the neuron's output would be zero. In any case, h2 is not activated.

Finally, we look at the output node. It receives a weighted input of +2 from h1, but receives no input from h2. Since the output node's bias is -3 (essentially requiring both h1 and h2 to be activated), the output node will return 0 or false. This is the expected result for XOR with both inputs being set to true or 1.

Let's similarly tabulate the results for the other XOR cases. The columns for h1, h2, and Out represent the weighted and biased input to the neuron, before being applied to an activation function (since we haven't chosen one). Just remember that each neuron will transmit values in [0, 1] to the next neuron; it will not send values such as -1 or 3 after the activation function is applied:

In 1	In 2	h1	h2	Out
0	0	-1	3	-1
0	1	1	1	1
1	0	1	1	1
1	1	3	-1	-1

The preceding table proves that the handcrafted ANN works for all XOR test cases. It also gives us a little insight into the inner workings of a network. The hidden h1 and h2 neurons have specific roles. The h1 neuron is off by default but easily satisfied and will become activated if any of the inputs are active; h1 is essentially a typical OR operation. On the other hand, h2 is on by default and can only be deactivated if both inputs are on; h2 is essentially a NAND operation. The output neuron requires both h1 and h2 to be active, therefore the output neuron is an AND operator.

Let's now use the `TensorFlow.js` library and see whether we can achieve the same success. On your computer, create a new folder called Ch8-ANN. Add the following `package.json` file and then issue `yarn install`:

```
{
  "name": "Ch8-ANN",
  "version": "1.0.0",
  "description": "ML in JS Example for Chapter 8 - ANN",
  "main": "src/index.js",
  "author": "Burak Kanber",
  "license": "MIT",
  "scripts": {
    "build-web": "browserify src/index.js -o dist/index.js -t [ babelify --
presets [ env ] ]",
    "build-cli": "browserify src/index.js --node -o dist/index.js -t [
babelify --presets [ env ] ]",
    "start": "yarn build-cli && node dist/index.js"
  },
  "dependencies": {
    "@tensorflow/tfjs": "^0.9.1",
    "babel-core": "^6.26.0",
    "babel-plugin-transform-object-rest-spread": "^6.26.0",
    "babel-preset-env": "^1.6.1",
```

```
    "babelify": "^8.0.0",
    "browserify": "^15.1.0"
  }
}
```

Now add the src/index.js file and import TensorFlow:

```
import * as tf from '@tensorflow/tfjs';
```

TensorFlow is not simply an ANN library. The TensorFlow library provides a number of building blocks that are useful in both ANNs and general ML and linear algebra (that is, vector/matrix math) problems. Because TensorFlow is more of a toolbox than a singular tool, there will always be many ways to solve any given problem.

Let's start by creating a sequential model:

```
const model = tf.sequential();
```

TensorFlow *models* are high-level containers that essentially run functions; they are mapping from input to output. You can use TensorFlow's low-level operators (the linear algebra tools that come with the library) to build your model, or you can use one of the higher-level model classes. In this case, we are building a *sequential model*, which is a special case of TensorFlow's generic model. You may think of a sequential model as a neural network that only feeds forward, and does not involve any recurrences or feedback loops internally. A sequential model is essentially a vanilla neural network.

Next, let's add layers to the model:

```
model.add(tf.layers.dense({units: 4, activation: 'relu', inputDim: 2}));
model.add(tf.layers.dense({units: 4, activation: 'relu'}));
model.add(tf.layers.dense({units: 1, activation: 'sigmoid'}));
```

We are adding three layers to our model. All layers are **dense** layers, meaning they are fully connected to the next layer. This is what you'd expect from a vanilla neural network. We've specified the *units* for each layer—units is TensorFlow's name for neurons, since TensorFlow can be used outside of ANN contexts. I've set this example up with four neurons per layer rather than two, because I found that the extra neurons greatly improve the speed and resilience of the training process. We've specified inputDim in the first layer, telling the layer that it should expect two inputs per data point. The first and second layers use the ReLU activation function. The third layer, which is the output layer, has only one unit/neuron and uses the familiar sigmoid activation function, since I would like the results to snap more readily toward 0 or 1.

Now we must compile the model before we can use it. We will specify a loss function, which can be either a prebuilt loss function that ships with the library or a custom loss function that we provide. We will also specify our optimizer; we discussed gradient descent earlier in this chapter, but there are many other optimizers available, such as Adam, Adagrad, and Adadelta. In this case, we will use the stochastic gradient descent optimizer (typical for vanilla neural networks), however, we will choose the `binaryCrossentropy` loss function, which is more appropriate than mean squared error for our binary classification task:

```
const learningRate = 1;
const optimizer = tf.train.sgd(learningRate);
model.compile({loss: 'binaryCrossentropy', optimizer, metrics:
['accuracy']});
```

We've also set the learning rate for the gradient descent optimizer; the learning rate dictates how much the backpropagation training algorithm will modify the weights and biases in each training generation or epoch. A lower learning rate will result in a longer time to train the network, but will be more stable. A higher learning rate will train the network more quickly, but less reliably; your network may not converge at all if the learning rate is too high.

Finally, we've added `metrics: ['accuracy']` to the compilation step. This allows us to get a report on the network's accuracy when we eventually call `model.evaluate`.

Next we'll set up our training data, which is simply four data points. TensorFlow operates on *tensors*, which are essentially mathematical matrices. TensorFlow tensors are immutable, and all operations performed on tensors will return new tensors rather than modifying the existing tensor. If you need to modify tensors in place, you must use TensorFlow's *variables*, which are mutable wrappers around tensors. TensorFlow requires all math be performed through tensors so that the library can optimize calculations for GPU processing:

```
// XOR data x values.
const xs = tf.tensor([
    [0, 0],
    [0, 1],
    [1, 0],
    [1, 1]
],
// Shape of the tensor is 4 rows x 2 cols
[4, 2]);

// XOR data y values.
const ys = tf.tensor([ 0, 1, 1, 0 ], [4, 1]);
```

Because tensors are matrices, every tensor has a *shape*. Shape, for 2D tensors, is defined as *[rows, cols]*. For 3D tensors, shape is *[rows, cols, depth]*; image processing typically uses 3D tensors, where rows and cols represent pixel Y and X coordinates, and depth represents a color channel (for example, RGBA) for that pixel. Since we have four training examples, and each training example requires two fields for inputs, our input tensor has a shape of four rows by two columns. Similarly, our target values tensor has a shape of four rows by one column. TensorFlow will throw errors if you attempt to run calculations or train models with the wrong input and output shapes.

Our last step is to train the model with the data and then evaluate the model. TensorFlow's `model.fit` method is what trains the model, and once trained we can use `model.evaluate` to get statistics, such as accuracy and loss, and we can also use `model.predict` to run the model in feedforward or prediction mode:

```
model.fit(xs, ys, {epochs: 1000}).then(() => {
    console.log("Done training. Evaluating model...");
    const r = model.evaluate(xs, ys);

    console.log("Loss:");
    r[0].print();
    console.log("Accuracy:");
    r[1].print();

    console.log("Testing 0,0");
    model.predict(tf.tensor2d([0, 0], [1, 2])).print();
    console.log("Testing 0,1");
    model.predict(tf.tensor2d([0, 1], [1, 2])).print();
    console.log("Testing 1,0");
    model.predict(tf.tensor2d([1, 0], [1, 2])).print();
    console.log("Testing 1,1");
    model.predict(tf.tensor2d([1, 1], [1, 2])).print();
});
```

Once you've added the code, run `yarn start` from the command line. Running this model takes about 60 seconds for me. When the model finishes, you should see something similar to the following as output. Note that ANNs and the stochastic gradient descent optimizer use random values for initialization and processing, and therefore some runs of the model may be unsuccessful, depending on the specific random initial conditions. The following is the output that will be obtained:

```
Done training. Evaluating model...
Loss:
Tensor
0.00011571444338187575
Accuracy:
```

```
Tensor
1
Testing 0, 0
Tensor
[[0.0001664],]
Testing 0, 1
Tensor
[[0.9999378],]
Testing 1, 0
Tensor
[[0.9999322],]
Testing 1, 1
Tensor
[[0.0001664],]
```

The preceding output shows that the model has learned to emulate XOR. The loss value is very low, while the accuracy is 1.0, which is what's required for such a simple problem. In real-world problems, accuracies of 80-90% are more realistic. Additionally, the program's output shows the individual predictions for each of the four test cases. You can see the effect of the sigmoid activation function in that the values get very close to 0 and 1, but don't quite get there. Internally, TensorFlow is rounding these values in order to determine whether the classification was correct.

At this point, you should play with the network parameters a bit. What happens if you reduce the number of training epochs? What happens if you switch the ReLU layers to sigmoid layers? What happens if you reduce the number of units/neurons in the first two layers to two? Does it work if you increase the number of training epochs? What is the effect of the learning rate on the training process? These are things that are best discovered through trial and error rather than lecture. This is an infinitely flexible neural network model, capable of handling much more complex problems than the simple XOR example, so you should become intimately familiar with all of these properties and parameters through experimentation and research.

While this example was only a simple XOR sample, this approach can also be used for many other types of ANN problems. We've created a three-layered binary classifier that automatically trains and evaluates itself—it's the ultimate vanilla neural network. I will leave it to you to take these concepts and apply them to your real-world problems, though in the next chapter we'll try out some advanced neural models, such as convolutional and recurrent networks.

Summary

This chapter introduced and described the concept of artificial neural networks. We first discussed ANNs from a conceptual standpoint. You learned that neural networks are made of individual neurons, which are simple weighted adding machines that can apply an activation function to their output. You learned that neural networks can have many topologies, and it is the topology and the weights and biases between neurons in the network that do the actual work. You also learned about the backpropagation algorithm, which is the method by which neural networks are automatically trained.

We also looked at the classic XOR problem and looked at it through the lens of neural networks. We discussed the challenges and the approach to solving XOR with ANNs, and we even built—by hand!—a fully-trained ANN that solves the XOR problem. We then introduced the `TensorFlow.js` library and built a vanilla neural network with it, and successfully used that NN to train and solve the XOR problem.

In the next chapter, we're going to take a deeper look at the advanced ANN topologies. In particular, we'll discuss the **Convolutional Neural Network (CNN)**, which is widely used in image processing, and we'll also look at **recurrent neural networks (RNN)**, which are commonly used in artificial intelligence and natural language tasks.

Deep Neural Networks

9

In the previous chapter, we discussed neural networks and their basic operation. Specifically, we discussed the fully connected feedforward neural network, which is just one simple topology out of many possible ANN topologies. In this chapter, we're going to focus on two advanced topologies: the **Convolutional Neural Network (CNN)** and one form of **recurrent neural network (RNN)**, called the **Long Short-Term Memory (LSTM)** network. CNNs are used most often for image processing tasks, such as object detection and image classification. LSTM networks are often used in NLP or language-modeling problems.

These exotic ANN topologies are considered to be **deep neural networks (DNNs)**. While the term is not well-defined, DNNs are typically understood to be ANNs with multiple hidden layers between the input and output layers. Convolutional network architectures can become quite deep, with ten or more layers in the network. Recurrent architectures can be deep as well, however, much of their depth comes from the fact that information can flow either forward or backward through the network.

In this chapter, we're going to take a look at TensorFlow's capabilities in terms of CNN and RNN architectures. We will discuss TensorFlow's own examples of these topologies and take a look at how they are used in practice. In particular, we will discuss the following topics:

- CNNs
- Simple RNNs
- Gated recurrent unit networks
- LSTM networks
- CNN-LSTM networks for advanced applications

Let's get started by taking a look at a classic **machine learning (ML)** problem: identifying handwritten digits from images.

Convolutional Neural Networks

To make the case for CNNs, let's first imagine how we might approach an image classification task using a standard feedforward, fully connected ANN. We start with an image that's 600 x 600 pixels in size with three color channels. There are 1,080,000 pieces of information encoded in such an image (600 x 600 x 3), and therefore our input layer would require 1,080,000 neurons. If the next layer in the network contains 1,000 neurons, we'd need to maintain one billion weights between the first two layers alone. Clearly, the problem is already becoming untenable.

Assuming the ANN in this example can be trained, we'd also run into problems with scale and position invariance. If your task is to identify whether or not an image contains street signs, the network may have difficulty understanding that street signs can be located in any position in the image. The network may also have issues with color; if most street signs are green, it may have difficulty identifying a blue sign. Such a network would require many training examples to get around issues of scale, color, and position variance.

In the past, before CNNs became popular, many researchers viewed this problem as a dimensionality reduction problem. One common tactic was to convert all images to grayscale, reducing the amount of data by a factor of three. Another tactic is to downscale images to something more manageable, such as 100 x 100 pixels, or even smaller, depending on the type of processing required. Converting our 600 x 600 image to grayscale and to 100 x 100 would reduce the number of input neurons by a factor of 100, from one million to 10,000, and further reduce the number of weights between the input layer and a 1,000-neuron hidden layer down from 1 billion to only 10 million.

Even after employing these dimensionality reduction techniques, we would still require a very large network with tens of millions of weights. Converting images to grayscale before processing avoids issues with color detection, but still does not solve scale and position variance problems. We are also still solving a very complex problem, since shadows, gradients, and the overall variance of images would require us to use a very large training set.

Another common preprocessing tactic employed was to perform various operations on images, such as noise reduction, edge detection, and smoothing. By reducing shadows and emphasizing edges, the ANN gets clearer signals to learn from. The problem with this approach is that preprocessing tasks are typically unintelligent; the same edge detection algorithm gets applied to every image in the set, whether or not that specific edge detection algorithm is actually effective on a particular image.

The challenge, then, is to incorporate the image-preprocessing tasks directly in the ANN. If the ANN itself manages the preprocessing tasks, the network can learn the best and most efficient ways to preprocess the images in order to optimize the network's accuracy. Recall from `Chapter 8`, *Artificial Neural Network Algorithms* that we can use *any* activation function in a neuron, as long as we can differentiate the activation function and employ its gradient in the backpropagation algorithm.

In short, a CNN is an ANN with multiple—perhaps many—preprocessing layers that perform transformations on the image before ultimately reaching a final fully connected layer or two that performs the actual classification. By incorporating the preprocessing tasks into the network, the backpropagation algorithm can tune the preprocessing tasks as part of the network training. The network will not only learn how to classify images, it will also learn how to preprocess the images for your task.

Convolutional networks contain several distinct layer types in addition to the standard ANN layer types. Both types of network contain an input layer, an output layer, and one or more fully connected layers. A CNN, however, also incorporates convolution layers, ReLU layers, and pooling layers. Let's take a look at each in turn.

Convolutions and convolution layers

Convolutions are a mathematical tool that combine two functions into a new function; specifically, the new function represents the area under the curve created by the pointwise multiplication of one function as another function is swept over it. If this is difficult to visualize, don't worry; it's easiest to visualize as an animation, which unfortunately we can't print in a book. The mathematical details of convolutions will not be important in this chapter, but I do encourage you to do some additional reading on the topic.

Most image filters—such as blur, sharpen, edge detect, and emboss—can be accomplished with convolution operations. In an image context, convolutions are represented by a *convolution matrix*, which is typically a small matrix (3 x 3, 5 x 5, or something similar). The convolution matrix is much smaller than the image to be processed, and the convolution matrix is swept across the image so the output of the convolution applied to the entire image builds a new image with the effect applied.

Consider the following image of Van Gogh's *Water Lilies*. Here is the original:

I can use my image editor's *convolution matrix* filter to create a sharpening effect. This has the same effect as the image editor's *sharpen* filter, except that I'm writing the convolution matrix manually:

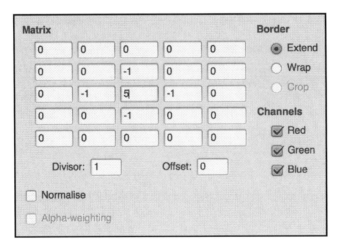

The result is a sharpened version of the original image:

I can also write a convolution matrix that blurs the image:

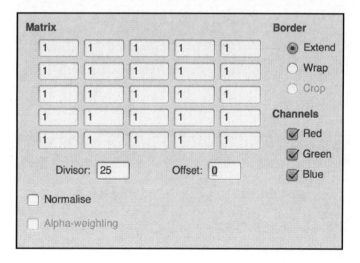

It results in the following image. The effect is subtle, as the oil panting itself is a little blurry, but the effect is there:

Convolutions can also be used to emboss or detect edges:

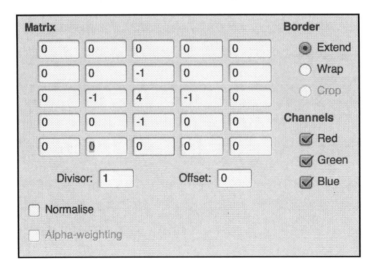

The preceding matrix results in the following:

A CNN uses multiple convolving layers, each with multiple convolution filters, to build a model of the image. The convolving layers and the convolution filters themselves are trained by the backpropagation algorithm, and the network will eventually discover the correct filters to use in order to enhance the features that the network is trying to identify. As with all learning problems, the types of filters the CNN develops may not necessarily be readily understood or interpretable by a human, but in many cases, you will find that your network develops a number of convolution filters that perform blur, edge detection, color isolation, and gradient detection.

In addition to extracting useful features from images, the convolution operations in effect provide for spatial and positional independence of features. The convolving layers are not fully connected, and therefore are able to inspect specific areas of the image. This reduces the dimensionality required of the weights in between layers and also helps us avoid reliance on the spatial positioning of features.

There is still a lot of data involved in these operations, so convolving layers are typically immediately followed by pooling layers, which essentially downsample an image. Most often you will employ something such as *2 x 2 max pooling*, which means that for every 2 x 2 area of pixels in the source feature, the pooling layer will downsample the 2 x 2 area to a single pixel that has the value of the maximum pixel in the source 2 x 2 area. A 2 x 2 pooling layer therefore reduces the image size by a factor of four; because the convolution operation (which may also reduce dimensionality) has already occurred, this downsampling will typically reduce the computation required without the loss of too much information.

In some cases, a CNN will employ simple ReLU activation functions immediately following the convolution operations and immediately preceding pooling; these ReLU functions help avoid oversaturation of the image or the feature maps that result from the convolution operations.

A typical architecture for a simple CNN would look like this:

- Input layer, with width x height x color depth neurons
- Convolving layer, with N convolution filters of an M x M size
- Max pooling layer
- Second convolving layer
- Second max pooling layer
- Fully connected output layer

More complex architectures for CNNs typically include several more groups of convolving and pooling layers, and may also involve two convolving layers in a row before reaching a pooling layer.

Each successive convolving layer in the network operates at a higher level than the convolving layers before it. The first convolving layer will only be able to perform simple convolutions, such as edge detection, smoothing, and blurring. The next convolving layer, however, is able to combine the results from previous convolutions into higher level features, such as basic shapes or color patterns. A third convolving layer can further combine information from previous layers to detect complex features, such as wheels, street signs, and handbags. The final fully connected layer, or layers, acts much like a standard feedforward ANN, and performs the actual classification of the image based on the high-level features that the convolving layers have isolated.

Let's now attempt to employ this technique in practice using `TensorFlow.js` on the MNIST handwritten digit dataset.

Example – MNIST handwritten digits

Rather than building an example from first principles, let's instead walk through an excellent `TensorFlow.js` MNIST example. The goal of this example is to train a CNN to classify images of handwritten digits. More specifically, the goal of this example is to achieve a high accuracy in classifications made against the MNIST handwritten digit dataset. In this section, we will aim to get an understanding of the code and the algorithm by performing experiments on the code and observing their results.

The current version of this example may be found on `TensorFlow.js`'s GitHub: `https://github.com/tensorflow/tfjs-examples/tree/master/mnist`. However, as the repository may be updated after this writing, I have also added the version that I am using as a Git submodule in this book's example repository. If you are using this book's repository and haven't already done so, please run `git submodule init; git submodule update` from the command line in the repository directory.

In the terminal, navigate to `Ch5-CNN`. This path is a symbolic link, so if it doesn't work on your system, you may alternately navigate to `tfjs-examples/mnist`.

Next, issue `yarn` from the command line to build the code, and finally issue `yarn watch`, which will start a local server and launch your browser to `http://localhost:1234`. If you have any other programs using that port, you will have to terminate them first.

The page will start by downloading MNIST images from Google's servers. It will then train a CNN for 150 epochs, periodically updating two graphs that show the loss and the accuracy. Recall that the loss is typically a metric, such as **mean square error** (**MSE**), while accuracy is the percentage of correct predictions. Finally, the page will display a few example predictions, highlighting correct versus incorrect predictions.

My test run of this page yielded a CNN with an accuracy of around 92%:

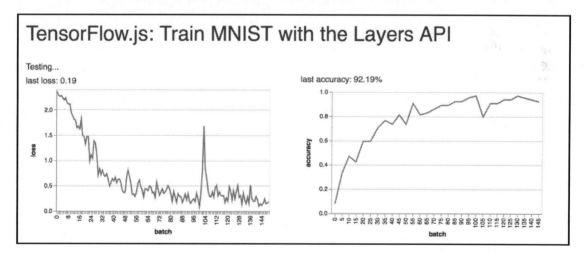

Often, the incorrect predictions are understandable. In this example, the digit 1 does seem to be shaped a bit like a 2. It is unlikely a human would have made this particular error, though I have encountered examples where I would have gotten the prediction wrong as well:

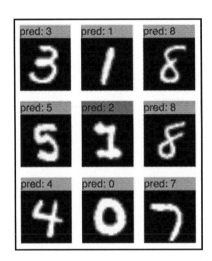

Opening `index.js`, we can see the topology of the network toward the top of the file:

```
model.add(tf.layers.conv2d({
    inputShape: [28, 28, 1],
    kernelSize: 5,
    filters: 8,
    strides: 1,
    activation: 'relu',
    kernelInitializer: 'varianceScaling'
}));
model.add(tf.layers.maxPooling2d({poolSize: [2, 2], strides: [2, 2]}));
model.add(tf.layers.conv2d({
    kernelSize: 5,
    filters: 16,
    strides: 1,
    activation: 'relu',
    kernelInitializer: 'varianceScaling'
}));
model.add(tf.layers.maxPooling2d({poolSize: [2, 2], strides: [2, 2]}));
model.add(tf.layers.flatten());
model.add(tf.layers.dense(
    {units: 10, kernelInitializer: 'varianceScaling', activation:
'softmax'}));
```

This network has two convolving layers with a pooling layer after each, and then a single fully connected layer that makes a prediction. Both the convolving layers use a kernelSize of 5, which means that the convolution filter is a 5 x 5 matrix. The first convolving layer uses eight filters, while the second uses 16. This means that the first layer will create and use eight different convolution filters, therefore identifying eight separate graphical features of the image. These features may be abstract, but in the first layer it is common to see features that represent edge detection, blurring or sharpening, or gradient identification.

The second convolving layer uses 16 features, which likely will be of a higher level than the first layer's features. This layer may try to identify straight lines, circles, curves, swoops, and so on. There are more high-level features than there are low-level features, so it makes sense that the first layer uses fewer filters than the second layer.

The final dense layer is a fully connected layer of 10 neurons, each representing a digit. The softmax activation function ensures that the output is normalized to 1. The input to this final layer is a flattened version of the second pooling layer. The data needs flattening because convolving and pooling layers are typically multidimensional. Convolving and pooling layers use matrices representing height, width, and color depth, which themselves are in turn stacked atop one another as the result of the convolution filters used. The output of the first convolving layer, for example, will be a volume that is [28 x 28 x 1] x 8 in size. The bracketed portion is the result of a single convolution operation (that is, a filtered image), and eight of them have been generated. When connecting this data to a vector layer, such as the standard dense or fully connected layer, it must also be flattened into a vector.

The data entering the final dense layer is much smaller than the data coming out of the first layer. The max-pooling layers serve to downscale the image. The poolSize parameter of [2, 2] means that a 2 x 2 window of pixels will be reduced to a single value; since we are using max-pooling, this will be the largest value (the lightest pixel) in the set. The strides parameter means that the pooling window will move in steps of two pixels at a time. This pooling will reduce both the height and width of the image by half, meaning that the image and the data is reduced in area by a factor of four. After the first pooling operation, images are reduced to 14 x 14, and after the second they are 7 x 7. Because there are 16 filters in the second convolving layer, this means that the flattened layer will have *7 * 7 * 16 = 784* neurons.

Let's see whether we can squeeze some more accuracy out of this model by adding another fully connected layer before the output. In the best case scenario, adding another layer will give us an improved ability to interpret the interplay of the 16 features that the convolutions generate.

However, adding another layer will increase the required training time, and it also may not improve results. It's perfectly possible that there is no more information to be discovered by adding another layer. Always remember that ANNs simply build and navigate a mathematical landscape, looking for shapes in the data. If the data isn't highly dimensional, adding another dimension to our capabilities may simply be unnecessary.

Add the following line, before the final dense layer in the code:

```
model.add(tf.layers.dense(
    {units: 100, kernelInitializer: 'varianceScaling', activation:
'sigmoid'}));
```

In context, the code should now look like this, with the new line highlighted:

```
model.add(tf.layers.maxPooling2d({poolSize: [2, 2], strides: [2, 2]}));
model.add(tf.layers.flatten());
model.add(tf.layers.dense(
    {units: 100, kernelInitializer: 'varianceScaling', activation:
'sigmoid'}));
model.add(tf.layers.dense(
    {units: 10, kernelInitializer: 'varianceScaling', activation:
'softmax'}));

const LEARNING_RATE = 0.15;
```

Since you have issued `yarn watch` from the command line, the code should automatically rebuild. Refresh the page and observe the results:

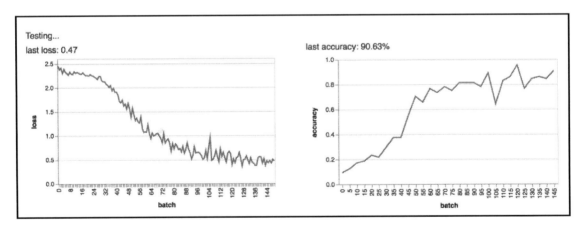

The algorithm is learning at a slower rate than the original version, which is expected because we have added a new layer and therefore more complexity to the model. Let's increase the training limit a little bit.

Find the `TRAIN_BATCHES` variable and update it to `300`. The line should now look like this:

```
const TRAIN_BATCHES = 300;
```

Save the file to trigger the rebuild and reload the page. Let's see whether we can beat the baseline:

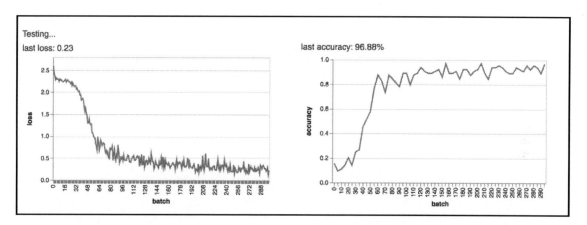

It does seem that we have indeed beaten the baseline score of 92%, however I would caution against too much optimism. It is possible we have overtrained and overfit the model, and there is a chance it will not perform so well in real life. Additionally, because training and validation are stochastic, it is possible that the true accuracy of this network is comparable to the baseline's. Indeed, 92% is already an excellent result and I would not expect much better from any model. However this is still an encouraging result, as the new layer was not too much of a burden to add.

At this point, revert your changes so that you are working with the original copy of the file. Let's run a different experiment. It would be interesting to see how small we can make the network without losing too much accuracy.

First, let's reduce the number of convolution filters the second convolving layer uses. My reasoning is that numerals use pretty simple shapes: circles, lines, and curves. Perhaps we don't need to capture 16 different features. Maybe eight will do. In the second convolving layer, change `filters: 8` to `filters: 2`. Your code should now read:

```
...
model.add(tf.layers.maxPooling2d({poolSize: [2, 2], strides: [2, 2]}));
model.add(tf.layers.conv2d({
  kernelSize: 5,
  filters: 2,
  strides: 1,
```

```
    activation: 'relu',
    kernelInitializer: 'varianceScaling'
}));
model.add(tf.layers.maxPooling2d({poolSize: [2, 2], strides: [2, 2]}));
...
```

Rerunning the code, we see that we still get decent accuracy, though the variance is a little higher than the baseline:

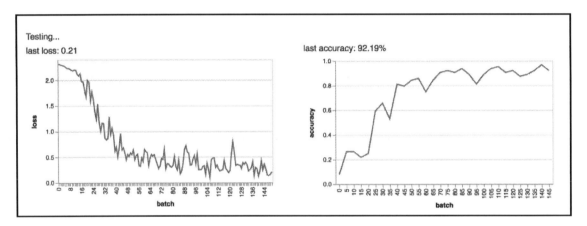

This supports the overall idea that the shapes and features used are relatively few. However, when we look at the test examples, we also find that the mistakes are less *understandable* than before. Perhaps we have not lost much accuracy, but our model has become more abstract:

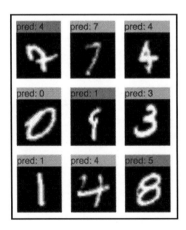

I encourage you to continue exploring and experimenting with this example, as there are many things you can learn by reading the code. One aspect of this example I would like to point out in particular is the `data.js` file, which manages the handling of the MNIST dataset. In your real-world applications, you will likely need to employ an approach similar to this, as your training data will not always be on the local machine. This file handles downloading data from a remote source, splitting it into testing and validation sets, and maintaining batches to be requested by the training algorithm. It is a good, lightweight approach to follow if you require training data from a remote source. We will discuss this topic in-depth in `Chapter 11`, *Using Machine Learning in Real-Time Applications*.

Here are some ideas for experiments you can try:

- Make the network as small as possible while maintaining 90%+ accuracy.
- Make the network as small as possible while maintaining 85%+ accuracy.
- Train the model to 90%+ accuracy in fewer than 50 epochs.
- Discover the fewest number of training examples required to achieve 90%+ accuracy (reduce the value of NUM_TRAIN_ELEMENTS in `data.js` to use fewer training examples)

In the next section, we will explore series prediction with recurrent neural networks.

Recurrent neural networks

There are many cases where memory is required of neural networks. For instance, when modeling natural language context is important, that is, the meaning of a word late in a sentence is affected by the meaning of words earlier in the sentence. Compare this to the approach used by Naive Bayes classifiers, where only the bag of words is considered but not their order. Similarly, time series data may require some memory in order to make accurate predictions, as a future value may be related to current or past values.

RNN are a family of ANN topologies in which the information does not necessarily flow in only one direction. In contrast to feedforward neural networks, RNNs allow the output of neurons to be fed backward into their input, creating a feedback loop. Recurrent networks are almost always time-dependent. The concept of time is flexible, however; ordered words in a sentence can be considered time-dependent, as one word must follow another. It is not necessary for the time-dependence of RNNs to be related to the actual passage of time on a clock.

In the simplest case, all that is required of an RNN is for the output value of a neuron to be connected - typically with a weight or decay factor—not just to neurons in the next layer, but also back to its own input. If you are familiar with **finite impulse response (FIR)** filters in digital signal processing, this style of neuron can be considered a variant of an FIR filter. This type of feedback results in a sort of memory, as the previous activation value is partially preserved and used as an input to the neuron's next cycle. You can visualize this as an echo created by the neuron, becoming more and more faint until the echo is no longer audible. Networks designed in this manner will therefore have a finite memory, as ultimately the echo will fade away to nothing.

Another style of RNN is fully recurrent RNNs, in which every neuron is connected to every other neuron, whether in the forward or backward direction. In this case, it is not just a single neuron that can hear its own echo; every neuron can hear the echoes of every other neuron in the network.

While these types of networks are powerful, in many cases a network will need memory that persists longer than an echo will last. A very powerful, exotic topology, called **LSTM**, was invented to solve the problem of long-term memory. The LSTM topology uses an exotic form of neuron called an LSTM unit, which is capable of storing all previous input and activation values and recalling them when calculating future activation values. When the LSTM network was first introduced, it broke an impressive number of records, particularly in speech recognition, language modeling, and video processing.

In the next section, we will briefly discuss three different types of RNN topologies provided by TensorFlow.js: the SimpleRNN (or fully recurrent RNN), the **gated recurrent unit (GRU)** network, and the LSTM network.

SimpleRNN

The first RNN layer provided out-of-the-box by `TensorFlow.js` is the SimpleRNN layer type, which is a layer composed of a SimpleRNNCell neuron. This is an exotic neuron that can feed its output back to its input. The input to such a neuron is a vector of time-dependent values; the activation output of each input value is fed back into the input of the next value, and so on. A *dropout* factor between 0 and 1 may be specified; this value represents the strength of each echo. A neuron designed in this manner is similar in many ways to an FIR filter.

In fact, this type of RNN architecture is made possible by earlier work in digital signal processing concerning FIR filters. The advantage of this architecture is that the mathematics are well-understood. It is possible to *unroll* an RNN, meaning that it is possible to create a feedforward ANN of many layers that generates the same results as an RNN with fewer layers. This is because the echoes of the neurons' feedback are finite. If a neuron is known to echo 20 times, then that neuron can be modeled as 21 feedforward neurons (including the source neuron). Initial efforts in training these networks were inspired by work on FIR filters, as the analysis is much the same.

Consider the following image, created by François Deloche (own work, CC BY-SA 4.0), which illustrates the unrolling of a recurrent neuron:

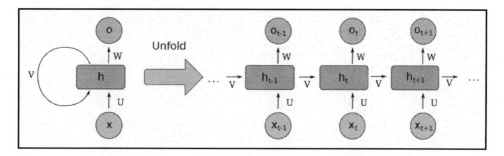

The loop labeled **V** represents the feedback operation of the neuron. As future input values (**X**) are given to the neuron, the output from the previous activation reaches the input and becomes an input factor. As the graphic illustrates, this can be modeled as a linear series of simple neurons.

From TensorFlow's perspective, the operation of recurrent layers are abstracted away by the TensorFlow layers API. Let's look at another of TensorFlow.js's examples that illustrates the interchangeability of various RNN architectures.

From this book's GitHub repository, navigate to the Ch9-RNN directory, which is once again a symbolic link to the tfjs-examples/addition-rnn directory. (If you still have the previous RNN example running, you will need to stop it by pressing *Ctrl* + *C* in the terminal that is running the yarn watch command.) First, issue the yarn command to build the code, then run yarn watch to once again start a local server and navigate to http://localhost:1234.

This particular example is meant to teach an RNN integer addition by example. The training data will be a list of questions, such as 24 + 22 or 14 + 54, represented in string form, and the network will need to be able to decode the string, represent it numerically, learn the answers, and be able to extend the knowledge to new examples.

When the page loads, you'll see the following form. Keep the defaults and click the **Train Model** button:

Digits:	2
Training Size:	5000
RNN Type:	SimpleRNN
RNN Layers:	1
RNN Hidden Layer Size:	128
Batch Size:	128
Train Iterations:	100
# of test examples:	20
Train Model	

You'll see loss and accuracy graphs similar to the following, which show that after 100 epochs of training, the accuracy for this model was 93.8%:

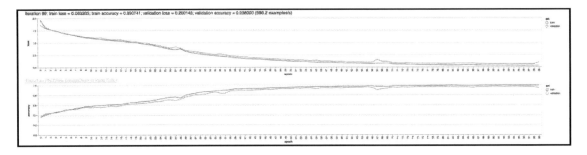

The loss and similarity graph

You'll also see test results from a random test input that the model validates against:

```
69+41 = 110
11+57 = 68
67+8 = 75
77+80 = 157
41+29 = 70
29+74 = 103
1+71 = 62
86+98 = 184
7+72 = 89
49+13 = 62
32+93 = 125
31+49 = 80
73+89 = 162
31+21 = 52
7+39 = 46
20+17 = 37
82+0 = 82
73+82 = 155
56+54 = 110
63+17 = 80
```

Let's take a closer look at how this is working under the hood. Open the index.js file and find the createAndCompileModel function. I will assume that you selected the SimpleRNN network type for this example, and omit the switch/case statements that handle GRU and LSTM topologies:

```
function createAndCompileModel(
    layers, hiddenSize, rnnType, digits, vocabularySize) {
    const maxLen = digits + 1 + digits;

    const model = tf.sequential();
    model.add(tf.layers.simpleRNN({
        units: hiddenSize,
        recurrentInitializer: 'glorotNormal',
        inputShape: [maxLen, vocabularySize]
    }));
    model.add(tf.layers.repeatVector({n: digits + 1}));
    model.add(tf.layers.simpleRNN({
        units: hiddenSize,
```

```
            recurrentInitializer: 'glorotNormal',
            returnSequences: true
    }));
    model.add(tf.layers.timeDistributed(
        {layer: tf.layers.dense({units: vocabularySize})}));
    model.add(tf.layers.activation({activation: 'softmax'}));
    model.compile({
        loss: 'categoricalCrossentropy',
        optimizer: 'adam',
        metrics: ['accuracy']
    });
    return model;
}
```

This code builds a model with two recurrent layers, a time-distributed, fully connected layer and an output layer. The `vocabularySize` parameter represents the total number of unique characters involved, which are the numerals 0-9, the plus sign, and the space character. The `maxLen` parameter represents the maximum length an input string could be; for two-digit addition problems, `maxLen` will be five characters, because the plus sign must be included.

Of particular note in this example is the `timeDistributed` layer type. This is a layer wrapper in TensorFlow's API, meant to create a volume of neurons in the layer where each slice represents one slice of time. This is similar in spirit to the volumes used by CNNs in the previous example, where the depth of the volume represented an individual convolution operation. In this example, however, the depth of the volume represents a time slice.

The `timeDistributed` wrapper allows each time slice to be handled by an individual dense or fully connected layer, rather than attempting to interpret the time-dependent data with only a single vector of neurons, in which case the temporal data may be lost. The `timeDistributed` wrapper is required because the previous *simpleRNN* layer uses the `returnSequences: true` parameter, which causes the layer to output not only the current time step, but all time steps encountered in the layer's history.

Next, let's take a look at the GRU topology.

Gated recurrent units

The GRU topology comprises specialized, exotic neurons that use several internal mechanisms to control the memory and feedback of the neuron. The GRU is a recent invention, being developed only in 2014 as a simplified version of the LSTM neuron. While the GRU is newer than the LSTM, I present it first as it is slightly simpler.

In both GRU and LSTM neurons, the input signal is sent to multiple activation functions. Each internal activation function can be considered a standard ANN neuron; these internal neurons are combined in order to give the overall neuron its memory capabilities. From the outside, GRU and LSTM neurons both look like neurons capable of receiving time-dependent inputs. On the inside, these exotic neurons use simpler neurons to control how much of the feedback from a previous activation is attenuated or amplified, as well as how much of the current signal is stored into memory.

GRU and LSTM neurons have two major advantages over simple RNN neurons. First, the memories of these neurons do not decay over time like the echoes of a simple RNN neuron do. Second, the memory is configurable and self-learning, in the sense that the neuron can learn through training how important specific memories are to the current activation.

Consider the following illustration, also by François Deloche (own work, CC BY-SA 4.0):

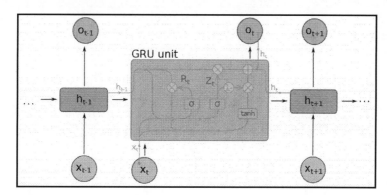

The flowchart may be a little difficult to interpret at first. The Z_t signal is a vector that controls how much of the activation gets stored into memory and passed to future values, while the R_t signal controls how much of the prior values should be forgotten from memory. Each of these signals are attached to standard activation functions, which in turn have their own weights. In a sense, the GRU is itself a tiny neural network.

At this point, it might be tempting to ask why the memory of neurons can't simply be programmed, for example, with a key/value store that the neuron can make lookups against. The reason these architectures are used is due to the fact that the backpropagation algorithm requires mathematical differentiability. Even exotic topologies like RNNs are still trained using mathematical methods such as gradient descent, so the entire system must be mathematically representable. For this reason, researchers need to use the preceding techniques in order to create a network whose every component is mathematically analyzable and differentiable.

On the test page at `http://localhost:1234`, change the *RNN Type* parameter to GRU while keeping all other parameters the same, and click **Train Model** again. The graphs will update and you should see something like the following:

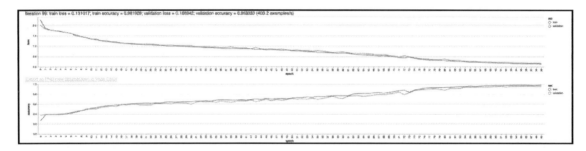

In this case, the training process has taken longer, but the accuracy has improved from 92% to 95% over the SimpleRNN type. The increased training time is not surprising, as the GRU architecture essentially triples the number of activation functions employed by the network.

While many factors affect the accuracy of the network, two obvious ones stand out. First, the GRU topology has long-term memory, unlike the SimpleRNN that will eventually forget previous values as their echoes decay. Second, the GRU has more precise control over how much of an activation signal is fed into future activations as well as how much of the information is retained. These parameters of the network are trained by the backpropagation algorithm, so the forgetfulness of neurons itself is optimized by the training.

Next, let's take a look at the topology that inspired the GRU and opened up entire new fields of research: the LSTM.

Long Short-Term Memory

The LSTM was introduced in 1997 and made waves throughout the academic ANN community due to its impressive accuracy at solving historically difficult problems. In particular, the LSTM excelled at many natural language-processing tasks, handwriting recognition, and speech recognition. In many cases, LSTM networks beat the previous accuracy records by a wide margin. Many systems at the forefront of speech recognition and language modeling use LSTM networks. Most likely, systems such as Apple's Siri and Google's Assistant, use LSTM networks both in their speech recognition and language-parsing models.

The LSTM network gets its name due to the fact that it can retain short-term memory (for example, memory of a word used earlier in a sentence) for long periods of time. When training, this avoids a problem known as the **disappearing gradient**, which is what simple RNNs suffer from as the echoes of previous activations fade away.

Like the GRU, an LSTM neuron is an exotic neuron cell with sophisticated inner workings. Specifically, the LSTM neuron has three *gates* it uses internally: an *input gate*, which controls how much of a value is allowed to enter the neuron, a *forget gate*, which manages the memory of the neuron, and an *output gate*, which controls how much of a signal is allowed in the output of the neuron. The combination of gates, along with the fact that the neurons are all connected to each other, gives the LSTM very fine-grained control over which signals a neuron remembers and how they are used. Like the gates in a GRU, the gates in an LSTM can also be thought of as individual standard neurons, each with their own weights.

Consider the following graphic by François Deloche (own work, CC BY-SA 4.0):

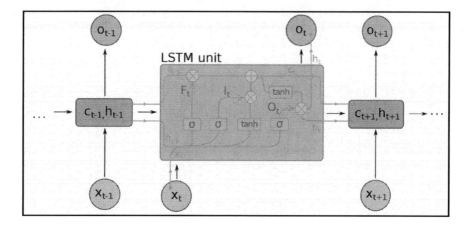

The I_t signal controls the proportion of the input signal that is allowed into the cell. The O_t signal controls how much of the output is allowed out of the cell, and the F_t signal controls how much of the previous value is retained by the cell. Keep in mind that these are all vector quantities, so that the input, output, and memory can be controlled on a per-element basis.

The LSTM excels at tasks that require memory and knowledge of prior values, though the sophisticated inner workings of the cell (there are five distinct activation functions involved) lead to much longer training times. Returning to the test page in your browser, switch the **RNN Type** to LSTM and click **Train Model:**

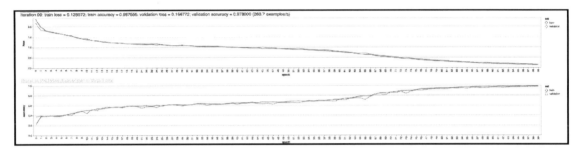

The LSTM has achieved an accuracy of nearly 98%, exceeding both the SimpleRNN and GRU RNN topologies. Of course, this network took longer to train than either of the others, due to the simple fact that there are more neurons (internal to the LSTM cells) that need to be trained.

There are many state-of-the-art uses for LSTM networks. They are very popular in audio analysis, such as speech recognition, as audio is heavily time-dependent. A single audio sample on its own is meaningless; it is only when many thousands of audio samples are taken together in context that an audio clip starts to make sense. An LSTM trained to recognize speech would first be trained to decode short audio clips (on the order of 0.1-0.25 seconds) into *phonemes*, or textual representations of phonetic sounds. Another LSTM layer would then be trained to connect sequences of phonemes together in order to determine the most likely phrase that was uttered. The first LSTM layer relies on time dependence in order to interpret the raw audio signal. The second LSTM layer relies on time dependence to bring context to natural language—for instance, using context and grammar to figure out whether the word *where* or *we're* was spoken.

Another state-of-the-art use case for LSTM is the CNN-LSTM. This network topology combines a CNN with an LSTM; a typical application would be action detection in a video clip. The CNN portion of the model analyzes individual video frames (as if they were independent images) to identify an object and its position or state. The LSTM portion of the model brings the individual frames together and generates a time-dependent context around them. Without an LSTM portion, a model would not be able to tell whether a baseball is stationary or in motion, for instance. It is the memory of the previous states of the object detected by the CNN that provides the context for determining the action occurring in the video. The CNN portion of the model identifies a baseball, and then the LSTM portion is what understands that the ball is moving and likely has been thrown or hit.

Another variation of the CNN-LSTM is used for the automated description of images. One can present a CNN-LSTM with an image of a woman standing on a pier by a lake. The CNN portion of the model individually identifies the woman, the pier, and the lake as objects in the image. The LSTM portion can then generate a natural language description of the image based on the information gathered by the CNN; it is the LSTM portion that grammatically compiles the description, *woman on a pier by a lake*. Remember that natural language descriptions are time-dependent, as the order of words matters.

One final note about LSTM networks relates to the *gates* used in the LSTM cell. While the input, forget, and output gates are usually standard activation neurons, it is also possible to use entire neural networks as gates themselves. In this manner, an LSTM can use *other* models as part of their knowledge and memory. A typical use case for this approach would be automated language translation. Individual LSTMs can be used to model the English and French languages, for instance, while an overall LSTM can manage translations between the two.

It is my personal belief that LSTM networks, or some variation thereof, such as the GRU topology, will be a key player in the road toward AGI. Having a robust memory is essentially a requirement when attempting to emulate general human intelligence, and LSTM fits the use case very nicely. These network topologies are at the forefront of ANN research, so expect to see major advances over the next couple of years.

Summary

In this chapter, we discussed two advanced neural network topologies: the CNN and the RNN. We discussed the CNN in the context of image recognition, specifically the problem of handwritten digit identification. While exploring the CNN, we also discussed the convolution operation itself in the context of image filtering.

We also discussed how neural networks can be made to retain memory through the RNN architecture. We learned that RNNs have many applications, ranging from time-series analysis to natural language modeling. We discussed several RNN architecture types, such as the simple fully recurrent network and the GRU network. Finally, we discussed the state-of-the-art LSTM topology, and how it can be used for language modeling and other advanced problems, such as image captioning or video annotation.

In the next chapter, we'll take a look at some practical approaches to natural language processing, particularly the techniques that are most commonly used in conjunction with ML algorithms.

10
Natural Language Processing in Practice

Natural language processing is the science (and art) of parsing, analyzing, and reconstructing natural language, such as written or spoken English, French, or German. It's not an easy task; **natural language processing** (**NLP**) is an entire field of research with a vibrant academic research community and significant financial backing from major tech firms. Every time companies such as Google, Apple, Amazon, and Microsoft invest in their Google Assistant, Siri, Alexa, and Cortana products, the field of NLP gets a little more funding. In short, NLP is why you can talk to your phone and your phone can talk back to you.

Siri is a lot more than NLP. We, as consumers, like to criticize our **artificial intelligence** (**AI**) assistants when they get something laughably wrong. But they are truly marvels of engineering, and the fact that they get *anything* right is a wonder!

If I look at my phone and say, *Ok Google, give me directions to 7-Eleven*, my phone will automatically wake up and respond to me, *Ok, going to 7-Eleven on Main Ave, make the next right*. Let's think about what that takes to accomplish:

- My sleeping phone is monitoring for my pre-trained OK Google catchphrase.
- The audio buffer gets an audio hash match on the OK Google soundwaves that I trained, and wakes up the phone.
- The phone starts capturing audio, which is just a time-series vector of numbers (representing sound wave intensity).
- The speech audio is decoded to phonemes, or textual representation of phonetic sounds. Several candidates for each utterance are generated.

- The candidate phonemes are combined together to try to make words. The algorithm uses a max-likelihood or other estimator to figure out which of the combinations is most likely to be a real sentence that would be used in the current context.
- The resultant sentence must be parsed for meaning, so many types of preprocessing are performed, and each word is tagged with its possible **parts of speech (POS)**.
- A learning system (typically an ANN) will try to determine intent given the phrase's subject, object, and verb.
- The actual intent must be carried out by a subroutine.
- A response to the user must be formulated. In the case where the response can't be scripted, it must be generated algorithmically.
- A text-to-speech algorithm decodes the response into phonemes and must then synthesize natural-sounding speech, which then plays over your phone's speakers.

Congratulations, you're on your way to getting your Slurpee! Your experience is powered by several ANNs, many different uses of various NLP tools, giant corpuses of data, and millions of engineer-hours of effort to build and maintain. This experience also explains the close relationship between NLP and ML—they are not the same thing, but they're partnered together at the forefront of technology.

Obviously, there's more to NLP than the topics we can cover in 25 pages. This chapter doesn't aim to be comprehensive; its aim is to familiarize you with the most common tactics you'll employ when solving ML problems that involve natural language. We'll take a whirlwind tour of seven NLP-related concepts:

- Measuring string distance
- The TF-IDF metric
- Tokenizing text
- Stemming words
- Phonetics
- Parts of speech tagging
- Word embedding with Word2vec

Don't worry if those topics look daunting. We'll introduce each one in turn and show lots of examples. There's a lot of jargon involved in NLP, and many edge cases, so the topic seems unapproachable at first glance. But the topic is *natural language* after all: we speak it every day! Once we learn the jargon, the topic becomes quite intuitive, because we all have a very strong intuitive understanding of language.

We'll start our discussion with a simple question: how do you measure the distance between *quit* and *quote*? We already know that we can measure the distance between two points in space, so now let's take a look at measuring the distance between two words.

String distance

It is always convenient to be able to measure some form of distance between two points. In previous chapters, we used the distance between points to aid in clustering and classification. We can do the same for words and passages in NLP. The problem, of course, is that words are made up of letters, and distances are made up of numbers—so how do we make a number out of two words?

Enter Levenshtein distance—a simple metric that measures the number of single-character edits it would take to transform one string into the other. The Levenshtein distance allows insertions, deletions, and substitutions. A modification of the Levenshtein distance, called the **Damerau-Levenshtein distance**, also allows transpositions, or the swapping of two neighboring letters.

To illustrate this concept with an example, let's try transforming the word **crate** into the word **plate**:

- Replace the **r** with **l** to get **clate**
- Replace the **c** with a **p** to get **plate**

The Levenshtein distance between crate and plate is therefore 2.

The distance between **plate** and **laser** is 3:

- Delete the **p** to get **late**
- Insert an **r** to get **later**
- Replace the **t** with an **s** to get **laser**

Let's confirm these examples in code. Create a new directory called `Ch10-NLP` and add the following `package.json` file:

```
{
  "name": "Ch10-NLP",
  "version": "1.0.0",
  "description": "ML in JS Example for Chapter 10 - NLP",
  "main": "src/index.js",
  "author": "Burak Kanber",
  "license": "MIT",
```

```
  "scripts": {
    "start": "node src/index.js"
  },
  "dependencies": {
    "compromise": "^11.7.0",
    "natural": "^0.5.6",
    "wordnet-db": "^3.1.6"
  }
}
```

Then issue `yarn install` from the command line to install the dependencies. This `package.json` file is a little different from the one in previous chapters, because the `wordnet-db` dependency is not compatible with the Browserify bundler. We will therefore have to omit some advanced JavaScript features in this chapter.

Create a directory called `src` and add to it an `index.js` file to which you'll add the following:

```
const compromise = require('compromise');
const natural = require('natural');
```

You'll use these imports for the rest of the chapter, so keep them in the `index.js` file. However, the rest of the code we use in this chapter will be fungible; you may delete old irrelevant code as you work through the examples in this chapter if you wish.

Let's take a look at Levenshtein distance using the `natural.js` library:

```
[
    ['plate', 'laser'],
    ['parachute', 'parasail'],
    ['parachute', 'panoply']
]
    .forEach(function(pair) {
        console.log("Levenshtein distance between '"+pair[0]+"' and
'"+pair[1]+"': "
            + natural.LevenshteinDistance.apply(null, pair)
        );
    });
```

Run `yarn start` from the command line and you'll see the following output:

```
Levenshtein distance between 'plate' and 'laser': 3
Levenshtein distance between 'parachute' and 'parasail': 5
Levenshtein distance between 'parachute' and 'panoply': 7
```

Try experimenting with a few pairs of words and see if you can calculate the distances in your head to get an intuitive feel for it.

The Levenshtein distance has many uses, since it is a metric and not any specific tool. Other systems, such as spellcheckers, suggester's, and fuzzy matcher's, use Levenshtein, or edit distance metrics in their own algorithms.

Let's take a look at a more advanced metric: the TF-IDF score, which represents how interesting or important a particular word is among a set of documents.

Term frequency - inverse document frequency

One of the most popular metrics used in search relevance, text mining, and information retrieval is the **term frequency-inverse document frequency (TF-IDF)** score. In essence, TF-IDF measures how significant a word is to a particular document. The TF-IDF metric therefore only makes sense in the context of a word in a document that's part of a larger corpus of documents.

Imagine you have a corpus of documents, such as blog posts on varying topics, that you want to make searchable. The end user of your application runs a search query for *fashion style*. How do you then find matching documents and rank them by relevance?

The TF-IDF score is made of two separate but related components. The first is *term frequency*, or the relative frequency of a specific term in a given document. If a 100-word blog post contains the word *fashion* four times, then the term frequency of the word *fashion* is 4% for that one document.

 Note that term frequency only requires a single term and a single document as parameters; the full corpus of documents is not required for the term frequency component of TF-IDF.

Term frequency by itself is not sufficient to determine relevance, however. Words such as *this* and *the* appear very frequently in most text and will have high term frequencies, but those words are not typically relevant to any search.

We therefore introduce a second metric to our calculation: inverse document frequency. This metric is essentially the inverse of the percentage of documents that a given word appears in. If you have 1,000 blog posts, and the word *fashion* appears in 50 of them, the (non-inverse) document frequency of that word is 5%. The inverse document frequency is an extension of this concept, given by taking the log of the inverse document frequency.

If $n_{fashion}$ is the number of documents containing the word *fashion* and N is the total number of documents, then the inverse document frequency is given by $log(N / n_{fashion})$. In our example, the inverse document frequency of the word *fashion* is roughly 1.3.

If we now consider the word *the*, which may appear in 90% of documents, we find that the inverse document frequency of *the* is 0.0451, much smaller than the 1.3 we got for *fashion*. The inverse document frequency therefore measures how rare or unique a given word is across a set of documents; higher values mean the word is more rare. The parameters required to calculate inverse document frequency are the term itself and the corpus of documents (unlike term frequency, which only requires one document).

The TF-IDF score is calculated by multiplying the term frequency and inverse document frequency together. The result is a single metric that encapsulates how significant or interesting a single term is to a specific document, considered across all documents that you've seen. Words such as *the* and *that* may have high term frequencies in any one document, but because they are prevalent across all documents, their overall TF-IDF score will be very low. Words, such as *fashion*, that exist only in a subset of documents will have a higher TF-IDF score. When comparing two separate documents that both contain the word *fashion*, the document that uses it more often will have a higher TF-IDF score, as the inverse document frequency portion will be the same for both documents.

When scoring search results for relevance, the most common approach is to calculate the TF-IDF scores for each term in the search query and for each document in the corpus. The individual TF-IDF scores for each query term can be added together, and the resultant sum can be called the **relevance score** of that particular document. Once all matching documents are scored in this manner, you can sort by relevance and display them in that order. Most full-text search systems, such as Lucene and Elasticsearch, use this sort of approach to relevance scoring.

Let's see this in practice, using the `natural.js` TF-IDF tool. Add the following to `index.js`:

```
const fulltextSearch = (query, documents) => {
    const db = new natural.TfIdf();
    documents.forEach(document => db.addDocument(document));
    db.tfidfs(query, (docId, score) => {
        console.log("DocID " + docId + " has score: " + score);
```

```
    });
};

fulltextSearch("fashion style", [
    "i love cooking, it really relaxes me and makes me feel at home",
    "food and restaurants are basically my favorite things",
    "i'm not really a fashionable person",
    "that new fashion blogger has a really great style",
    "i don't love the cinematic style of that movie"
]);
```

This code defines a fulltextSearch function that accepts a search query and an array of documents to be searched. Each document is added to the TF-IDF database object, where it is automatically tokenized by natural.js. Run the program with yarn start and you'll see the following output:

```
DocID 0 has score: 0
DocID 1 has score: 0
DocID 2 has score: 0
DocID 3 has score: 3.4271163556401456
DocID 4 has score: 1.5108256237659907
```

The first two documents, which have nothing to do with fashion or style, return scores of zero. The term frequency component for both *fashion* and *style* in those documents is zero, so the overall score becomes zero. The third document also has a score of zero. This document does make a reference to fashion, however, the tokenizer was not able to reconcile the word *fashionable* with *fashion*, as no stemming has been performed. We'll discuss both tokenization and stemming in depth in the later sections of this chapter, but for now it's sufficient to know that *stemming* is an operation that reduces a word to its root form.

Documents three and four have non-zero scores. Document three has a higher score because it includes both the words *fashion* and *style*, whereas document four only includes the word *style*. This simple metric has done a surprisingly good job of capturing relevance, which is why it's so widely used.

Let's update our code to add a stemming operation. After applying stemming to the text, we would expect document two to also have a non-zero relevance score, since *fashionable* should be transformed to *fashion* by the stemmer. Add the following code to index.js:

```
const stemmedFulltextSearch = (query, documents) => {
    const db = new natural.TfIdf();
    const tokenizer = new natural.WordTokenizer();
    const stemmer = natural.PorterStemmer.stem;
    const stemAndTokenize = text => tokenizer.tokenize(text).map(token =>
```

```
stemmer(token));

    documents.forEach(document =>
db.addDocument(stemAndTokenize(document)));
    db.tfidfs(stemAndTokenize(query), (docId, score) => {
        console.log("DocID " + docId + " has score: " + score);
    });
};

stemmedFulltextSearch("fashion style", [
    "i love cooking, it really relaxes me and makes me feel at home",
    "food and restaurants are basically my favorite things",
    "i'm not really a fashionable person",
    "that new fashion blogger has a really great style",
    "i don't love the cinematic style of that movie"
]);
```

We have added a `stemAndTokenize` helper method and applied it both to the documents added to the database and to the search query. Run the code with `yarn start` and you'll see the updated output:

```
DocID 0 has score: 0
DocID 1 has score: 0
DocID 2 has score: 1.5108256237659907
DocID 3 has score: 3.0216512475319814
DocID 4 has score: 1.5108256237659907
```

As expected, document two now has a non-zero score because the stemmer was able to transform the word *fashionable* into *fashion*. Documents two and four have the same score, but only because this is a very simple example; with a much larger corpus we would not expect the inverse document frequencies of the terms *fashion* and *style* to be equivalent.

Search relevance and ranking is not the only application for TF-IDF. This metric is widely used across many use cases and problem domains. One interesting use for TF-IDF is article summarization. In article summarization, the goal is to reduce a written passage to only a few sentences that effectively summarize the passage.

One approach to the article summarization problem is to consider each sentence or paragraph in an article to be a separate document. After indexing each sentence for TF-IDF, you then evaluate each individual word's TF-IDF score and use that to score each sentence as a whole. Pick the top three or five sentences and display them in their original order, and you will have a decent summary.

Let's see this in action, using both `natural.js` and `compromise.js`. Add the following code to `index.js`:

```
const summarize = (article, maxSentences = 3) => {
    const sentences = compromise(article).sentences().out('array');
    const db = new natural.TfIdf();
    const tokenizer = new natural.WordTokenizer();
    const stemmer = natural.PorterStemmer.stem;
    const stemAndTokenize = text => tokenizer.tokenize(text).map(token =>
stemmer(token));
    const scoresMap = {};

    // Add each sentence to the document
    sentences.forEach(sentence =>
db.addDocument(stemAndTokenize(sentence)));

    // Loop over all words in the document and add that word's score to an
overall score for each sentence
    stemAndTokenize(article).forEach(token => {
        db.tfidfs(token, (sentenceId, score) => {
            if (!scoresMap[sentenceId]) scoresMap[sentenceId] = 0;
            scoresMap[sentenceId] += score;
        });
    });

    // Convert our scoresMap into an array so that we can easily sort it
    let scoresArray = Object.entries(scoresMap).map(item => ({score:
item[1], sentenceId: item[0]}));
    // Sort the array by descending score
    scoresArray.sort((a, b) => a.score < b.score ? 1 : -1);
    // Pick the top maxSentences sentences
    scoresArray = scoresArray.slice(0, maxSentences);
    // Re-sort by ascending sentenceId
    scoresArray.sort((a, b) => parseInt(a.sentenceId) <
parseInt(b.sentenceId) ? -1 : 1);
    // Return sentences
    return scoresArray
        .map(item => sentences[item.sentenceId])
        .join('. ');

};
```

The preceding `summarize` method implements the following procedure:

- Use `compromise.js` to extract sentences from the article
- Add each individual sentence to the TF-IDF database
- For each word in the article, calculate its TF-IDF score for each sentence
- Add each word's TF-IDF score to a list of total scores for each sentence (the `scoresMap` object)
- Convert `scoresMap` into an array to make sorting easier
- Sort `scoresArray` by descending relevance score
- Remove all but the top-scoring sentences
- Re-sort `scoresArray` by the chronological order of sentences
- Build the summary by joining the top sentences together

Let's add a simple article to the code and try out both a three-sentence and a five-sentence summary. In this example, I'll use the first few paragraphs of this section, but you can replace the text with anything you like. Add the following to `index.js`:

```
const summarizableArticle = "One of the most popular metrics used in search
relevance, text mining, and information retrieval is the term frequency -
inverse document frequency score, or tf-idf for short. In essence, tf-idf
measures how significant a word is to a particular document. The tf-idf
metric therefore only makes sense in the context of a word in a document
that's part of a larger corpus of documents. Imagine you have a corpus of
documents, like blog posts on varying topics, that you want to make
searchable. The end user of your application runs a search query for
fashion style. How do you then find matching documents and rank them by
relevance? The tf-idf score is made of two separate but related components.
The first is term frequency, or the relative frequency of a specific term
in a given document. If a 100-word blog post contains the word fashion four
times, then the term frequency of the word fashion is 4% for that one
document. Note that term frequency only requires a single term and a single
document as parameters; the full corpus of documents is not required for
the term frequency component of tf-idf. Term frequency by itself is not
sufficient to determine relevance, however. Words like this and the appear
very frequently in most text and will have high term frequencies, but those
words are not typically relevant to any search.";

console.log("3-sentence summary:");
console.log(summarize(summarizableArticle, 3));
console.log("5-sentence summary:");
console.log(summarize(summarizableArticle, 5));
```

When you run the code with `yarn start`, you'll see the following output:

```
3-sentence summary:
  the tf idf metric therefore only makes sense in the context of a word in a
document that's part of a larger corpus of documents. if a 100-word blog
post contains the word fashion four times then the term frequency of the
word fashion is 4% for that one document. note that term frequency only
requires a single term and a single document as parameters the full corpus
of documents is not required for the term frequency component of tf idf


 5-sentence summary:
  one of the most popular metrics used in search relevance text mining and
information retrieval is the term frequency inverse document frequency
score or tf idf for short. the tf idf metric therefore only makes sense in
the context of a word in a document that's part of a larger corpus of
documents. the first is term frequency or the relative frequency of a
specific term in a given document. if a 100-word blog post contains the
word fashion four times then the term frequency of the word fashion is 4%
for that one document. note that term frequency only requires a single term
and a single document as parameters the full corpus of documents is not
required for the term frequency component of tf idf
```

The quality of these summaries illustrates both the power and flexibility of the `tf-idf` `metric`, while also highlighting the fact that you don't always need advanced ML or AI algorithms to accomplish interesting tasks. There are many other uses of TF-IDF, so you should consider using this metric any time you need the relevance of a word or term as it pertains to a document in a corpus.

In this section, we made use of tokenizers and stemmers without formally introducing them. These are core concepts in NLP, so let's now introduce them formally.

Tokenizing

Tokenizing is the act of transforming an input string, such as a sentence, paragraph, or even an object such as an email, into individual *tokens*. A very simple tokenizer might take a sentence or paragraph and split it by spaces, thus generating tokens that are individual words. However, tokens do not necessarily need to be words, nor does every word in an input string need to be returned by the tokenizer, nor does every token generated by the tokenizer need to be present in the original text, nor does a token need to represent only one word. We therefore use the term *token* rather than *word* to describe the output of a tokenizer, as tokens are not always words.

The manner in which you tokenize text before processing it with an ML algorithm has a major effect on the performance of the algorithm. Many NLP and ML applications use a *bag-of-words* approach, in which only the words or tokens matter but their order does not, as in the Naive Bayes classifier we explored in Chapter 5, *Classification Algorithms*. However, a tokenizer that generates *bigrams*, or pairs of words found next to each other, will actually preserve some of the positional and semantic meaning of the original text even when used with a bag-of-words algorithm.

There are many ways to tokenize text. As mentioned, the simplest method is to split a sentence by spaces to generate a *token stream* of individual words. There are numerous problems with the simple approach, however. For one, the algorithm will treat capitalized words as being distinct from their lowercase versions; Buffalo and buffalo are considered two separate words or tokens. Sometimes this is desirable, other times it's not. Oversimplified tokenization will also treat contractions such as *won't* as being distinct and separate from the words *will not*, which will get split into two separate tokens, *will and not*.

In most cases, that is, in 80% of applications, the simplest tokenization that one should consider is a tokenizer that converts all text to lowercase, removes punctuation and newlines, removes formatting and markup such as HTML, and even removes *stopwords* or common words such as *this* or *the*. In other cases, more advanced tokenization is necessary, and in some cases, simpler tokenization is desired.

In this section, I've been describing the act of tokenization as a compound process, including case transformations, removing non-alphanumeric characters, and stopword filtering. However, tokenizer libraries will each have their own opinion as to what the roles and responsibilities of the tokenizer are. You may need to combine a library's tokenization tool with other tools in order to achieve the desired effect.

First, let's build our own simple tokenizer. This tokenizer will convert a string to lowercase, remove non-alphanumeric characters, and also remove words that are fewer than three characters in length. Add the following to your `index.js` file, either replacing the Levenshtein distance code or adding beneath it:

```
const tokenizablePhrase = "I've not yet seen 'THOR: RAGNAROK'; I've heard
it's a great movie though. What'd you think of it?";

const simpleTokenizer = (text) =>
    text.toLowerCase()
        .replace(/ (\w)'(\w)/g, '$1$2')
        .replace(/\W/g, ' ')
        .split(' ')
        .filter(token => token.length > 2);

console.log(simpleTokenizer(tokenizablePhrase));
```

This `simpleTokenizer` will convert the string to lowercase, remove apostrophes in the middle of a word (so that *won't* becomes *wont*), and filter out all other non-word characters by replacing them with spaces. It then splits the string by the space character, returning an array, and finally removes any items that have fewer than three characters.

Run `yarn start` and you'll see the following:

```
[ 'ive', 'not', 'yet', 'seen', 'thor',
  'ragnarok', 'ive', 'heard', 'its',
  'great', 'movie', 'though',
  'whatd', 'you', 'think' ]
```

This token stream can then be given to an algorithm, either in an ordered or unordered fashion. A classifier, such as Naive Bayes, will ignore the order and analyze each word as if it were independent.

Let's compare our simple tokenizer to two tokenizers provided by `natural.js` and `compromise.js`. Add the following to your `index.js` file:

```
console.log("Natural.js Word Tokenizer:");
console.log((new natural.WordTokenizer()).tokenize(tokenizablePhrase));
```

Running the code with `yarn start` will yield the following output:

```
Natural.js Word Tokenizer:
  [ 'I', 've', 'not', 'yet', 'seen',
  'THOR', 'RAGNAROK', 'I', 've',
  'heard', 'it', 's', 'a', 'great', 'movie',
  'though', 'What', 'd', 'you', 'think',
  'of', 'it' ]
```

As you can see, short words have been preserved, and contractions, such as *I've*, have been split up into separate tokens. Additionally, capitalization has been preserved.

Let's try another one of `natural.js` tokenizers:

```
console.log("Natural.js WordPunct Tokenizer:");
console.log((new
natural.WordPunctTokenizer()).tokenize(tokenizablePhrase));
```

This will result in:

```
Natural.js WordPunct Tokenizer:
  [ 'I', '\'', 've', 'not', 'yet', 'seen',
  '\'', 'THOR', ': ', 'RAGNAROK', '\'', '; ',
  'I', '\'', 've', 'heard', 'it', '\'', 's',
  'a', 'great', 'movie', 'though', '.', 'What',
```

```
'\'', 'd', 'you', 'think', 'of',
'it', '?' ]
```

This tokenizer continues to split on punctuation, however, the punctuation itself is preserved. In applications where punctuation is important, this may be desired.

Other tokenizer libraries, such as the one in `compromise.js`, take a more intelligent approach and even perform POS tagging in order to parse and understand the sentence while tokenizing. Let's try a number of `compromise.js` tokenizing techniques:

```
console.log("Compromise.js Words:");
console.log(compromise(tokenizablePhrase).words().out('array'));
console.log("Compromise.js Adjectives:");
console.log(compromise(tokenizablePhrase).adjectives().out('array'));
console.log("Compromise.js Nouns:");
console.log(compromise(tokenizablePhrase).nouns().out('array'));
console.log("Compromise.js Questions:");
console.log(compromise(tokenizablePhrase).questions().out('array'));
console.log("Compromise.js Contractions:");
console.log(compromise(tokenizablePhrase).contractions().out('array'));
console.log("Compromise.js Contractions, Expanded:");
console.log(compromise(tokenizablePhrase).contractions().expand().out('arra
y'));
```

Run the new code with `yarn start` and you'll see the following:

```
Compromise.js Words:
 [ 'i\'ve', '', 'not', 'yet', 'seen',
 'thor', 'ragnarok', 'i\'ve', '', 'heard',
 'it\'s', '', 'a', 'great', 'movie', 'though',
 'what\'d', '', 'you', 'think', 'of', 'it' ]
Compromise.js Adjectives:
 [ 'great' ]
Compromise.js Nouns:
 [ 'thor', 'ragnarok', 'movie' ]
Compromise.js Questions:
 [ 'what\'d you think of it' ]
Compromise.js Contractions:
 [ 'i\'ve', 'i\'ve', 'it\'s', 'what\'d' ]
Compromise.js Contractions, Expanded:
 [ 'i have', 'i have', 'it is', 'what did' ]
```

The `words()` tokenizer does not split contractions apart like the `natural.js` tokenizer did. Additionally, `compromise.js` gives you the capability to extract specific entity types from the text. We can separately extract adjectives, nouns, verbs, questions, contractions (even with the capability to expand contractions); we can also use `compromise.js` to extract dates, hashtags, lists, clauses, and numerical values.

It is also not a requirement that your tokens must map directly to words and phrases in the input text. For instance, when developing a spam filter for an email system, you might find that including some data from the email header in the token stream gives you a huge accuracy improvement. Whether the email passes SPF and DKIM checks may be a very strong signal to your spam filter. You might also find that differentiating body text from the subject line is also advantageous; it may also be the case that words that appear as hyperlinks are stronger signals than plaintext.

Often, the simplest way to tokenize this type of semi-structured data is to prefix the tokens with a character or set of characters that normally would not be allowed by the tokenizer. For example, tokens in the subject line of an email may be prefixed by _SUBJ: and tokens that appear in hyperlinks may be prefixed by _LINK:. To illustrate this, here's an example of what a token stream might look like for an email:

```
['_SPF:PASS',
 '_DKIM:FAIL',
 '_SUBJ:buy',
 '_SUBJ:pharmaceuticals',
 '_SUBJ:online',
 '_LINK:pay',
 '_LINK:bitcoin',
 'are',
 'you',
 'interested',
 'buying',
 'medicine',
 'online']
```

Even if a Naive Bayes classifier has never seen references to pharmaceuticals before, it may see that most spam emails have failed their DKIM check and still flag this message as spam. Or perhaps you work closely with the accounting department and they often get emails about payments, but almost never receive a legitimate email with the word `pay` in a hyperlink to an external site; the differentiation of the *pay* token appearing in plaintext versus the `_LINK:pay` token appearing in a hyperlink may make all the difference between an email being classified as spam or not.

In fact, one of the earliest spam filtering breakthroughs, developed by Paul Graham, of Y Combinator fame, used this approach of annotated email tokens to mark a significant improvement in the accuracy of early spam filters.

Another approach to tokenization is *n-gram* tokenization, which splits an input string into N-sized groups of neighboring tokens. In fact, all tokenization is n-gram tokenization, however, in the preceding examples, N is set to 1. More typically, n-gram tokenization refers to schemes where N > 1. Most commonly, you'll encounter *bigram* and *trigram* tokenization.

The purpose of bigram and trigram tokenization is to preserve some context around individual words. An example related to sentiment analysis is an easy visualization. The phrase *I did not love the movie* will be tokenized (with a *unigram* tokenizer, or n-gram tokenizer where N = 1) to *I, did, not, love, the, movie*. When using a bag-of-words algorithm, such as Naive Bayes, the algorithm will see the word *love* and guess that the sentence has a positive sentiment, as bag-of-words algorithms do not consider the relationships between words.

A bigram tokenizer, on the other hand, can trick a naive algorithm into considering the relationships between words, because every *pair* of words becomes a token. The preceding phrase, processed with a bigram tokenizer, will become *I did, did not, not love, love the, the movie*. Even though each token is composed of two individual words, the algorithm operates on tokens and therefore will treat *not love* differently from *I love*. A sentiment analyzer will therefore have more context around each word and will be able to distinguish negations (*not love*) from positive phrases.

Let's try out the `natural.js` bigram tokenizer on our earlier example sentence. Add the following code to `index.js`:

```
console.log("Natural.js bigrams:");
console.log(natural.NGrams.bigrams(tokenizablePhrase));
```

Running the code with `yarn start` will yield:

```
Natural.js bigrams:
 [ [ 'I', 've' ],
 [ 've', 'not' ],
 [ 'not', 'yet' ],
 [ 'yet', 'seen' ],
 [ 'seen', 'THOR' ],
 [ 'THOR', 'RAGNAROK' ],
 [ 'RAGNAROK', 'I' ],
 [ 'I', 've' ],
 [ 've', 'heard' ],
```

```
[ 'heard', 'it' ],
[ 'it', 's' ],
[ 's', 'a' ],
[ 'a', 'great' ],
[ 'great', 'movie' ],
[ 'movie', 'though' ],
[ 'though', 'What' ],
[ 'What', 'd' ],
[ 'd', 'you' ],
[ 'you', 'think' ],
[ 'think', 'of' ],
[ 'of', 'it' ] ]
```

The biggest issue with n-gram tokenization is that it dramatically increases the entropy of the data domain. When training an algorithm on n-grams, you're not just on the hook for making sure the algorithm learns all the significant words, but also all the significant *pairs* of words. There are many more pairs of words than there are unique words, so n-gram tokenization will only work when you have a very large and comprehensive training set.

One clever way around the n-gram entropy issue, particularly for dealing with negations in sentiment analysis, is to transform the token immediately following the negation in the same way we handled email headers and subject lines. For example, the phrase *not love* can be tokenized as *not, _NOT:love,* or *not, !love,* or even just *!love* (discarding *not* as an individual token).

Under this scheme, the phrase *I did not love the movie* will get tokenized as *I, did, not, _NOT:love, the, movie.* The advantage of this approach is that the contextual negation still gets preserved, but in general we are still using low-entropy unigrams that can be trained with a smaller dataset.

There are many ways to tokenize text, and each has its advantages and disadvantages. As always, the approach you choose will depend on the task at hand, the training data available, and the problem domain itself.

Keep the topic of tokenization in mind throughout the next few sections, as those topics can also be applied to the tokenization process. For example, you can stem words after tokenizing to further reduce entropy, or you can filter your tokens by their TF-IDF score, therefore only using the most interesting words in a document.

In order to continue our discussion about entropy, let's take a moment to discuss *stemming*.

Stemming

Stemming is a type of transformation that can be applied to a single word, though typically the stemming operation occurs right after tokenizing. Stemming after tokenizing is so common that `natural.js` offers a `tokenizeAndStem` convenience method that can be attached to the `String` class prototype.

Specifically, stemming reduces a word to its root form, for instance by transforming *running* to *run*. Stemming your text after tokenizing can significantly reduce the entropy of your dataset, because it essentially de-duplicates words with similar meanings but different tenses or inflections. Your algorithm will not need to learn the words *run, runs, running,* and *runnings* separately, as they will all get transformed into *run*.

The most popular stemming algorithm, the *Porter stemmer*, is a heuristic algorithm that defines a number of staged rules for the transformation. But, in essence, it boils down to cutting the standard verb and noun inflections off the end of the word and dealing with specific edge cases and common irregular forms as they arise.

In one sense, stemming is a sort of compression algorithm that discards information about inflections and specific word forms, but retains the conceptual information left behind by the word root. Stemming should therefore not be used in cases where the inflection or form of the language itself is important.

For the same reason, stemming excels in situations where the conceptual information is more important than the form. Topic extraction is a good example: it doesn't matter if someone is writing about their own experiences as a runner versus their experience watching track races—they're still writing about running.

Because stemming reduces data entropy, it is very effectively employed when the dataset is small or modest in size. Stemming cannot be applied carelessly, however. A very large dataset may incur an accuracy penalty if you use stemming unnecessarily. You destroy information when you stem text, and models with very large training sets may have been able to use that extra information to generate better predictions.

In practice, you should never have to guess whether your model will perform better with or without stemming: you should try both ways and see which performs better. I can't tell you *when* to use stemming, I can only tell you why it works and why it sometimes doesn't.

Let's try out the `natural.js` Porter stemmer, and we'll combine it with our tokenization from earlier. Add the following to `index.js`:

```
console.log("Tokenized and stemmed:");
console.log(
    (new natural.WordTokenizer())
        .tokenize(
            "Writing and write, lucky and luckies, part parts and parted"
        )
        .map(natural.PorterStemmer.stem)
```

Run the code with `yarn start` and you'll see the following:

```
Tokenized and stemmed:
 [ 'write', 'and', 'write',
 'lucki', 'and', 'lucki',
 'part', 'part', 'and', 'part' ]
```

This simple example illustrates how words with different forms get reduced into their conceptual meanings. It also illustrates that there is no guarantee that the stemmer will create *real* words (you won't find `lucki` in the dictionary), only that it will reduce entropy for a set of similarly constructed words.

There are other stemmer algorithms that try to approach the problem more linguistically. That type of stemming is called **lemmatization**, and the analog to stems is called the **lemma**, or the dictionary form of a word. In essence, a lemmatizer is a stemmer that first determines the part of speech of the word (typically requiring a dictionary, such as *WordNet*), and then applies in-depth rules for that specific part of speech, potentially involving more lookup tables. As an example, the word *better* is unchanged by stemming, but it is transformed into the word *good* by lemmatization. Lemmatization is not necessary in most everyday tasks, but may be useful when your problem requires more precise linguistic rules or drastically reduced entropy.

We can't discuss NLP or linguistics without also discussing the most common mode of communication: speech. How does a speech-to-text or text-to-speech system actually know how to say the hundreds of thousands of defined words in the English language, plus an arbitrary amount of names? The answer is *phonetics*.

Phonetics

Speech detection, such as those used in speech-to-text systems, is a surprisingly difficult problem. There are so many variations in styles of speaking, pronunciation, dialect, and accent, as well as variations in rhythm, tone, speed, and elocution, plus the fact that audio is a simple one-dimensional time-domain signal, that it's no surprise that even today's state-of-the-art smartphone tech is *good, not great*.

While modern speech-to-text goes much deeper than what I'll present here, I would like to show you the concept of *phonetic algorithms*. These algorithms transform a word into something resembling a phonetic hash, such that it is easy to identify words that sound similar to one another.

The *metaphone* algorithm is one such phonetic algorithm. Its aim is to reduce a word down to a simplified phonetic form, with the ultimate goal of being able to index similar pronunciations. Metaphone uses an alphabet of 16 characters: 0BFHJKLMNPRSTWXY. The 0 character represents the *th* sound, X represents a *sh* or *ch* sound, and the other letters are pronounced as usual. Nearly all vowel information is lost in the transformation, though some are preserved if they are the first sound in a word.

A simple example illustrates where phonetic algorithms can be useful. Imagine that you're in charge of a search engine and people keep searching for *knowledge is power, France is bacon*. You, having familiarity with art history, would understand that it was actually Francis Bacon who said *knowledge is power*, and that your users have simply misheard the quote. You'd like to add a *Did you mean:* **Francis Bacon** link to your search results, but don't know how to approach the problem.

Let's take a look at how the Metaphone algorithm would phoneticize the terms France is Bacon and Francis Bacon. Add the following to index.js:

```
console.log(
    (new natural.WordTokenizer())
        .tokenize("Francis Bacon and France is Bacon")
        .map(t => natural.Metaphone.process(t))
);
```

When you run the code with yarn start, you'll see the following:

```
[ 'FRNSS', 'BKN', 'ANT', 'FRNS', 'IS', 'BKN' ]
```

Francis has transformed into FRNSS, France has transformed into FRNS, and Bacon has transformed into BKN. Intuitively, these strings represent the most distinguishable sounds used to pronounced the word.

After phoneticizing, we can use the Levenshtein distance to measure the similarity between two words. If you ignore the space, *FRNSS BKN* and *FRNS IS BKN* only have a Levenshtein distance of one between them (the addition of the *I*); these two phrases therefore sound very similar. You can use this information, combined with the rest of the search term and a reverse lookup, to determine that France is Bacon is a plausible mispronunciation of Francis Bacon, and that Francis Bacon is actually the correct topic to present in your search results. Phonetic misspellings and misunderstandings, such as France is Bacon, are so common that we even use them in some spellchecker tools.

A similar approach is used in speech-to-text systems. The recording system does its best to capture the specific vowel and consonant sounds you make and uses a phonetic index (a reverse lookup of phonetics mapped to various dictionary words) to come up with a set of candidate words. Typically, a neural network will then determine which is the most likely combination of words considering both the confidence of the phonetic form and the semantic meaningfulness or meaninglessness of the resultant statements. The set of words that makes the most sense is what is presented to you.

The natural.js library also provides a convenience method to compare two words, returning *true* if they sound alike. Try the following code:

```
console.log(natural.Metaphone.compare("praise", "preys"));
console.log(natural.Metaphone.compare("praise", "frays"));
```

When run, this will return true and then false.

You should consider using phonetic algorithms any time your problem involves pronunciation or working with similar-sounding words and phrases. This is usually restricted to more specialized fields, but speech-to-text and text-to-speech systems are becoming very popular, and you may find yourself needing to update your search algorithm for phonetic sound-alikes if users start interacting with your service by speech in the future.

Speaking of speech systems, let's now take a look at POS tagging and how it can be used to extract semantic information from phrases—such as commands you might issue to your smartphone assistant.

Part of speech tagging

A **part of speech** (POS) tagger analyzes a piece of text, such as a sentence, and determines each individual word's POS in the context of the sentence. The only way to accomplish this is with a dictionary lookup, so it is not an algorithm that can be developed from first principles alone.

A great use case for POS tagging is intent extraction from commands. For instance, when you say *Siri, please order me a pizza from John's pizzeria*, the AI system will tag the command with parts of speech in order to extract the subject, verb, object, and any other relevant details from the command.

Additionally, POS tagging is often used as a supporting tool for other NLP operations. Topic extraction, for instance, makes heavy use of POS tagging in order to separate people, places, and topics from verbs and adjectives.

Keep in mind that POS tagging is never perfect, due to the ambiguity of the English language in particular. Many words can be used both as a noun and a verb, so many POS taggers will return a list of candidate parts of speech for a given word. Libraries that perform POS tagging have a wide range of sophistication, ranging from simple heuristics, to dictionary lookups, to advanced models that attempt to determine the POS based on context.

The `compromise.js` library has a flexible POS tagger and matching/extraction system. The `compromise.js` library is unique in that it aims to be *good enough* but not comprehensive; it is trained on only the most common words in the English language, which is enough to give 80-90% accuracy for most cases while still being a fast and small library.

Let's see the `compromise.js` POS tagging and matching in action. Add the following code to `index.js`:

```
const siriCommand = "Hey Siri, order me a pizza from John's pizzeria";
const siriCommandObject = compromise(siriCommand);

console.log(siriCommandObject.verbs().out('array'));
console.log(siriCommandObject.nouns().out('array'));
```

Using `compromise.js` allows us to extract just the verbs, or just the nouns (and other parts of speech) from the command. Running the code with `yarn start` will yield:

```
[ 'order' ]
[ 'siri', 'pizza', 'john\'s pizzeria' ]
```

The POS tagger has identified `order` as the sole verb in the sentence; this information can then be used to load up the correct subroutine for making orders that's built into Siri's AI system. The extracted nouns can then be sent to the subroutine in order to determine what type of order to make and from where.

Impressively, the POS tagger has also identified `John's pizzeria` as a single noun, rather than considering the words `John's` and `pizzeria` to be separate nouns. The tagger has understood that `John's` is a possessive, and therefore applies to the word following it.

We can also use `compromise.js` to write parsing and extraction rules for common commands. Let's try one out:

```
console.log(
    compromise("Hey Siri, order me a pizza from John's pizzeria")
        .match("#Noun [#Verb me a #Noun+ *+ #Noun+]").out('text')
);

console.log(
    compromise("OK Google, write me a letter to the congressman")
        .match("#Noun [#Verb me a #Noun+ *+ #Noun+]").out('text')
);
```

Running the code with `yarn start` will yield:

```
order me a pizza from John's
write me a letter to the congressman
```

The same matching selector is able to capture both of these commands, ignoring the addressee of the command (Siri or Google) through match groups (denoted with `[]`). Because both commands follow the verb-noun-noun pattern, both will match the selector.

Of course, this selector by itself is not enough to build a full AI system such as Siri or Google Assistant. This tool would be used near the beginning of the AI system process in order to determine the user's overall intent, based on predefined but flexible command formats. You could program a system to respond to phrases such as *Open my #Noun*, where the noun can be `calendar` or `email` or `Spotify`, or *Write an email to #Noun*, and so on. This tool can be used as a first step toward building your own speech or natural language command system, as well as for various topic-extraction applications.

Throughout this chapter, we've discussed the foundational tools used in NLP. Many advanced NLP tasks use an ANN as part of the learning process, but for many novice practitioners, it's unclear exactly how words and natural language should be sent to the input layer of an ANN. In the next section, we will discuss *word embedding*, particularly the Word2vec algorithm, which can be used to feed words into an ANN and other systems.

Word embedding and neural networks

Throughout this chapter, we've discussed various NLP techniques, particularly with regards to preprocessing text. In many use cases, we will need to interact with an ANN to perform the final analysis. The type of analysis is not relevant to this section, but imagine you're developing a sentiment analysis ANN. You appropriately tokenize and stem your training text, then, as you attempt to train your ANN on your preprocessed text, you realize you have no idea how to get words into a neural network.

The simplest approach is to map each input neuron in the network to an individual unique word. When processing a document, you can set the input neuron's value to the term frequency (or absolute count) of that word in the document. You'll have a network where one input neuron responds to the word *fashion*, another neuron responds to *technology*, another neuron responds to *food*, and so on.

This approach will work, but it has several drawbacks. The topology of an ANN must be defined in advance, so you must know how many unique words are in your training set before you start training the network; this will become the size of the input layer. This also means that your network is not capable of learning new words after it has been trained. To add a new word to the network, you must essentially build and train a new network from scratch.

Additionally, throughout a corpus of documents, you may encounter tens of thousands of unique words. This has a huge negative impact on the efficiency of the ANN, as you will need an input layer with, say, 10,000 neurons. This will dramatically increase the training time required by the network as well as the memory and processing requirements of the system.

The approach of one-word-per-neuron also intuitively feels inefficient. While your corpus contains 10,000 unique words, most of them will be rare and only appear in a few documents. For most documents, only a few hundred input neurons will be activated, with the others set to zero. This amounts to what is called a **sparse matrix** or **sparse vector**, or a vector where most of the values are zero.

A more evolved approach is therefore required when natural language interacts with ANNs. A family of techniques called *word embedding* can analyze a corpus of text and transform each word into a fixed-length vector of numerical values. The vector is a fixed-length representation of a word in much the same way that a hash (such as md5 or sha1) is a fixed-length representation of arbitrary data.

Word embedding confers several advantages, particularly when used with ANNs. Because the word vectors are fixed in length, the topology of the network can be decided beforehand and can also handle the appearance of new words after the initial training.

The word vectors are also *dense vectors*, meaning that you don't need 10,000 input neurons in your network. A good value for the size of a word vector (and the size of the input layer) is somewhere between 100-300 items. This factor alone significantly reduces the dimensionality of your ANN and will allow for much faster training and convergence of the model.

There are many word embedding algorithms to choose from, but the current state-of-the-art choice is the Word2vec algorithm, developed at Google. This particular algorithm also has another desirable trait: similar words will be clustered close to one another in terms of their vector representations.

Earlier in this chapter, we saw that we can use string distance to measure the typographical distance between two words. We can also use the string distance between two phonetic representations of words to measure how similar they sound. When using Word2vec, you can measure the distance between two word vectors to get the *conceptual* distance between two words.

The Word2vec algorithm is itself a shallow neural network that trains itself on your corpus of text. The algorithm uses n-grams to develop a sense of the context between words. If the words *fashion* and *blogger* often appear next to each other in your corpus, Word2vec will assign similar vectors to those words. If *fashion* and *mathematics* rarely appear together, their resultant vectors will be separated by some distance. The distance between two word vectors therefore represents their conceptual and contextual distance, or how alike two words are in terms of their semantic content and context.

This trait of the Word2vec algorithm also confers its own efficiency and accuracy advantage to the ANN that ultimately processes the data, as the word vectors will activate similar input neurons for similar words. The Word2vec algorithm has not only reduced the dimensionality of the problem, but it has also added contextual information to the word embedding's. This additional contextual information is exactly the type of signal that ANNs are highly proficient at picking up on.

The following is an example of a common workflow involving both natural language and ANNs:

- Tokenize and stem all text
- Remove stopwords from text
- Determine the appropriate ANN input layer size; use this value both for the input layer and the Word2vec dimensionality
- Use Word2vec to generate word embedding's for your text
- Use the word embedding's to train the ANN on your task
- When evaluating a new document, tokenize, stem, and vectorize the document before passing it to the ANN

Using a word-embedding algorithm such as Word2vec will not only improve the speed and memory performance of your model, but it will likely also increase the accuracy of your model due to the contextual information that the Word2vec algorithm preserves. It should also be noted that Word2vec is, like n-gram tokenization, one possible way to trick a naive bag-of-words algorithm into taking word context into account, as the Word2vec algorithm itself uses n-grams to develop the embedding's.

While word embedding is used primarily in NLP, the same approach can be used in other fields, such as genetics and biochemistry. In those fields, it is sometimes advantageous to be able to vectorize sequences of proteins or amino acids such that similar structures will have similar vector embedding's.

Summary

Natural language processing is a rich field of study with many advanced techniques and wide applications in ML, computational linguistics, and artificial intelligence. In this chapter, however, we focused on the specific tools and tactics that are most prevalent in everyday ML tasks.

The techniques presented in this chapter are building blocks that can be mixed and matched in order to achieve many different outcomes. Using the information in this chapter alone, you can build a simple full-text search engine, an intent extractor for spoken or written commands, an article summarizer, and many other impressive tools. However, the most impressive applications of NLP arise when these techniques are combined with advanced learning models, such as ANNs and RNNs.

In particular, you learned about word metrics, such as string distance and TF-IDF relevance scoring; preprocessing and dimensionality reduction techniques, such as tokenization and stemming; phonetic algorithms, such as the Metaphone algorithm; part of speech extraction and phrase parsing; and converting words to vectors using word embedding algorithms.

You have also been introduced, through numerous examples, to two excellent JavaScript libraries, `natural.js` and `compromise.js`, which can be used to easily accomplish most of the NLP tasks relevant to ML. You were even able to write an article summarizer in 20 lines of code!

In the next chapter, we'll discuss how everything you've learned so far can be put together in a real-time, user-facing JavaScript application.

11
Using Machine Learning in Real-Time Applications

Throughout this book, you have learned many ML algorithms and techniques. What remains, however, is to deploy these algorithms into real-world applications. This chapter is dedicated to those pieces of advice related to using ML in the real world, in real applications, and in production environments.

There are many differences between idealized usage of ML algorithms and real-world usage. In our examples, we both train and execute models in one step, in response to one command. We assume that the models do not need to be serialized, saved, or reloaded in any way. We have not thought about user interface responsiveness, executing on mobile devices, or building API interfaces between clients and servers.

Real applications may also have a scope several orders of magnitude larger than the examples we've discussed. How do you train an ANN with billions of data points in a dataset? How do you collect, store, and process that amount of information?

In this chapter, we'll discuss the following topics:

- Frontend architecture
- Backend architecture
- Data pipelining
- Tools and services you can use to build a production ML system

Serializing models

Our examples throughout this book have built, trained, and tested models only to destroy them a millisecond later. We can get away with this because our examples use limited training data and, at worst, take only a few minutes to train. Production applications will typically use much more data and require more time to train. In production applications, the trained model itself is a valuable asset that should be stored, saved, and loaded on demand. In other words, our models must be serializable.

Serialization itself is typically not a difficult issue. Models are essentially a compressed version of the training data. Some models can indeed be very large, but they will still be a fraction of the size of the data that trained them. What makes the topic of serialization challenging is that it opens up many other architectural questions that you will have to consider, the first being the question of where and how to store the model.

Disappointingly, there's no right answer. Models can be stored nearly anywhere depending on their size, complexity, frequency of use, available technology, and so on. Naive Bayes classifiers require only the storage of token and document counts and use only key/value lookups with no advanced querying, so a single Redis server can host a huge classifier trained on billions of documents. Very large models can be serialized into a dedicated database, perhaps even a dedicated graph database cluster. Moderately sized models may be serialized as JSON or a binary format and stored in a database BLOB field, hosted on a file server or API such as Amazon S3, or stored in browser local storage if it is small enough.

Most ML libraries have serialization and deserialization built in, as ultimately this functionality is dependent on the implementation details of the library. Most libraries include methods such as `save()` and `load()`, though you will want to refer to the documentation of the specific library you're using.

Make sure to include serialization functionality when writing your own libraries. If you want to support multiple storage backends, it would be best to decouple the serialization functionality from the core logic and implement a driver and interface architecture instead.

This is just the first of the questions we'll need to answer now that we have a serializable model. Serializable models are also portable, which means they can be moved from machine to machine. You can download a pretrained model onto a smartphone for offline usage, for instance. Your JavaScript application can use a web worker to download and maintain a ready-to-use model for speech detection, ask for microphone permission, and make a website navigable solely by voice commands—all through a Chrome extension.

In this section, we'll discuss the various architectural considerations that arise once your model is serializable and portable.

Training models on the server

Due to the time, data, processing power, and memory requirements involved in training sophisticated models, it's often desirable to train models on the server rather than the client. Depending on the use case, even the evaluation of models may need to occur on the server.

There are a few paradigms to consider in terms of where to train and where to evaluate models. Your options, in general, will be to train and evaluate fully on the server, train and evaluate fully on the client, or to train on the server but evaluate on the client. Let's explore some examples of each paradigm.

The simplest implementation is to both train and evaluate models on the server. The main advantage of this approach is that you get to determine and control the entire execution environment of the model. You can easily analyze the server load required to train and execute a model and scale your servers as necessary. It's easier for a server you fully control to get access to a large corpus of training data, as the data is most likely in a database that you also control. You won't have to worry about which version of JavaScript your clients are running or whether you will have access to the client's GPU for training. Training and executing models on the server also means that there is no additional load on the client machine due to the model.

The primary downside of a fully server-side approach is that it requires a well-designed and robust API. If you have an application which requires quick response times for a model evaluation, you will need to ensure that your API can serve results quickly and reliably. This approach also means that offline evaluation of models is not possible; the client will require a connection to your server in order for anything to work. Most applications or products billed as **Software as a Service (SaaS)** will use the server-side model, and this approach should be the first one you consider if you are providing a paid service to customers.

Models can conversely be fully trained and evaluated on the client. In this case, the client itself will need access to the training data and it will need sufficient processing power to train a model. This approach is generally not appropriate for models that require large training sets or long training times, as there is no way to ensure that the client's device will be able to process the data. You will also have to contend with older devices which may not have a GPU or the processing power to train even simple models.

However, client-side training and evaluation is a good approach for applications which require a high level of data privacy or data ownership in cases where the training data originates from the device itself. Restricting the processing to the client device ensures that the user's data is not transmitted to any third-party server and can be deleted directly by the user. Applications such as fingerprint scanning, biometrics analysis, location data analysis, phone call analysis, and so on, are good candidates for a fully client-side approach. This approach also ensures that models can be trained and evaluated offline, with no need for an internet connection.

A hybrid approach can blend the best of both worlds in some cases. Advanced models that require a lot of training data can be trained on a server and serialized. A client, when it first connects to your application, can download and store the trained model for offline usage. The client itself becomes responsible for evaluating the model, but does not need to train the model in this case.

The hybrid approach allows you to train and periodically update sophisticated models on the server. A serialized model is much smaller than the original training data, and therefore can be delivered to a client for offline evaluation. As long as both the client and the server use compatible libraries or algorithms (that is, `TensorFlow.js` on both sides), the client can take advantage of the processing power of the server for training but use its own offline processing capabilities for the much less demanding evaluation step.

An example use case for the hybrid model is speech or image recognition, perhaps for an AI assistant or **Augmented Reality (AR)** application. In the case of an AR application, the server is responsible for maintaining millions of training images and training (for example) an RNN to classify objects. Once the training is complete, this model can be serialized, stored, and downloaded by the client.

Let's imagine an AR application that connects to the device's camera and displays an annotated video feed that identifies objects. When the application first starts, the client downloads the AR RNN model and stores it in the device's local storage along with version information. When the video feed first starts, the application retrieves the model from storage and deserializes it into the client's own RNN implementation. Ideally, the client's RNN implementation will use the same library and version as the library on the server.

In order to classify and annotate every frame of the video, the client would need to do all the necessary work in just 16 ms (for 60 FPS video). This is achievable, but in practice not every frame is used for classification; 1 of every 3 frames (50 ms apart) would suffice. The hybrid approach shines here; the application would suffer a major performance penalty if each frame of a video had to be uploaded to a server, evaluated, and then returned. Even with a fantastic model performance—a model that evaluates in, say, 5 ms—you could experience an additional 100 ms lag due to the round-trip time required by an HTTP request.

Under the hybrid approach, the client does not need to ship the image to a server for evaluation but instead can evaluate the image immediately, based on the previously trained model now loaded into memory. A well-designed client will periodically check the server for updates to the model and update it when necessary, but will still allow outdated models to run offline. Users are happiest when applications *just work*, and the hybrid model gives you both performance and resilience. Servers are relied upon only for tasks that can happen asynchronously, such as downloading updated models or sending information back to the server.

The hybrid approach, therefore, is best for use cases where a large, sophisticated model is needed but the evaluation of the model either needs to happen very quickly or offline. This is not a hard-and-fast rule, of course. There are many other situations where a hybrid approach makes the most sense; if you have many clients and cannot afford the server resources to process all their evaluations, you might use the hybrid approach to offload your processing responsibilities.

Care must be taken when designing a client application that performs model training or evaluation. While evaluation is a lot faster than training, it is still nontrivial and may cause UI performance issues on the client if not implemented correctly. In the next section, we'll look at a modern web browser feature called **web workers** that can be used to perform processing in a standalone thread, keeping your UI responsive.

Web workers

If you're developing for a web browser application, you'll certainly want to use a web worker to manage the model in the background. Web workers are a browser-specific feature intended to allow background processing, which is exactly what we want when we're dealing with large models.

Web workers can interact with XMLHttpRequest, IndexedDB, and postMessage. A web worker can download a model from the server with XMLHttpRequest, store it locally with IndexedDB, and communicate with the UI thread with postMessage. These three tools, used together, provide a complete foundation for a responsive, performant, and potentially offline experience. Other JavaScript platforms, such as React Native, also have similar faculties for HTTP requests, data storage, and interprocess communication.

Web workers can be combined with other browser-specific features such as **service workers** and device APIs to provide a full offline experience. Service workers can cache specific assets for offline use or intelligently switch between online and offline evaluation. The browser extension platforms, as well as mobile platforms such as React Native, also provide a number of mechanisms for supporting cached data, background threads, and offline use.

Regardless of the platform, the concepts are the same: the application should download and upload data asynchronously when an internet connection is available; the application should cache (and version) everything it needs to function, like a pretrained model; and the application should evaluate the model independently of the UI.

It would be easy to mistakenly assume that a model is small and fast enough to run in the same thread as the UI. If your average evaluation time is only 5 ms and you only need one evaluation every 50 ms, it's tempting to become complacent and skip the additional detail of evaluating your model in a separate thread. However, the range of devices on the market today make it so you cannot even assume an order-of-magnitude similarity in performance. If you've tested your application on a modern phone with a GPU, for example, you may not be able to accurately assess how it will perform on an older phone's CPU. The evaluation time might jump from 5 ms to 100 ms. In a poorly designed application this will result in UI lag or freezing, but in a well-designed application, the UI will remain responsive but with less frequent updates.

Fortunately, web workers and the postMessage API are simple to use. The IndexedDB API is a low-level API and may be daunting to use initially, but there are many user-friendly libraries that abstract the details away. The specific manner in which you download and store the pretrained model is solely dependent on the implementation details of your application and the specific ML algorithm you've chosen. Smaller models can be serialized as JSON and stored in IndexedDB; more advanced models can be integrated directly into IndexedDB. Make sure to include a mechanism for comparing version information in your server-side API; you should have a way to ask the server what the current version of the model is and be able to compare that to your own copy so that you can invalidate and update the model.

Put some thought into the design of your web worker's message-passing API as well. You will use the `postMessage` API (available in all major browsers) for communication between the UI thread and the background thread. This communication should, at the very least, include some way to check on the status of the model and a way to send a data point to the model for evaluation. But you'll also want to look forward to future functionality and make your API flexible and future-proof.

Two examples of functionality you might want to plan for are continually improving models, that retrain themselves based on user feedback, and per-user models that learn the behaviors or preferences of individual users.

Continually improving and per-user models

Throughout the life cycle of your application, it's likely that the end user is going to interact with your model in some way. Often, this interaction can be used as feedback to further train the model. The interaction may also be used to customize the model to the user, tailoring it to their own interests and behaviors.

A good example of both concepts is the spam filter. A spam filter should continually improve as users mark messages as spam. Spam filters are most powerful when they have lots of data points to train against, and this data can come from other users of the application. Any time a user marks a message as spam, that knowledge should be applied to the model and other users should also be able to enjoy the automatic improvement in their own spam filtering.

Spam filters are also a good example of models that should be customizable per user. What I think is spam may not be the same as what you think is spam. I aggressively mark marketing emails and newsletters that I haven't signed up for as spam, but other users may want to see those types of messages in their own inbox. At the same time, there are messages that everyone agrees are spam, so it would be good to design our application to use a central, continually updating model that can be locally refined to better fit the behavior of the specific user.

Bayesian classifiers fit this description very well, as Bayes' theorem is designed to be updated by new information. In `Chapter 5`, *Classification Algorithms*, we discussed an implementation of the Naive Bayes classifier that handles rare words gracefully. In that scheme, a weight factor skewed word probabilities towards neutral so that rare words wouldn't influence the model too strongly. A per-user spam filter can use this same technique but instead of skewing words towards neutrality, we can skew them towards the central model's probability.

The rare word weight factor, in this usage, becomes a weight factor that balances the central model against the local model. The larger you make the weight factor, the more important the central model becomes and the longer it will take for the user to affect the local model. A smaller weight factor will be more responsive to user feedback, but may also cause irregularities in performance. In a typical rare word implementation the weight factor is in the range from 3 to 10. In a per-user model, however, the weight factor should be larger—perhaps 50 – 1,000—in consideration of the fact that the central model is trained by millions of examples and should not be easily overridden by just a handful of local examples.

Care must be taken when sending data back to the server for continual model improvements. You should not transmit the email message back to the server, as that would create an unnecessary security risk—*especially* if your product is not an email hosting provider but only an email client. If you are also the email hosting provider, then you can simply send the email ID back to the server to be marked as spam and given to the model for training; the client and the server will maintain their own models separately. If you are not the email hosting provider, then you should take extra care to secure your user's data. If you must transmit a token stream back to the server, then you should encrypt it in transit as well as anonymize it. You may also consider using a tokenizer that salts and hashes the tokens (for example, with sha1 or hmac) after tokenizing and stemming the content. The classifier will work just as well with hashed data as it does with readable data, but will add an additional layer of obfuscation. Finally, make sure that the HTTP request and raw token data is not logged. Once the data enters the model (in the form of token counts) it is sufficiently anonymized, but make sure there is no way a spy can relate a specific token stream to a specific user.

Naive Bayes classifiers are not the only models that can be continually updated or customized per user, of course. Continual updating of a model is possible with most ML algorithms. If a user indicates that an RNN got an image classification wrong, that user's data point can be added to the model's training set and the model can either be fully retrained at periodic intervals, or can be batch-updated with newer training examples.

Some algorithms support truly live updates of the model. The Naive Bayes classifier requires only an update to token and document counts, which might even be stored in memory. The knn and k-means algorithms similarly allow data points to be added to the model at any time. Some ANNs, like those used in reinforcement learning, also rely on live feedback.

Other algorithms are better updated periodically in batches. These algorithms typically rely on gradient descent or stochastic methods and require a feedback loop over many examples during training; examples are ANNs and random forests. An ANN model can indeed be retrained with a single data point, but batch training is far more effective. Be careful not to overfit models as you update them; too much training is not always a good thing.

In some cases, it is better to fully retrain a model based on the updated training set. One reason to do this is to avoid overfitting short-term trends in training data. By fully retraining a model, you ensure that recent training examples have the same weight as old training examples; this may or may not be desired. If models are periodically and automatically retrained, make sure that the training algorithm is looking at the right signals. It should be able to balance accuracy, loss, and variance in order to develop reliable models. As much of ML training is stochastic in nature, there is no guarantee that two training runs will finish to the same level of quality or in similar amounts of time. Your training algorithm should control for these factors and be able to discard bad models if necessary, for instance if a target accuracy or loss was not achieved within a maximum limit on the number of training epochs.

A new question arises at this point: how do you collect, store, and process gigabytes or terabytes of training data? How and where do you store and distribute serialized models to clients? How do you collect new training examples from millions of users? This topic is called data pipelining, which we'll discuss next.

Data pipelines

When developing a production ML system, it's not likely that you will have the training data handed to you in a ready-to-process format. Production ML systems are typically part of larger application systems, and the data that you use will probably originate from several different sources. The training set for an ML algorithm may be a subset of your larger database, combined with images hosted on a **Content Delivery Network** (**CDN**) and event data from an Elasticsearch server. In our examples, we have been given an isolated training set, but in the real world we will need to generate the training set in an automated and repeatable manner.

The process of ushering data through various stages of a life cycle is called **data pipelining**. Data pipelining may include data selectors that run SQL or Elasticsearch queries for objects, event subscriptions which allow data to flow in from event-or log-based data, aggregations, joins, combining data with data from third-party APIs, sanitization, normalization, and storage.

In an ideal implementation, the data pipeline acts as an abstraction layer between the larger application environment and the ML process. The ML algorithm should be able to read the output of the data pipeline without any knowledge of the original source of the data, similar to our examples. Under this approach, the ML algorithm will not need to understand the implementation details of the application; it is the pipeline itself that is responsible for knowing how the application is built.

As there are many possible data sources and infinite ways to architect an application, there is no one-size-fits-all data pipeline. However, most data pipelines will contain these components, which we will discuss in the following sections:

- Data querying and event subscription
- Data joining or aggregation
- Transformation and normalization
- Storage and delivery

Let's take a look at each of these concepts and introduce some tools and techniques that can achieve them.

Data querying

Imagine an application such as Disqus, which is an embeddable comment form that website owners can use to add comment functionality to blog posts or other pages. The primary functionality of Disqus is to allow users to like or leave comments on posts, however, as an additional feature and revenue stream, Disqus can make content recommendations and display them alongside sponsored content. The content recommendation system is an example of an ML system that is only one feature of a larger application.

A content recommendation system in an application such as Disqus does not necessarily need to interact with the comment data, but might use the user's likes history to generate recommendations similar to the current page. Such a system would also need to analyze the text content of the liked pages and compare that to the text content of all pages in the network in order to make recommendations. Disqus does not need the post's content in order to provide comment functionality, but does need to store metadata about the page (like its URL and title) in its database. The post content may therefore not reside in the application's main database, though the likes and page metadata would likely be stored there.

A data pipeline built around Disqus's recommendation system needs first to query the main database for pages the user has liked—or pages that were liked by users who liked the current page—and return their metadata. In order to find similar content, however, the system will need to use the text content of each liked post. This data might be stored in a separate system, perhaps a secondary database such as MongoDB or Elasticsearch, or in Amazon S3 or some other data warehouse. The pipeline will need to retrieve the text content based on the metadata returned by the main database, and associate the content with the metadata.

This is an example of multiple data selectors or data sources in the early stages of a data pipeline. One data source is the primary application data, which stores post and likes metadata. The other data source is a secondary server which stores the post's text content.

The next step in this pipeline might involve finding a number of candidate posts similar to the ones the user has liked, perhaps through a request to Elasticsearch or some other service that can find similar content. Similar content is not necessarily the correct content to serve, however, so these candidate articles will ultimately be ranked by an (hypothetical) ANN in order to determine the best content to display. In this example, the input to the data pipeline is the current page and the output from the data pipeline is a list of, say, 200 similar pages that the ANN will then rank.

If all the necessary data resides in the primary database, the entire pipeline can be achieved with an SQL statement and some JOINs. Even in this case, care should be taken to develop a degree of abstraction between the ML algorithm and the data pipeline, as you may decide to update the application's architecture in the future. In other cases, however, the data will reside in separate locations and a more considered pipeline should be developed.

There are many ways to build this data pipeline. You could develop a JavaScript module that performs all the pipeline tasks, and in some cases, you could even write a bash script using standard Unix tools to accomplish the task. On the other end of the complexity spectrum, there are purpose-built tools for data pipelining such as *Apache Kafka* and *AWS Pipeline*. These systems are designed modularly and allow you to define a specific data source, query, transformation, and aggregation modules as well as the workflows that connect them. In AWS Pipeline, for instance, you define *data nodes* that understand how to interact with the various data sources in your application.

The earliest stage of a pipeline is typically some sort of data query operation. Training examples must be extracted from a larger database, keeping in mind that not every record in a database is necessarily a training example. In the case of a spam filter, for instance, you should only select messages that have been marked as spam or not spam by a user. Messages that were automatically marked as spam by a spam filter should probably not be used for training, as that might cause a positive feedback loop that ultimately causes an unacceptable false positive rate.

Similarly, you may want to prevent users that have been blocked or banned by your system from influencing your model training. A bad actor could intentionally mislead an ML model by taking inappropriate actions on their own data, so you should disqualify these data points as training examples.

Alternatively, if your application is such that recent data points should take precedence over older training points, your data query operation might set a time-based limit on the data to use for training, or select a fixed limit ordered reverse chronologically. No matter the situation, make sure you carefully consider your data queries as they are an essential first step in your data pipeline.

Not all data needs to come from database queries, however. Many applications use a *pub/sub* or event subscription architecture to capture streaming data. This data could be activity logs aggregated from a number of servers, or live transaction data from a number of sources. In these cases, an event subscriber will be an early part of your data pipeline. Note that event subscription and data querying are not mutually exclusive operations. Events that come in through a pub/sub system can still be filtered based on various criteria; this is still a form of data querying.

One potential issue with an event subscription model arises when it's combined with a batch-training scheme. If you require 5,000 data points but receive only 100 per second, your pipeline will need to maintain a buffer of data points until the target size is reached. There are various message-queuing systems that can assist with this, such as RabbitMQ or Redis. A pipeline requiring this type of functionality might hold messages in a queue until the target of 5,000 messages is achieved, and only then release the messages for batch processing through the rest of the pipeline.

In the case that data is collected from multiple sources, it most likely will need to be joined or aggregated in some manner. Let's now take a look at a situation where data needs to be joined to data from an external API.

Data joining and aggregation

Let's return to our example of the Disqus content recommendation system. Imagine that the data pipeline is able to query likes and post metadata directly from the primary database, but that no system in the applications stores the post's text content. Instead, a microservice was developed in the form of an API that accepts a post ID or URL and returns the page's sanitized text content.

In this case, the data pipeline will need to interact with the microservice API in order to get the text content for each post. This approach is perfectly valid, though if the frequency of post content requests is high, some caching or storage should probably be implemented.

The data pipeline will need to employ an approach similar to the buffering of messages in the event subscription model. The pipeline can use a message queue to queue posts that still require content, and make requests to the content microservice for each post in the queue until the queue is depleted. As each post's content is retrieved it is added to the post metadata and stored in a separate queue for completed requests. Only when the source queue is depleted and the sink queue is full should the pipeline move on to the next step.

Data joining does not necessarily need to involve a microservice API. If the pipeline collects data from two separate sources that need to be combined, a similar approach can be employed. The pipeline is the only component that needs to understand the relationship between the two data sources and formats, leaving both the data sources and the ML algorithm to operate independently of those details.

The queue approach also works well when a data aggregation is required. An example of this situation is a pipeline in which the input is streaming input data and the output is token counts or value aggregations. Using a message queue is desirable in these situations as most message queues ensure that a message can be consumed only once, therefore preventing any duplication by the aggregator. This is especially valuable when the event stream is very high frequency, such that tokenizing each event as it comes in would lead to backups or server overload.

Because message queues ensure that each message is consumed only once, high-frequency event data can stream directly into a queue where messages are consumed by multiple workers in parallel. Each worker might be responsible for tokenizing the event data and then pushing the token stream to a different message queue. The message queue software ensures that no two workers process the same event, and each worker can operate as an independent unit that is only concerned with tokenization.

As the tokenizers push their results onto a new message queue, another worker can consume those messages and aggregate token counts, delivering its own results to the next step in the pipeline every second or minute or 1,000 events, whatever is appropriate for the application. The output of this style of pipeline might be fed into a continually updating Bayesian model, for example.

One benefit of a data pipeline designed in this manner is performance. If you were to attempt to subscribe to high-frequency event data, tokenize each message, aggregate token counts, and update a model all in one system, you might be forced to use a very powerful (and expensive) single server. The server would simultaneously need a high-performance CPU, lots of RAM, and a high-throughput network connection.

By breaking up the pipeline into stages, however, you can optimize each stage of the pipeline for its specific task and load condition. The message queue that receives the source event stream needs only to receive the event stream but does not need to process it. The tokenizer workers do not necessarily need to be high-performance servers, as they can be run in parallel. The aggregating queue and worker will process a large volume of data but will not need to retain data for longer than a few seconds and therefore may not need much RAM. The final model, which is a compressed version of the source data, can be stored on a more modest machine. Many components of the data pipeline can be built of commodity hardware simply because a data pipeline encourages modular design.

In many cases, you will need to transform your data from format to format throughout the pipeline. That could mean converting from native data structures to JSON, transposing or interpolating values, or hashing values. Let's now discuss several types of data transformations that may occur in the data pipeline.

Transformation and normalization

As your data makes its way through a pipeline, it may need to be converted into a structure compatible with your algorithm's input layer. There are many possible transformations that can be performed on the data in the pipeline. For example, in order to protect sensitive user data before it reaches a token-based classifier, you might apply a cryptographic hashing function to the tokens so that they are no longer human readable.

More typically, the types of transformations will be related to sanitization, normalization, or transposition. A sanitization operation might involve removing unnecessary whitespace or HTML tags, removing email addresses from a token stream, and removing unnecessary fields from the data structure. If your pipeline has subscribed to an event stream as the source of the data and the event stream attaches source server IP addresses to event data, it would be a good idea to remove these values from the data structure, both in order to save space and to minimize the surface area for potential data leaks.

Similarly, if email addresses are not necessary for your classification algorithm, the pipeline should remove that data so that it interacts with the fewest possible servers and systems. If you've designed a spam filter, you may want to look into using only the domain portion of the email address instead of the fully qualified address. Alternately, the email addresses or domains may be hashed by the pipeline so that the classifier can still recognize them but a human cannot.

Make sure to audit your data for other potential security and privacy issues as well. If your application collects the end user's IP address as part of its event stream, but the classifier does not need that data, remove it from the pipeline as early as possible. These considerations are becoming ever more important with the implementation of new European privacy laws, and every developer should be aware of privacy and compliance concerns.

A common category of data transformation is normalization. When working with a range of numerical values for a given field or feature, it's often desirable to normalize the range such that it has a known minimum and maximum bound. One approach is to normalize all values of the same field to the range [0,1], using the maximum encountered value as the divisor (for example, the sequence *1, 2, 4* can be normalized to *0.25, 0.5, 1*). Whether data needs to be normalized in this manner will depend entirely on the algorithm that consumes the data.

Another approach to normalization is to convert values into percentiles. In this scheme, very large outlying values will not skew the algorithm too drastically. If most values lie between 0 and 100 but a few points include values such as 50,000, an algorithm may give outsized precedence to the large values. If the data is normalized as a percentile, however, you are guaranteed to not have any values exceeding 100 and the outliers are brought into the same range as the rest of the data. Whether or not this is a good thing depends on the algorithm.

The data pipeline is also a good place to calculate derived or second-order features. Imagine a random forest classifier that uses Instagram profile data to determine if the profile belongs to a human or a bot. The Instagram profile data will include fields such as the user's followers count, friends count, posts count, website, bio, and username. A random forest classifier will have difficulty using those fields in their original representations, however, by applying some simple data transformations, you can achieve accuracies of 90%.

In the Instagram case, one type of helpful data transformation is calculating ratios. Followers count and friends count, as separate features or signals, may not be useful to the classifier since they are treated somewhat independently. But the friends-to-followers *ratio* can turn out to be a very strong signal that may expose bot users. An Instagram user with 1,000 friends doesn't raise any flags, nor would an Instagram user with 50 followers; treated independently, these features are not strong signals. However, an Instagram user with a friends-to-followers ratio of 20 (or 1,000/50) is almost certainly a bot designed to follow other users. Similarly, a ratio such as posts-versus-followers or posts-versus-friends may end up being a stronger signal than any of those features independently.

Text content such as the Instagram user's profile bio, website, or username is made useful by deriving second-order features from them as well. A classifier may not be able to do anything with a website's URL, but perhaps a Boolean *has_profile_website* feature can be used as a signal instead. If, in your research, you notice that usernames of bots tend to have a lot of numbers in them, you can derive features from the username itself. One feature can calculate the ratio of letters to numbers in the username, another Boolean feature can represent whether the username has a number at the end or beginning, and a more advanced feature could determine if dictionary words were used in the username or not (therefore distinguishing between `@themachinelearningwriter` and something gibberish like `@panatoe234`).

Derived features can be of any level of sophistication or simplicity. Another simple feature could be whether the Instagram profile contains a URL in the profile bio field (as opposed to the dedicated website field); this can be detected with a regex and the Boolean value used as the feature. A more advanced feature could automatically detect whether the language used in the user's content is the same as the language specified by the user's locale setting. If the user claims they're in France but always writes captions in Russian it may indeed be a Russian living in France, but when combined with other signals like a friends-to-followers ratio far from 1, this information may be indicative of a bot user.

There are lower level transformations that may need to be applied to the data in the pipeline as well. If the source data is in an XML format but the classifier requires JSON formatting, the pipeline should take responsibility for the parsing and conversion of formats.

Other mathematical transformations may also be applied. If the native format of the data is row-oriented but the classifier needs column-oriented data, the pipeline can perform a vector transposition operation as part of the processing.

Similarly, the pipeline can use mathematical interpolation to fill in missing values. If your pipeline subscribes to events emitted by a suite of sensors in a laboratory setting and a single sensor goes offline for a couple of measurements, it may be reasonable to interpolate between the two known values in order to fill in the missing data. In other cases, missing values can be replaced with the population's mean or median value. Replacing missing values with a mean or median will often result in the classifier deprioritizing that feature for that data point, as opposed to breaking the classifier by giving it a null value.

In general, there are two things to consider in terms of transformation and normalization within a data pipeline. The first is the mechanical details of the source data and the target format: XML data must be transformed to JSON, rows must be converted to columns, images must be converted from JPEG to BMP formats, and so on. The mechanical details are not too tricky to work out, as you will already be aware of the source and target formats required by the system.

The other consideration is the semantic or mathematical transformation of your data. This is an exercise in feature selection and feature engineering, and is not as straightforward as the mechanical transformation. Determining which second-order features to derive is both art and science. The art is coming up with new ideas for derived features, and the science is to rigorously test and experiment with your work. In my experience with Instagram bot detection, for instance, I found that the letters-to-numbers ratio in Instagram usernames was a very weak signal. I abandoned that idea after some experimentation in order to avoid adding unnecessary dimensionality to the problem.

At this point, we have a hypothetical data pipeline that collects data, joins and aggregates it, processes it, and normalizes it. We're almost done, but the data still needs to be delivered to the algorithm itself. Once the algorithm is trained, we might also want to serialize the model and store it for later use. In the next section, we'll discuss a few considerations to make when transporting and storing training data or serialized models.

Storing and delivering data

Once your data pipeline has applied all the necessary processing and transformations, it has one task left to do: deliver the data to your algorithm. Ideally, the algorithm will not need to know about the implementation details of the data pipeline. The algorithm should have a single location that it can interact with in order to get the fully processed data. This location could be a file on disk, a message queue, a service such as Amazon S3, a database, or an API endpoint. The approach you choose will depend on the resources available to you, the topology or architecture of your server system, and the format and size of the data.

Models that are trained only periodically are typically the simplest case to handle. If you're developing an image recognition RNN that learns labels for a number of images and only needs to be retrained every few months, a good approach would be to store all the images as well as a manifest file (relating image names to labels) in a service such as Amazon S3 or a dedicated path on disk. The algorithm would first load and parse the manifest file and then load the images from the storage service as needed.

Similarly, an Instagram bot detection algorithm may only need to be retrained every week or every month. The algorithm can read training data directly from a database table or a JSON or CSV file stored on S3 or a local disk.

It is rare to have to do this, but in some exotic data pipeline implementations you could also provide the algorithm with a dedicated API endpoint built as a microservice; the algorithm would simply query the API endpoint first for a list of training point references, and then request each in turn from the API.

Models which require online updates or near-real-time updates, on the other hand, are best served by a message queue. If a Bayesian classifier requires live updates, the algorithm can subscribe to a message queue and apply updates as they come in. Even when using a sophisticated multistage pipeline, it is possible to process new data and update a model in fractions of a second if you've designed all the components well.

Returning to the spam filter example, we can design a highly performant data pipeline like so: first, an API endpoint receives feedback from a user. In order to keep the user interface responsive, this API endpoint is responsible only for placing the user's feedback into a message queue and can finish its task in under a millisecond. The data pipeline in turn subscribes to the message queue, and in another few milliseconds is made aware of a new message. The pipeline then applies a few simple transformations to the message, like tokenizing, stemming, and potentially even hashing the tokens.

The next stage of the pipeline transforms the token stream into a hashmap of tokens and their counts (for example, from *hey hey there* to *{hey: 2, there: 1}*); this avoids the need for the classifier to update the same token's count more than once. This stage of processing will only require another couple of milliseconds at worst. Finally, the fully processed data is placed in a separate message queue which the classifier subscribes to. Once the classifier is made aware of the data it can immediately apply the updates to the model. If the classifier is backed by Redis, for instance, this final stage will also require only a few milliseconds.

The entire process we have described, from the time the user's feedback reaches the API server to the time the model is updated, may only require 20 ms. Considering that communication over the internet (or any other means) is limited by the speed of light, the best-case scenario for a TCP packet making a round-trip between New York and San Francisco is 40 ms; in practice, the average cross-country latency for a good internet connection is about 80 ms. Our data pipeline and model is therefore capable of updating itself based on user feedback a full 20 ms before the user will even receive their HTTP response.

Not every application requires real-time processing. Managing separate servers for an API, a data pipeline, message queues, a Redis store, and hosting the classifier might be overkill both in terms of effort and budget. You'll have to determine what's best for your use case.

The last thing to consider is not related to the data pipeline but rather the storage and delivery of the model itself, in the case of a hybrid approach where a model is trained on the server but evaluated on the client. The first question to ask yourself is whether the model is considered public or private. Private models should not be stored on a public Amazon S3 bucket, for instance; instead, the S3 bucket should have access control rules in place and your application will need to procure a signed download link with an expiration time (the S3 API assists with this).

The next consideration is how large the model is and how often it will be downloaded by clients. If a public model is downloaded frequently but updated infrequently, it might be best to use a CDN in order to take advantage of edge caching. If your model is stored on Amazon S3, for example, then the Amazon CloudFront CDN would be a good choice.

Of course, you can always build your own storage and delivery solution. In this chapter, I have assumed a cloud architecture, however if you have a single dedicated or collocated server then you may simply want to store the serialized model on disk and serve it either through your web server software or through your application's API. When dealing with large models, make sure to consider what will happen if many users attempt to download the model simultaneously. You may inadvertently saturate your server's network connection if too many people request the file at once, you might overrun any bandwidth limits set by your server's ISP, or you might end up with your server's CPU stuck in I/O wait while it moves data around.

As mentioned previously, there's no one-size-fits-all solution for data pipelining. If you're a hobbyist developing applications for fun or just a few users, you have lots of options for data storage and delivery. If you're working in a professional capacity on a large enterprise project, however, you will have to consider all aspects of the data pipeline and how they will impact your application's performance.

I will offer one final piece of advice to the hobbyists reading this section. While it's true that you don't need a sophisticated, real-time data pipeline for hobby projects, you should build one anyway. Being able to design and build real-time data pipelines is a highly marketable and valuable skill that not many people possess, and if you're willing to put in the practice to learn ML algorithms then you should also practice building performant data pipelines. I'm not saying that you should build a big, fancy data pipeline for every single hobby project—just that you should do it a few times, using several different approaches, until you're comfortable not just with the concepts but also the implementation. Practice makes perfect, and practice means getting your hands dirty.

Summary

In this chapter, we discussed a number of practical matters related to ML applications in production. Learning ML algorithms is, of course, central to building an ML application, but there's much more to building an application than simply implementing an algorithm. Applications ultimately need to interact with users across a variety of devices, so it is not enough to consider only what your application does — you must also plan for how and where it will be used.

We began the chapter with a discussion about serializable and portable models, and you learned about the different architectural approaches to the training and evaluation of models. We discussed the fully server-side approach (common with SaaS products), the fully client-side approach (useful for sensitive data), and a hybrid approach by which a model is trained on the server but evaluated on the client. You also learned about web workers, which are a useful browser-specific feature that you can use to ensure a performant and responsive UI when evaluating models on the client.

We also discussed models which continually update or get periodically retrained, and various approaches to communicating feedback between the client and the server. You also learned about per-user models, or algorithms which can be trained by a central source of truth but refined by an individual user's specific behaviors.

Finally, you learned about data pipelines and various mechanisms that manage the collection, combining, transformation, and delivery of data from one system to the next. A central theme in our data pipeline discussion was the concept of using the data pipeline as a layer of abstraction between ML algorithms and the rest of your production systems.

The final topic I'd like to discuss is one that many ML students are curious about: how exactly do you choose the right ML algorithm for a given problem? Experts in ML typically develop an intuition that guides their decisions, but that intuition can take years to form. In the next chapter, we'll discuss practical techniques you can use to narrow in on the appropriate ML algorithm to use for any given problem.

12
Choosing the Best Algorithm for Your Application

There are three distinct phases in the software-engineering process: conception, implementation, and deployment. This book has primarily focused on the implementation phase of the process, which is when a software engineer develops the core functionality (that is, a **machine learning (ML)** algorithm) and features of the project. In the last chapter, we discussed matters concerning the deployment phase. Our learning is nearly complete.

In this final chapter, we'll turn to the conception phase in order to round out our understanding of the full ML development process. Specifically, we'll discuss how to choose the best algorithm for a given problem. The ML ecosystem is evolving, intimidating, and full of jargon unfamiliar even to experienced software developers. I often see students of ML get stuck at the beginning of the process, not knowing where to start in a vast and unfamiliar landscape. What they don't know yet is that once you get past the initial hurdle of choosing an algorithm and decrypting the jargon, the rest of the journey is much easier.

The goal of this chapter is to provide a compass, a simple guide one can use to find a way around the landscape. It's not always easy to select the right algorithm, but sometimes it is. The first sections of this chapter will teach you four simple decision points—essentially four multiple-choice questions—that you can use to focus in on the most suitable algorithms for your project. Most of the time, you'll end up with only one or two algorithms to choose from after going through this process.

We'll then continue our education by discussing other topics related to planning an ML system. We'll discuss the telltale signs that you've chosen the wrong algorithm so that you can identify mistakes early on. You'll also learn how to tell the difference between using the wrong algorithm versus a bad implementation of one.

I'll also show you an example of combining two different ML models, so that you can compose larger systems out of individual models that are best suited to their own tasks. This approach can yield great results if designed carefully.

I called this chapter a compass—not a map—for a reason. It is not a comprehensive guide that covers every ML algorithm known to computer scientists. As with a compass, you must also use your guile and skills to find your way. Use this chapter to find your own project's starting point, and then follow up with your own research. While the 20 or so algorithms and techniques we've discussed in this book give you a pretty wide view of the landscape, they're only a fraction of the ecosystem.

As we come to the beginning of the end of this book, I'd like to give you one final piece of advice. To become an expert at something requires a consistent dedication to *both* practice and play. If you want to become a world-class pianist, you must spend countless hours doing meticulous rote practice with a metronome, practicing fingering exercises and learning challenging *études*.

But you also have to *play*, which is where exploration happens and creativity is developed. After thirty minutes of running drills, a pianist might spend thirty minutes improvising jazz and experimenting with melody and counterpoint, learning the *je ne sais quoi* or the emotive essence of the scales and patterns in the music. That playful exploration, the experimentation involved in creativity, develops the intuitive sense of music in a way that rote practice does not. Rote practice—meticulous work and study—in turn develops the mechanical sense and skill that play cannot. Practice and play elevate each other in a virtuous cycle. The skilled are able to explore farther and deeper than the unskilled, and the excitement of what lies even deeper still is what motivates the practice that develops the skill. Time and patience, practice and play, motivation and discipline are the only things you need to go from being a novice to an expert.

ML is the opposite of jazz piano, but the path to expertise is the same. The rote practice of ML—the equivalent of practicing scales—is building and implementing algorithms. I particularly recommend writing algorithms from scratch as practice; that's the only true way to understand what's really going on inside. Don't just write an algorithm from scratch once to prove to yourself that you can. Write the algorithm several times, in different environments, different programming languages, different architectures, with different datasets, and keep doing that until you can write nearly the whole thing off the top of your head. I'm fairly certain I can write a Naive Bayes classifier blindfolded in any of three programming languages, just as you would be able to after you've written dozens of them.

The play of ML lies in experimentation. This chapter is about choosing the best algorithm for your application, but it isn't rule of law. If you never experiment you'll never develop a rich intuition for the algorithms or data. Experiment with other approaches, parameters, or variations on algorithms and learn from the experimentation. You'll be surprised at how often an experiment can end up successful, but more importantly than that, experimentation should be part of your practice and education.

Let's kick the chapter off by discussing the four major decision points you can use to hone your skills on an algorithm:

- Mode of learning
- The task at hand
- The format or form of the data
- Available resources

Also we'll discuss what to do when it all goes wrong, and finally we'll discuss combining multiple models together.

Mode of learning

The first decision point to visit when choosing an ML algorithm is the mode of the learning process: supervised, unsupervised, or reinforcement learning. These modes have very little overlap; in general an algorithm is either supervised or unsupervised but not both. This narrows your choices down by roughly half, and fortunately it is very easy to tell which mode of learning applies to your problem.

The difference between supervised and unsupervised learning is marked by whether or not you need labeled training examples to teach the algorithm. If all you have is data points, and not labels or categories to associate them with, then you are only able to perform unsupervised learning. You must therefore choose one of the unsupervised learning algorithms, such as k-means clustering, regressions, **Principal Component Analysis (PCA)**, or singular value decomposition.

Another telltale difference between supervised and unsupervised learning is whether or not there is a way to judge semantic accuracy. If the concept of judging accuracy doesn't make sense in your application (because you don't have labeled training or reference data), then you are facing an unsupervised learning problem.

In some cases, however, you will not have training data but the problem is best solved by a supervised learning problem. It's important to recognize the difference between having training data and *needing* training data. When you need training data, you are likely looking at a supervised learning problem. If you need training data but don't have it, you'll have to figure out some way to get the training data.

The simplest way to generate training data for a problem is to generate it yourself. In an image classification task you can simply label a few hundred images by hand to generate your training data. This is time consuming but will work for small training sets.

A more scalable approach is to use a service like Amazon Mechanical Turk, through which you pay human workers $0.05-$0.10 to label each image. The Mechanical Turk approach has become very popular with ML researchers and data scientists, as it is a fast and scalable way to generate a large volume of training data at a reasonable cost. Generating labels for 5,000 images might cost $250 and take a day or two on Mechanical Turk. If you think $250 is expensive, consider the cost of the time it would take for you to label those 5,000 images personally.

There are more clever ways to generate training data, such as shifting the responsibility to your application's users. Years ago, when Facebook first introduced the ability to tag people in photos, they required the photo's uploader to draw a box around each subject's face and tag them. After billions of photo uploads, Facebook has a huge training set that not just identifies facial forms but also specific people in photos. Nowadays, there is no need to draw boxes around peoples' faces when tagging photos, and typically Facebook is able to figure out who each subject in the photo is automatically. We, the users, provided them with this massive training set.

Supervised learning is made apparent by the act of training an algorithm on prelabeled data, with the goal of algorithm learning from the labels, and by being able to extend that knowledge and apply it to new, unseen examples. If you find yourself in a situation where you have a lot of data points and some, but not all, have the correct answers or labels available, you likely want a supervised learning algorithm. If you have a million emails, 5,000 of which were manually filtered as spam or not spam, and if the goal is to extend that knowledge to the other 995,000 messages, you're looking for a supervised learning algorithm.

If you have a situation where you need to judge the semantic accuracy of the algorithm, you must also use a supervised learning algorithm. An unsupervised algorithm has no source of truth; those algorithms will cluster or smooth or extrapolate data, but without a canonical reference, there is no way to judge the algorithm's accuracy. A supervised learning algorithm, on the other hand, can be judged in terms of semantic accuracy as the prelabeled training data serves as the source of truth.

While we haven't covered reinforcement learning algorithms in this book, they are marked by situations where the algorithm must affect its environment in an attempt to optimize behavior. There is a degree of separation between the algorithm's output and the results of the action, since the environment itself is a factor. An example of reinforcement learning is teaching an AI to play a video game by scanning the screen and using mouse and keyboard controls. An AI playing *Super Mario Bros.* can only interact with the environment by hitting combinations of up, down, left, right, A, and B on the control pad. The algorithm's output takes an action in the environment, and the environment will either reward or punish those actions. The algorithm therefore tries to maximize its reward, for instance by collecting coins, making progress through the level, defeating enemies, and not falling into bottomless pits.

Reinforcement learning algorithms are a major topic in applied robotics, control system design, simulation-based optimization, hardware-in-the-loop simulation, and many other fields that blend the physical world with the algorithmic world. Reinforcement learning is most effective when the system you're studying—the environment—is a sophisticated black box that cannot be directly modeled. Reinforcement learning is used, for instance, to optimize control strategies for systems that will be used in arbitrary environments, such as a robot that must autonomously navigate unknown terrain.

Finally, there are tasks that require only the optimization of a system whose model is either known or directly observable. These are only tangentially considered ML problems, and are more appropriately called **optimization problems**. If you must choose the best driving route from Point A to Point B based on current traffic conditions, you can use a genetic algorithm, for instance. If you must optimize a small number of parameters that configure a different model, you might try a grid search. If you must determine the boundary conditions of a complex system, Monte Carlo methods might be able to help. If you must find the global optimum of a continuous system, then stochastic gradient descent might serve your purpose.

Optimization algorithms are often used to solve problems with ML algorithms. Indeed, the backpropagation algorithm used to train ANNs uses gradient descent as its optimizer. The parameters given to k-means or other unsupervised algorithms can be tuned automatically through grid search in order to minimize variance. We have not discussed optimization algorithms in-depth in this book, but you should be aware of them and their use cases.

When choosing an algorithm for your application, start with the simplest question: Do I need supervised or unsupervised learning? Determine whether you have or can generate training data; if you cannot, you are forced to use unsupervised algorithms. Ask yourself whether you need to judge the accuracy of the algorithm's output (supervised learning), or whether you are simply exploring data (unsupervised).

After you've identified the mode of learning, which will cut your available choices roughly in half, you can further hone in on the algorithm you need by thinking about the specific task at hand, or the goal of your research.

The task at hand

The most effective way to partition the world of ML algorithms is to consider the task at hand, or the desired results and purpose of the algorithm. If you can identify the goal of your problem—that is, whether you need to predict continuous values based on inputs, categorize data, classify text, reduce dimensionality, and so on—you'll be able to reduce your choices to only a handful of algorithms.

For example, in cases where you need to predict a continuous output value—such as a prediction for server load at a future date—you will likely need a regression algorithm. There are only a handful of regression algorithms to choose from, and the other decision points in this guide will help to reduce those options further.

In cases where you need to inspect data and identify data points that look similar to one another, a clustering algorithm would be the most appropriate. The specific clustering algorithm you choose will depend on the other decision points, such as the format or form of the data, the linearity or nonlinearity of the relationships, and the resources available to you (time, processing power, memory, and so on).

If the purpose of your algorithm is to categorize a data point with one of a dozen possible labels, you must choose from one of a handful of classification algorithms. Again, selecting the correct algorithm from the family of classification algorithms available to you will depend on the form of the data, your requirements for accuracy and any resource limitations imposed upon you.

One common issue novice researchers face at this stage is a lack of clarity of the actual goal of the project versus the capabilities of individual algorithms. Sometimes, the business goal of a problem is abstract and only partially defined. It is often the case in those situations that the business goal is only achievable through the use of several individual algorithms. A student of ML may have difficulty identifying the concrete technical steps that must be composed in order to achieve the goal.

An illustrative example is the business goal of writing an application that analyzes an image and returns a natural language description of the image's contents. For instance, when uploading a picture of a path through a park, the goal might be to return the text *a park bench and trash pail on a path with trees in the background*. It would be easy to fixate on the singular business goal of the project and assume that a single business goal maps to a single algorithm.

However, this example requires at least two or three ML algorithms. First, a **Convolutional Neural Network (CNN)** must be able to identify objects in an image. Another algorithm must then be able to determine the spatial relationships between the objects. Finally, an NLP or ML algorithm must be able to take the output of the first two algorithms and compose a natural language representation from that information.

The ability to understand a business goal and translate it into concrete technical steps takes time and experience to develop. You must be able to parse the business goal and work backwards in order to decompose it into individual subtasks. Once you've identified the subtasks, determining which algorithm best fits each subtask becomes a straightforward exercise in this decision-making process. We'll discuss the topic of composing algorithms shortly, but for now the important take-away is that some business goals will require multiple ML algorithms.

In some cases, the task at hand will narrow your choices down to just a single algorithm. Object detection in images, for instance, is best achieved by a CNN. There are, of course, many different specialized subtypes of CNNs that can perform object detection (RCNN, Fast RCNN, Mask RCNN, and so on), but in this case we are able to narrow the playing field down to just CNNs.

In other cases, the task at hand can be achieved with several or many algorithms, in which case you must use additional decision points in order to choose the best one for your application. Sentiment analysis, for instance, can be achieved with many algorithms. Naive Bayes classifiers, maximum entropy models, random forests, and ANNs (particularly RNNs) can all solve the sentiment analysis problem.

You may also be required to compose multiple algorithms in order to achieve the best accuracy for your sentiment analyzer. Therefore, the decision of which approach to use will depend not only on the task at hand, but also the form and format of the data used by the other algorithms in your composition. Not every algorithm is compatible for use in composition with all other algorithms, so the form and format decision point is effectively recursive, and you will need to apply it to each of the subtasks that you have identified in pursuit of your business goal.

Format, form, input, and output

What I've been describing as the format and form of data encapsulates several concepts. Most superficially, the *format* of the data relates to the specific data types (for example, integers, continuous numbers/floats, text, and discrete categories) of both the input and output of the application. The *form* of the data encapsulates the relationships between the data structures and the overall shape of the problem or solution space. These factors can help you select the appropriate algorithm even when the task at hand has given you several choices for an algorithm.

When dealing with text (the format), for instance, you must consider how the text is treated in terms of its relationship to the problem space and the task at hand; I call this the form of the data. When filtering spam it is generally not necessary to map the relationships between individual words. When analyzing text for sentiment it may indeed be necessary to map some relationships between words (for example, to deal with negations or other language modifiers), and this will require an additional level of dimensionality. When parsing text in order to build a knowledge graph you will need to map the relationships between not only the individual words but their conceptual meanings meticulously, requiring an even higher level of dimensionality.

In these examples, the format of the data is the same—all three examples deal with text—but the form is different. The shape of the problem space is different. The spam filter has a simpler problem space with lower dimensionality and linearly separable relationships; each word is treated independently. The sentiment analyzer has a different form, requiring some additional dimensionality in the problem space in order to encode the relationships between some words, but not necessarily all relationships between all words. The knowledge graph problem requires a highly dimensional space into which the complex semantic and spacial relationships between words must be mapped.

In these text analysis cases, you can often ask yourself a series of simple questions that helps you narrow in on the correct algorithm: can each word be treated independently? Do we need to consider words being modified by other words (*like* versus *not like*, or *good* versus *very good*)? Do we need to maintain relationships between words separated by large distances (for example, a Wikipedia article that introduces a subject in the first paragraph but continues to refer to the subject many paragraphs later)?

Each relationship you keep track of adds a level of dimensionality to the problem space, so you must choose an algorithm that can work effectively in the dimensionality of the problem. Using a low-dimensionality algorithm such as naive Bayes on a high-dimensional problem such as a knowledge graph problem would not yield good results; this is akin to a person who lives their whole life in three dimensions trying to visualize the ten-dimensional space of superstring theory in physics.

Conversely, a highly dimensional algorithm such as a **Long Short-Term Memory (LSTM)** RNN can solve low-dimensional problems such as spam filtering, but it comes with a cost: the time and resources required to train a highly dimensional algorithm. They are incongruous with the difficulty of the problem. A Bayesian classifier can be trained on millions of documents in dozens of seconds, but an LSTM RNN might require hours of training for the same task and be slower to evaluate a data point by an order of magnitude. Even then, there is no guarantee that the LSTM RNN will outperform the Bayesian classifier in terms of accuracy.

You must also consider the form and dimensionality when working with numerical data. Compared to statistical analysis, time-series analysis requires an additional dimension in order to capture the ordinality of the data in addition to the value of the data. This is analogous to the difference between a bag-of-words text algorithm such as Naive Bayes versus one that preserves sequential ordering of text such as an LSTM RNN.

Finally, the structural format of the data might be a consideration, though formats can often be successfully converted into more amenable formats. In `Chapter 10`, *Natural Language Processing in Practice*, we discussed the Word2vec word-embedding algorithm which converts text into numerical vectors so that they can be used as the inputs to a neural network (which requires numerical inputs). Format conversion actually makes our decision-making process more difficult, as it allows us to choose from a wider array of algorithms. Using Word2vec means that we can use text as an input to algorithms that don't normally accept text, therefore giving us many more options to choose from.

Another common format conversion is the quantization or bucketing of continuous numerical values. For instance, a continuous numerical value ranging from 0–10 could be quantized into three buckets: small, medium, and large. This conversion allows us to use our continuous-value data in algorithms that only deal with discrete values or categories.

You should also consider the form and format of the output that you require from an algorithm. In a classification task the nominal output of the classifier will be a discrete label that describes the input. But not all classifiers are created equally. A decision tree classifier will yield one label as its output, whereas a Bayesian classifier will yield the probabilities of all possible labels as its output. In both cases the nominal output is a probable label, but the Bayesian classifier also returns the confidence of its guess along with a probability distribution over all possible guesses. In some tasks, the only thing you need from the algorithm is a single label; in other cases, the probability distribution is useful or even required.

The form of the output of an algorithm is closely related to the mathematical mechanism of the model. This means that, even without a deep understanding of the algorithm itself, you can evaluate the mathematical properties of a model by looking at the form of its output. If a classifier returns probabilities as part of its output, it is likely a probabilistic classifier that can be used for tasks where you suspect a nondeterministic approach would be more effective than a deterministic one.

Similarly, if an algorithm returns semantically ordered output (as opposed to unordered output), that's a clue that the algorithm itself models and remembers some form of ordering. Even if your application doesn't directly require ordered output, you might still choose this algorithm because you recognize that the form of your data contains information embedded in the ordinality of the data. If you know, on the other hand, that the ordinality of your data contains no relevant information, then an algorithm which returns ordered output (and therefore models ordinality as a dimension) may be overkill.

If you still have a few algorithms to choose from at this point, the last step to honing in on the best algorithm will be to consider the resources available to you and balance them against your requirements for accuracy and speed.

Available resources

It is often the case that there is no clear winner discernible from an array of algorithm options. In a sentiment analysis problem, for instance, there are several possible approaches and it is not often clear which to take. You can choose from a Naive Bayes classifier with embedded negations, a Naive Bayes classifier using bigrams, an LSTM RNN, a maximum entropy model, and several other techniques.

If the format and form decision point doesn't help you here—for instance, if you have no requirement for a probabilistic classifier—you can make your decision based on your available resources and performance targets. A Bayesian classifier is lightweight with quick training times, very fast evaluation times, a small memory footprint and comparatively small storage and CPU requirements.

An LSTM RNN, on the other hand, is a sophisticated model that takes a long time to train, a moderate amount of evaluation time, significant CPU/GPU requirements, especially during training, and steeper memory and storage requirements than the Bayesian classifier.

If no other factor gives you clear guidance on how to choose an algorithm, you can make your decision based on the resources available (CPU, GPU, memory, storage, or time) to you or your application's user. In this case, there is almost always a trade-off; more sophisticated models are typically more accurate than simple ones. This is not always true, of course, as naive Bayes classifiers consistently outperform other approaches to spam filtering; but this is because of the form and dimensionality of the spam detection problem space.

In some cases, the limiting factor for your application will be training or evaluation time. An application that requires evaluations in 1 ms or less may not be an appropriate use case for an ANN, whereas an application that tolerates 50 ms evaluations is much more flexible.

In other cases, the limiting factor or the resource available is the required accuracy of the algorithm. If you consider incorrect predictions to be a form of resource consumption, you may be able to determine a lower bound on the required accuracy of an algorithm. The world of ML is not too different from the world of high-performance sports, in that the difference between the gold medal and the bronze may only be a matter of a fraction of a second.

The same applies to ML algorithms: a state-of-the-art algorithm for a particular problem might have an accuracy of 94%, while a more commonplace algorithm might yield 90% accuracy. If the cost of an incorrect prediction is sufficiently high, that difference of four percentage points might be the deciding factor in which algorithm you choose and how much time and energy you invest in the problem. If, on the other hand, the cost of an incorrect prediction is low, the more common algorithm might be your best choice based on the resources, time, and effort required to implement it.

If you carefully consider these four decision points—the mode of learning, the task at hand, the format and form of the data, and the resources available to you—you will often find that the best algorithm to choose stands out clearly. This will not always be the case; sometimes you will be forced to make a judgment call based on the algorithms and processes you're most comfortable with.

Sometimes, after choosing an algorithm, you will find that your results are unacceptable. It can be tempting to throw out your algorithm immediately and choose a new one, but use caution here as it's often difficult to tell the difference between a bad choice of algorithm and a bad configuration of an algorithm. You must therefore be prepared to debug your system when it all goes wrong.

When it goes wrong

There is a wide range of possible undesirable outcomes in ML. These can range from models that simply don't work to models that do work but use an unnecessary amount of resources in the process. Negative outcomes can be caused by many factors, such as the selection of an inappropriate algorithm, poor feature engineering, improper training techniques, insufficient preprocessing, or misinterpretation of results.

In the best-case scenario—that is, the best-case scenario of a negative outcome—the problem will make itself apparent in the early stages of your implementation. You may find during the training and validation stage that your ANN never achieves an accuracy greater than 50%. In some cases, an ANN will quickly stabilize at a value like 25% accuracy after only a few training epochs and never improve.

Problems that make themselves obvious during training in this manner are the easiest to debug. In general, these are indications that you've selected the wrong algorithm for your problem. In the case of ANNs, which are rarely the *wrong* choice because they are so flexible, this type of plateau can indicate that you've designed the wrong network topology (too few layers or too few hidden neurons) or selected the wrong activation functions for your layers (for example, using tanh when sigmoid is more appropriate). In this case, you have made a reasonable decision to use an ANN, but have configured it incorrectly.

Sometimes the problem is more difficult to debug, particularly when you have not written the algorithm from first principles. In `Chapter 5`, *Classification Algorithms*, I introduced you to the random forest classifier and we found that its accuracy was unacceptably low for our example problem. Was the decision to use a random forest simply a poor decision? Or was it a reasonable decision that was hindered by the incorrect selection of parameters? In that case, the answer was **neither**. I was confident of my choice of using a random forest as well as my parameter selection, so I ran the same data and parameters through a random forest library in a different programming language and got results more in line with my expectations. This pointed to a third likely possibility: there must be something wrong with the specific implementation of the random forest algorithm in the library that I chose to demonstrate.

Unfortunately, without the confidence that experience brings, it would be easy to assume that random forest was simply a poor choice of algorithm for that problem. This is why I encourage both practice and play, theory and experimentation. Without a thorough understanding of the concepts that underlie random forests I may have been tricked into believing that the algorithm itself was to blame, and without a tendency to experiment I may never have confirmed that the algorithm and parameters were indeed appropriate.

When things go wrong, my advice is to return to first principles. Go back to the very beginning of your engineering design process, and consider each step in turn. Is the selection of the algorithm appropriate? Is the form and format of the data appropriate? Is the algorithm able to resolve the dimensionality of the problem space sufficiently? Have I trained the algorithm appropriately? Ask yourself these questions until you've identified the one that you have the least confidence in, and then start exploring and experimenting.

From my perspective, the worst-case scenario for ML is an algorithm that *fails silently*. These are cases where an algorithm achieves its training and validation successfully, is deployed into a real application, but generates poor results from real-world data. The algorithm has not been able to generalize its knowledge and has only memorized the training data well enough to pass validation. The silent failure occurs because the algorithm lulls you into a false sense of security by showing good accuracy during validation. You then deploy the algorithm into production, trusting its results, only to find a month or a year later that the algorithm has been grossly underperforming and making poor decisions affecting real people or processes that now need to be corrected.

For that reason, you must always monitor the performance of your algorithms under real-world workloads. You should periodically spot-check the algorithm's work to make sure that its real-world accuracy is comparable to what you've observed during training. If an algorithm shows 85% accuracy during training, and a production spot-check of 20 data points yields 15 correct answers (75%), that algorithm is probably working as expected. However, if you find that only 50% of real-world evaluations are correct, you should expand your audit of the algorithm and potentially retrain it based on an updated training set drawn from your more realistic data points.

These silent failures are often caused by over-training or poor training. Even if you have followed best practices for training and split your prelabeled data set into separate training and validation sets, it is still possible to overtrain and undergeneralize. In some cases the source data itself can be blamed. If your entire training and validation set was generated from survey results of college students, for instance, the model may not be able to accurately evaluate survey results from senior citizens. In this case, even though you have validated your model on an independent data set, the training and validation data itself is not an appropriate random sampling of real-world conditions. In real-world usage you will see a lower accuracy than the validation results, as the source data you used to train the model has been compromised by selection bias.

A similar thing can happen with other types of classification tasks. A sentiment analysis algorithm trained on movie reviews may not be able to generalize to restaurant reviews; the jargon and tone—the form of the data—may be different between those two data sources.

If your model is underperforming and you are truly lost as to what to do next, turn to experimentation and exploration. Test out a different algorithm with the same training set and compare results. Try generating a new training set, either one more broad or more narrow. Experiment with different tokenization techniques, different preprocessing techniques, and potentially even different implementations of the same algorithm. Search the web to see how other researchers approach similar problems, and most importantly, never give up. Frustration is part of the learning process.

Combining models

Sometimes, in order to achieve a singular business goal, you'll need to combine multiple algorithms and models and use them in concert to solve a single problem. There are two broad approaches to achieving this: combining models in series and combining them in parallel.

In a series combination of models, the outputs of the first model become the inputs of the second. A very simple example of this is the Word2vec word-embedding algorithm used before a classifier ANN. The Word2vec algorithm is itself an ANN whose outputs are used as the inputs to another ANN. In this case, Word2vec and the classifier are trained separately but evaluated together, in series.

You can also consider a CNN to be a serial combination of models; the operation of each of the layers (convolution, max pooling, and fully connected) each has a different purpose and is essentially a separate model whose output provides the input to the next layer. In this case, however, the entire network is both evaluated and trained as a single unit.

Models run in parallel are often called **ensembles**, with the random forest being a straightforward example. In a random forest many individual decision trees are run in parallel and their outputs combined. More generally, however, there is no requirement for models run in parallel to be of the same type of algorithm. When analyzing sentiment, for instance, you can run both a bigram Naive Bayes classifier and an LSTM RNN in parallel, and use a weighted average of their outputs in order to produce more accurate results than either would return individually.

In some cases, you can combine models in order to better handle heterogeneous data. Let's imagine a business goal where a user should be classified into one of ten psychometric categories based on both their written content and also a number of other features derived from their profile. Perhaps the goal is to analyze a user on Twitter in order to determine which marketing vertical to place them in: *fashionista, weekend warrior, sports junkie,* and so on. The data available to you is the text content of their tweet history, their list of friends and content interactions, and a number of derived metrics such as average post frequency, average Flesch-Kincaid reading ease, friends-to-followers ratio, and so on.

This problem is a classification task, but it is a business goal that requires multiple technical steps to achieve. Because the input data is not homogeneous, we must split the problem up into parts and solve each separately. We then combine the parts to compose an accurate and performant ML system.

First, we can take text content of the user's tweets and pass that through a naive Bayes classifier in order to determine which of the 10 categories the content best fits. The classifier will return a probability distribution like *5% fashionista, 60% sports junkie, and 25% weekend warrior*. This classifier alone is probably not sufficient to solve the problem; weekend warriors and sports junkies tend to write about similar topics, and the Bayesian classifier cannot tell the difference between the two because there's so much overlap.

Fortunately, we can combine the text classification with other signals, such as how often the user posts images to Twitter, how often they tweet on weekends versus weekdays, and so on. An algorithm like random forest, which can deal with heterogeneous input data, would be useful here.

The approach we can take is to use the 10 probabilities generated by the Bayesian classifier, combine them with another 10 features derived directly from the user's profile data, and feed the combined list of 20 features to the random forest classifier. The random forest will learn when to trust the Bayesian classifier's output and when to lean more heavily on other signals. In cases where the Bayesian classifier has difficulty discerning between sports junkies and weekend warriors, for instance, the random forest may be able to draw distinctions between the two based on the additional context.

Furthermore, the random forest will be able to learn when to trust the Bayesian probabilities and when not to. A random forest might learn that the Bayesian classifier is often correct when it judges *fashionista* with a 90% probability. It might similarly learn that the Bayesian classifier is unreliable when judging *weekend warrior* even at high probabilities, and that for a significant proportion of the time a weekend warrior might be mistaken for a sports junkie.

From an intuitive perspective, the random forest is a good algorithm to choose for this use case. Because it is based on decision trees, it is able to create decision points based on the values of specific attributes. A random forest might generate a logical structure like this:

- If *bayes_fashionista_probability* > 85%, return *fashionista*
- If *bayes_weekend_warrior_probability* > 99%, return *weekend warrior*
- If *bayes_weekend_warrior_probability* < 99%, continue to:
    - If *twitter_weekend_post_frequency* > 70%, return *weekend warrior*
    - Else, if *bayes_sports_junkie_probability* > 60%, return *sports junkie*

In this simplified example, the random forest has learned to trust the Bayesian classifier's judgment for the *fashionista* category. However, the forest will only trust the Bayesian classifier's judgement of weekend warriors if the probability is very high. If the Bayesian classifier is less than certain about the weekend warrior classification, then the random forest can turn to the user's frequency of tweets on the weekend as a separate signal used to discriminate between weekend warriors and sports junkies.

When designed thoughtfully, composed models like this one can be very powerful tools capable of handling many situations. This technique allows you to decompose a business goal into multiple technical goals, choose the best algorithm for each type of data or classification, and combine the results into one coherent and confident response.

Summary

Most of this book has focused on the implementation of ML algorithms used to solve specific problems. However, the implementation of an algorithm is only one part of the software-engineering design process. An engineer must also be skilled in choosing the right algorithm or system for her problem and be able to debug issues as they arise.

In this chapter, you learned a simple four-point decision-making process that can help you choose the best algorithm or algorithms for a specific use case. Using the process of elimination, you can progressively reduce your options by disqualifying algorithms based on each of those decision points. Most obviously, you should not use an unsupervised algorithm when you're facing a supervised learning problem. You can further eliminate options by considering the specific task at hand or business goal, considering the format and form of the input and output data or the problem space, and doing a cost-benefit analysis with regards to the resources available to you.

We also discussed some problems that can arise when using ML models in the real world, such as the insidious issue of silent failures caused by poor training practices, or the more obvious failures caused by inappropriate algorithm selection or network topology.

Finally, we discussed the idea of composing models in either series or parallel, in order to leverage the particular strengths of algorithms, especially when presented with heterogeneous data. I showed an example of a random forest classifier that uses both direct signals and the outputs of a separate Bayesian classifier as its inputs; this approach helps to disambiguate confusing signals coming from the Bayesian classifier, which on its own may not be able to resolve overlapping categories accurately.

There is much more I wish I could teach you. This book has simply been an overview, a whirlwind introduction to the central concepts and algorithms of ML. Each one of the algorithms I've shown you is its own field of research that goes much deeper than what can be taught in just 10 or 20 pages.

I do not expect this book to solve all your ML problems, and neither should you. I hope, however, that this book has given you a solid foundation of understanding on top of which you can build your future education. In a field like ML, both esoteric and full of jargon, the biggest challenge is often knowing where to start. Hopefully the information in these pages has given you enough understanding and clarity to be able to navigate the wider world of ML on your own.

As you finish reading these final pages, I do not expect you to be fluent in the language of ML yet, but hopefully you are now conversational. While you may not yet be able to design exotic ANN topologies on your own, you should at least be comfortable with the core concepts, be able to communicate with other researchers, and find your own way to resources for continued in-depth learning. You can also solve many types of problems that you may not have been able to previously, and if that is the case then I have achieved my goal.

I have one final request of you: if you do continue your ML education, particularly in the JavaScript ecosystem, please contribute back to the community. As you have seen, there are many high-quality JavaScript ML libraries and tools available today, but there are also major gaps in the ecosystem. Some algorithms and techniques simply do not exist in the JavaScript world yet, and I would encourage you to seek out opportunities to fill in these gaps as best as you can, whether by contributing to open source software or writing educational materials for others to use.

Thank you for taking the time to read this humble introduction to machine learning in JavaScript—I hope it has served you well.

Other Books You May Enjoy

If you enjoyed this book, you may be interested in these other books by Packt:

Learning JavaScript Data Structures and Algorithms - Third Edition
Loiane Groner

ISBN: 978-1-78862-387-2

- Declare, initialize, add, and remove items from arrays, stacks, and queues
- Create and use linked lists, doubly linked lists, and circular linked lists
- Store unique elements with hash tables, dictionaries, and sets
- Explore the use of binary trees and binary search trees
- Sort data structures using algorithms such as bubble sort, selection sort, insertion sort, merge sort, and quick sort
- Search elements in data structures using sequential sort and binary search

Practical Internet of Things with JavaScript
Arvind Ravulavaru

ISBN: 978-1-78829-294-8

- Integrate sensors and actuators with the cloud and control them for your Smart Weather Station.
- Develop your very own Amazon Alexa integrating with your IoT solution
- Define custom rules and execute jobs on certain data events using IFTTT
- Build a simple surveillance solutions using Amazon Recognition & Raspberry Pi 3
- Design a fall detection system and build a notification system for it.
- Use Amazon Rekognition for face detection and face recognition in your Surveillance project

Leave a review - let other readers know what you think

Please share your thoughts on this book with others by leaving a review on the site that you bought it from. If you purchased the book from Amazon, please leave us an honest review on this book's Amazon page. This is vital so that other potential readers can see and use your unbiased opinion to make purchasing decisions, we can understand what our customers think about our products, and our authors can see your feedback on the title that they have worked with Packt to create. It will only take a few minutes of your time, but is valuable to other potential customers, our authors, and Packt. Thank you!

Index

3

3D data
  k-means algorithm, implementing 114, 117

4

4-6-2 network 225

A

activation function 225
algorithms
  categories 82
  classification 83
  clustering 82
  dimensionality reduction 83
  image processing 85
  natural language processing 84
  optimization 84
  regression 83
Amazon Web Services (AWS) 12
Amazon
  URL 183
arrow functions 23
Artificial General Intelligence (AGI) 223
artificial intelligence (AI) 13, 269
Artificial Neural Networks (ANNs)
  about 223
  overview 224, 226, 228
association rule learning
  about 177, 179
  algorithmic perspective 182, 183, 184
  applications 178, 184, 185
  mathematical perspective 179, 180, 182
  retail data example 186, 187, 188, 189, 190, 191
  support, for itemset 180

association rule
  about 180
  confidence 180
async function
  URL 27
Augmented Reality (AR) 300
average 89

B

Backbone.js 17
backpropagation 228, 229, 232
bias 79
bigrams 144

C

centroids
  locations, updating 102
  points, assigning 100
Chocolatey 29
classes 21
classification algorithm 77, 83
classification
  versus regression 194
cluster 87
clustering algorithm 82, 87
CommonJS initiative 15
conditional probability 142
Convolutional Neural Network (CNN)
  about 13, 36, 70, 243, 244, 245, 325
  convolution layers 245, 247, 248, 249, 250
  convolutions 245, 247, 248, 249, 250
  MNIST handwritten digits example 250, 252, 253, 254, 255, 257
curse of dimensionality 39

D

Damerau-Levenshtein distance 271
data pipelines
    about 305
    components 306
    data aggregation 309, 310
    data, delivering 314, 316
    data, joining 309, 310
    data, querying 306, 307, 308
    data, storing 314, 316
    normalization 310, 311, 313
    transformation 310, 311, 313
data pipelining 305
data
    missing data, handling 48
    noise, handling 49, 55
    normalizing 59, 64
    outliers, handling 55, 59
    preparing 47
    transforming 59, 64
database-as-a-service (DBaaS) 17
deep neural networks (DNNs) 243
degree 210
dense layers 237
development environment
    Hello World project, creating 30, 33
    Node.js, installing 29
    preparing 28
    project, creating 6, 30
    project, initializing 6, 30
    Yarn, optionally installing 29
dimensionality 41
dimensionality reduction 83
disappearing gradient 265
distance 89
distance map 129
Document Object Model (DOM) 10

E

ECMAScript 2015 14
electron 14
embedded methods 43
ensembles 332
ES6

arrow functions 23
async/await functions 27
classes 21
const 20
enhancements 19
for..of function 26
let 20
module imports 22
object literals 25
promises 26
exponential regression 204, 206, 210

F

Fast Fourier Transform (FFT) 220
feature extraction 41
feature identification
    about 38
    curse of dimensionality 39
feature selection 41
filtering 214
finite impulse response (FIR) 258
flowcharts 169
for..of function 26
Fourier analysis 219, 221
fully-recurrent RNNs 258

G

gamma 163
gated recurrent unit (GRU) 258, 263, 264
gini impurity 170
Google Cloud Platform (GCP) 13
growth constant 206

H

ham 69
heuristics 68
high-pass filters 214
hockey-stick growth 205
Homebrew 29

I

image processing algorithm 85
inference 69
isomorphic applications 17

itemset 179

J

JavaScript
  advantages 14
  challenges 14
  using 9, 11

K

k-means algorithm
  about 88
  average 89
  centroid locations, updating 102, 105
  development environment, setting up 92
  distance 89
  extending 117, 119, 121, 123
  implementing, on 2D data 107, 112, 114
  implementing, on 3D data 114, 117
  initializing 93, 97
  main loop 106
  points, assigning to centroids 100
  random centroid generation, testing 98
  writing 91
k-Nearest Neighbors (KNN) algorithm
  about 125, 126
  building 127, 132
  examples 132, 135, 136, 139, 141
kernel trick 162

L

lemma 287
lemmatization 287
Levenshtein distance 273
lift 181
linear regression 200, 202, 204
locale 65
logistic curve 231
logistic function 231
Long Short-Term Memory (LSTM) 243, 265, 266,
  267, 327
low-pass filters 214
LSTM RNN 327

M

machine learning (ML) algorithm, selecting
  based on available resources 328, 329
  based on data form 326, 327, 328
  based on data format 326, 327, 328
  based on data input 326, 327, 328
  based on data output 326, 327, 328
  based on mode of learning 321, 322, 323, 324
  based on performance 330, 331
  based on task 324, 325
machine learning (ML)
  about 9, 35, 67, 68, 141, 182, 193, 223
  overview 35, 37
  using 12, 13
MacPorts 29
main loop 106
MDN web docs 20
mean square error (MSE) 229, 251
measurements 61
metaphone algorithm 288
MeteorJS 17
missing data
  handling 48
  missing categorical data, handling 48
  missing numerical data, handling 49
MNIST handwritten digits example
  reference 251
models
  combining 332, 333, 334
  improving 303, 304, 305
  per-user models 303, 304, 305
  serializing 298, 299
  training, on server 299, 301
  web workers 301, 303
module imports 22
Mozilla Developer Network
  URL 20
Mustache 17

N

Naive Bayes classifier
  about 141, 143
  building 145, 147, 150, 152, 154
  Movie review sentiment 155, 157, 159

tokenization 144
natural language processing (NLP) 40, 84, 223, 269
neural networks 292, 293, 294
Node Package Manager (npm) 14
Node.js
  about 16
  installing 29
noise
  handling 49, 55
npm registry 16

O

object literals 25
optimization algorithm 84
optimization problems 323
outliers
  handling 55, 59
overfitting 79

P

part of speech (POS) tagging 270, 290, 291
Pearson correlation
  example 44, 47
phonetics 288, 289
polynomial regression 210, 212
prediction mode 229
Principal Component Analysis (PCA) 44, 72, 321
promise 26
Prototype JavaScript Framework 9
prototypes 18

R

R2 value 199
random centroid generation
  testing 98
random forest algorithm 169, 171, 173, 175
rectified linear unit (ReLU) 231
recurrent neural networks (RNN)
  about 243, 257, 258
  fully-recurrent RNNs 258
  gated recurrent unit (GRU) 263, 264
  Long Short-Term Memory (LSTM) 265, 266, 267

SimpleRNN 258, 260, 261, 262
regression
  about 77, 83, 195, 197, 198, 200
  exponential regression 204, 206, 210
  linear regression 200, 202, 204
  polynomial regression 210, 212
  versus classification 194
reinforcement learning 69, 81
relevance score 274
RequireJS 17
root mean square error (RMSE) 95, 200

S

scikit-learn 11
seasonality analysis 217, 218
sentiment analysis 125
serialization 298
service workers 302
SimpleRNN 258, 260, 261, 262
Software as a Service (SaaS) 299
spam filter 303
sparse matrix 292
sparse vector 292
stemming 286, 287
stopword filtering 144
string distance
  measuring 271, 272, 273
subtractive processing 216
supervised learning
  about 68, 69, 73, 77, 80
  accuracy, measuring 74, 76
  classification 77
  regression 77
Support Vector Machines (SVMs) 125, 160, 163, 164, 167, 168

T

TensorFlow 13
TensorFlow.js
  used, for solving XOR problem 232, 235, 237
term frequency-inverse document frequency (tf-idf) 273, 274, 275, 276, 278
time-series analysis techniques
  about 213

filtering 214
Fourier analysis 219, 221
seasonality analysis 217, 218
tokenization 144
tokenizing 279, 280, 281, 283, 284, 285
topology 224
training data 69
training set 69
transactional database
  about 179
  items 179
  sessions 179
  supermarket example 179
trigram approach 41
trigrams 144
TypeScript language 18

U

unigram analysis 40
unsupervised learning
  about 68, 69, 70, 73

analysis 70
preprocessing 70

V

variance 79

W

web workers 301, 303
word crate 271
word embedding 292, 293, 294
word plate 271
Word2Vec algorithm 293

X

XOR problem
  solving, with TensorFlow.js 232, 235, 237, 240

Y

Yarn
  optionally installing 29